Life in the Lordship of Christ

Raniero Cantalamessa OFM Cap., born in 1934, was professor and director of the Religious Sciences Department of the Catholic University of
the Sacred Heart in Milan, and a member of the International Theological
Commission from 1975 to 1981. Since 1980, he has been the preacher to
the Papal Household where he delivers a weekly meditation, during Advent and Lent, in the presence of the Pope, the members of the Roman
Curia and the general superiors of religious orders. He leads numerous
formation sessions and retreats throughout the world. He is the author of
many books, including *The Mystery of Christmas: Commentary on the
Magnificat, Gloria and Nunc Dimittis* and *Obedience: The Authority of
the Word* (both St. Paul Publications).

Life in the Lordship of Christ

A Spiritual Commentary on the Letter to the Romans

Raniero Cantalamessa

Translated from the Italian
by
Frances Lonergan Villa

Darton, Longman and Todd
London

First published in Great Britain in 1992 by
Darton, Longman and Todd Ltd
89 Lillie Road, London SW6 1UD

First published in the USA in 1990 by
Sheed & Ward
115 E. Armour Blvd, P.O. Box 419492, Kansas City, MO 64141

Originally published in Italian in 1986 as *La Vita Nella Signoria di Cristo*
by Editrice Ancora, Milano
© 1990 Raniero Cantalamessa
English translation of the 4th revised Italian edition (1989)
© 1990 Raniero Cantalamessa

ISBN 0–232–52006–2

A catalogue record for this book is available from the British Library

The front cover illustration is a Russian Icon of the Novgorod School.
Design by Jeremy Dixon.

Printed and bound in Great Britain
at the University Press, Cambridge.

Contents

Contents

Introduction

"The Gospel is the power of God for salvation to everyone who has faith"

This work presents a way of re-evangelization and spiritual renewal based on St. Paul's letter to the Romans. It is therefore neither an exegetical comment nor a theological treatise, but an attempt to go straight to the heart of what animated the Apostle when he wrote this letter, which was of imparting to us some spiritual gift to strengthen us so that together with him we might be mutually encouraged by each other's faith (cf. Rom 1:11 f.). Down through the centuries the letter to the Romans has often been a privileged field of theological discussion and battle, whereas, in actual fact, it wasn't written for a narrow circle of scholars but for all the people "holy and loved by God" in Rome, made up, for the most part, of simple and illiterate people. Its aim was the edification of the faith.

The general scheme of the spiritual journey and the various stages that distinguish it, in order of progression, are taken from St. Paul's text as, and most important of all, are the words used to describe these stages which are the words of God and as such "living and eternal," efficacious in themselves, independent of all schemes and particular use.

The aim we have in view is to become new creatures in conformity with what the Apostle said: *If anyone is in Christ, he is a new creature; the old one has passed away, behold, the new has come* (2 Cor 5:17). The starting point might be different for each one of us: incredulity, sin, tepidness, a state of spiritual weakness, the need for greater strength and holiness. . . , but the goal, "a new life in the Spirit," is the same for all. If we obey God's word, it has the power to make us carry out the truest and deepest of conversions, that of "living for the Lord" instead of "living for ourselves." In fact, the whole effort of this present journey is to lead us to the point where we, too, can finally exclaim with St. Paul: *None of us lives for himself. If we live, we live for the Lord* (Rom 14:7 f.).

Our spiritual journey is divided into two parts: the first part, called *kerygma* or proclamation, presents the *work accomplished* by God for us in history, while the second part, called *parenesis* or exhortation, presents the work *to be accomplished* by man. The first part presents Jesus Christ to us as a *gift* to be accepted through faith, the second part presents Jesus Christ as the *model* to imitate through acquisition of the virtues. In this way we are helped to re-establish one of the most difficult balances to maintain in the spiritual life, the balance between the mysteric element and ascetic element, between the part played by grace and the part freedom plays. The most important teaching in the Letter to the Romans lies in its structure. The Apostle doesn't first deal with christian "duties" (charity, humility, obedience, service, etc.) and then with "grace" almost as if grace were a consequence of duty. On the contrary, he first deals with justification and grace and then with the duties that spring from these and which are made possible by justification and grace. The chapter on prayer has been inserted between the first and second part as a sort of link as prayer springs from the gift of the Spirit and serves as a tool for the acquisition of virtue.

The means and the tool St. Paul uses to accomplish all that has been said is the Gospel: *I am not ashamed of the Gospel; it is the power of God for salvation to every one who has faith* (Rom 1:16). We are given to seeing the Gospel as God's "truth" revealed by Jesus, but the Apostle encourages us to discover it also as the "power" of God. Here "Gospel" stands for the contents of the Gospel, for what is proclaimed in it and particularly the redemptive death of Christ and his resurrection. He therefore teaches us to count not so much on rational demonstration or rhetorical effectiveness as on the bare proclamation of divine facts. In it the believer experiences God's saving power without feeling the need to know the why and the wherefore.

The frequent recourse in these pages to renowned exponents of modern culture and to Church tradition, is not to prove or adorn God's word but, rather, to render a service to the Word. The principal reason why Scripture can be questioned in every epoch and deeper meanings drawn from it is that every epoch can question it at a different and deeper level of conscience and an ever richer experience of life compared with the past. In fact, in the meanwhile, the Church has produced other saints and humanity other geniuses. Secular geniuses, especially if they are strong believers, render an incomparable service to the word of God. They cause the level of the conscience of humanity to increase and thus help to create ever more stimulating and deeper questions and challenges to God's word. We are in a position to grasp something more than even Augustine, Thomas and Luther were from the Letter to the Romans and Scripture in general, even if they were greater than us, not only because of the great progress made in Biblical exegesis but also because meanwhile we've known other sufferings and had other teachers of humanity.

I. Loved by God!

The good news of God's love

The runner arriving breathlessly in the town square from the battlefield doesn't begin by giving an orderly account of the development of events and neither does he waste time on details. He goes straight to the point and in a few words gives the most vital piece of news which everyone is waiting to hear. Explanations can come later. If a battle has been won, he shouts: "Victory!" and if peace has been made, he shouts "Peace!" That's how I remember things the day the second world war ended. The news "Armistice! Armistice!" brought by someone returning from the city, flashed from house to house in the town and spread throughout the countryside. The people poured out on to the streets embracing one another with tears in their eyes after the terrible years of war.

St. Paul, chosen to announce the word of God, behaves in the same way at the beginning of his Letter to the Romans. He comes as the herald of the greatest event in the world, as the messenger of the most splendid of victories and hastens to tell us, in a few words, the most beautiful news ever told: *To all God's beloved people in Rome*—he says—*who are called to be saints: Grace to you and peace from God our Father and the Lord Jesus Christ!* (Rom 1:7). At a first reading this might seem just a simple greeting, like those at the beginning of each letter, whereas, in fact, it contains news. And what news! I announce, he is saying, that God loves you; that once and for all peace has been made between heaven and earth; I tell you that you "have grace"! Moreover, in such cases, more than the words themselves, it's the tone in which they are said that counts and this greeting by the Apostle inspires joyous confidence and trust. "Love," "grace," "peace" are words that contain "in synthesis" the whole of the evangelic message and not only have they the power to communicate news but also to create a state of mind. They recall the greeting of the heavenly messenger sent to announce the good

1

news to the shepherds: *Glory to God in the highest, and on earth peace among men with whom he is pleased* (Lk 2:14).

We start from the assumption that the Letter to the Romans, being God's "living and eternal" word, was written also for us and that at this moment in history, we are those for whom it was intended. It results, therefore, that this message is being addressed to us here and now. The love of God embraces us right from the beginning of this spiritual journey. We become witnesses to the first breaking of the good news to the world; we relive the moment in which the Gospel "exploded," in all its greatness and newness, for the first time in history. No other consideration, not even that of our unworthiness, must be allowed to disturb our hearts and distract them from this joyous certainty until they have been filled with this first and most important message: that God loves us and is offering us this very day his peace and grace as fruits of this love. As soon as we withdraw into ourselves a little and set about reforming our lives, we quickly realize how much time, conflict and bad habits have hardened us; we can see ourselves perfectly described in the words God pronounced through the prophet Isaiah: *Your neck is an iron sinew and your forehead brass* (Is 48:4). We are like iron sinews which must be bent. But how can this be done? If iron is hammered when it is cold it either doesn't bend at all or it breaks; it must first be heated by fire to soften it. That's what we want to do in this first meditation: warm ourselves in God's love. We will then be able to bear the hammering of God's word without hardening our hearts because it's possible to bear anything when we feel loved.

Let us welcome and accept the message of God's love through three wonderful phrases in the Epistle to the Romans: we are "God's beloved" (1:7); "God's love has been poured into our hearts" (5:5); "nothing will be able to separate us from the love of God" (8:39). These short phrases are linked one to the other and form something like a single message that runs throughout the whole Epistle—almost a message within a message—recognizable even from the style which passes each time from a simple and conversational tone to a spiritually elevated and almost enthusiastic one.

1. "Loved by God"

The expression "the love of God" has two different meanings: in one God is the object and in the other God is the subject; one indicates our love for God and the other God's love for us. Human reason, which naturally tends to being more active than passive, has always given more importance to the first meaning, that is, to our "duty" to love God. Christian preaching has often followed this line, speaking at certain times almost only about the "commandment" to love God and about the degrees of this love ("De diligendo Deo"). But revelation gives more importance to the second meaning, to God's love for us rather than to our love for God. Aristotle said that God moves the world in so far as he is loved, that is, in so far as he is the object of love and the final cause of all its creatures (*Metaf.* XII, 7, 1072b); but the Bible says the exact opposite, that God creates and moves the world in so far as he loves the world. Concerning God's love, therefore, the most important thing is not that man should love God but that God loves man and that he loved him first. *In this is love, not that we loved God but that he loved us* (1 Jn 4:10). Our purpose in this meditation is to re-establish the order revealed by the Word of God, placing anew the gift before the commandment and putting the simple and overwhelming message that "God loves us" at the head of every consideration. Everything else depends on this including our own chance of loving God: *We love, because he first loved us* (1 Jn 4:19).

Our spirit is so made that if a thought is to leave a lasting sign, we need to be exposed to that thought for some time. Nothing of what just quickly strikes the spirit really makes any lasting impression or brings about any change. Just as the soil is daily exposed to the sun to get light, warmth and life from it, so we must now expose ourselves to the idea of God's love. This can take place only by questioning divine revelation. Who else, in fact, other than God himself could assure us that he loves us? The whole Bible, St. Augustine observes, does nothing but tell of God's love (*Cat.rud.* I,8,4; PL 40,319); it is, so to say, full of it. This is the message that supports and explains all the other messages. The love of God is the answer to all the "why's" in the Bible; the why of Creation, the why of the Incarnation, the why of Redemption. . . If the written word of the Bible could be changed into a spoken word and become one single voice, this voice, more powerful than the roaring of the sea would cry out: *The Father loves you*! (Jn 16:27). Everything that God does and says in the Bible is love, even God's anger is nothing but love. God "is" love! It has been said that it is not so important to know whether God exists or not; what is important is to know whether he is love (Kierkegaard, *The Gospel of suffering*, IV). And the Bible assures us that he is love!

We have a way called "spiritual reading" for finding out more about the Bible as it teaches us to read the words of the New Testament in the light of the Old Testament. It teaches us to reconstruct the resonance the words held for Jesus and the Apostles when they uttered them for the first time. They thought and spoke with the whole of Scripture in mind and we must do the same when listening to their words if we don't want to deprive ourselves of much of their richness and depth. The Old Testament is like a marvellous sound-box in which the words of the New Testament find their full meaning just as, on the other hand, the New Testament is even more so for the Old Testament. This principle will help us understand the message enclosed in the words "loved by God." "The expression 'loved by God' (*agapemenoi tou Theou*) tells us that the Roman Christians are the Israel of fulfillment; in fact Israel is the people loved by God" (H. Schlier, *Der Römerbrief*, Freiburg i.B., 1977, p. 31). In using this expression to designate christians, like the expressions "chosen" and "holy," it's as if the Apostle is transferring to the Church all the prerogatives of the love of God which Israel enjoyed in the Old Testament, not in the sense that Israel no longer enjoys these privileges but in the sense that we are also allowed to share in them. We who were strangers and sojourners have become fellow citizens with the Saints and members of the household of God (cf. Ep 2:19).

The Gospel, says St. Paul, was promised by God in the Scriptures, "by means of his prophets" (Rom 1:2). Let us therefore turn to the prophets to learn from them the first great revelation of the love of God. They were the first "friends of the Spouse," charged with declaring the love of God to humanity. God prepared those men "right from the maternal womb" so that they might be up to their calling; he gave them immense hearts open to all the great human sentiments having decided to reach man's heart by speaking the same language and making use of the same experiences.

God talks to us of his love through his prophets, making use, above all, of the image of paternal love: *When Israel was a child*—he says in Hosea—*I loved him. . . It was I who taught Ephraim to walk, I took them up in my arms; I led them with cords of compassion, with the bands of love; and I became to them as one who eases the yoke of their jaws and I bent down to them and fed them* (Hos 11:1-4). These are familiar images which each of us has often contemplated in our lives. Now, however, because of the mysterious power that symbols possess when they are associated with the things of God, these images are capable of arousing in man the vivid sentiment of God's fatherly love. The people, Hosea continues, are not easy to convert; the more God draws men to himself, the less they understand and they turn to idols. What should God do in such a case? Abandon them? Destroy them? God shared this intimate drama with the prophet, this sort of weakness and impotence he finds himself facing because of his passionate love for his creatures. God's heart misses a beat at the thought that his people can be destroyed: *My heart recoils within me, my compassion grows warm and tender. . . I am God and not man* (Hos 11:8-9). A man might give vent to his anger and usually does so, but God doesn't, for he is "holy," he is different; if we are faithless, he is faithful still, for he cannot disown his own self (cf. 2 Tm 2:13). Jeremiah speaks the same language: *Is Ephraim, then, so dear a son to me, a child so favoured, that whenever I mention him, I remember him loving still? That is why I yearn for him, why I must take pity on him* (Jer 31:20).

In these oracles God's love simultaneously expresses itself as both paternal and maternal love. *Paternal love* is made up of care and encouragement; the father wants to bring up his son and guide him towards maturity. A father is reluctant to praise his son too highly in his presence in case he should think too much of himself and make no further effort. In fact a father often disciplines his son and it is written: *For what son is there whom his father doesn't discipline?* (Heb 12:7) and the Lord *disciplines him whom he loves* (Heb 12:6). But not only this. The father also gives a sense of security and protection and throughout the Bible God presents himself to man as "his rock, his fortress and his deliverer" (Ps 18:2-3). *Maternal love* instead is all embracing and full of tenderness; it's a visceral love coming from the deepest fibre of the mother's being where the child was formed, gripping her whole person and "filling her with compassion." Whatever a child has done, however dreadful, a mother's first reaction is to open wide her arms and welcome her child back. If a son who has run away from home returns, it is the mother who begs and persuades the father to welcome him back and not to reprimand him too severely. In man these two types of love, maternal and paternal, are almost always separate; in God they are always united. That's why God's love is sometimes explicitly expressed through the image of maternal love: *Can a mother forget her child, that she should have no compassion on the son of her womb?* (Is 49:15); *As one whom his mother comforts, so I will comfort you* (Is 66:13). In the parable of the prodigal son, Jesus united in the figure of the father the traits of this God who is at the same time both father and mother. Actually, the father of the parable acts more like a mother than a father.

Man has the experience of another kind of love which is said to be "as strong as death and whose flashes are flashes of fire" (cf. Song 8:6), and God also had recourse to this kind of love in the Bible to give us an idea of his passionate love for us. All the different stages and difficulties of nuptial love are evoked and used to this end: the magic of love during the betrothal: *I remember the devotion of your youth, your love as a bride* (Jer 2:2); the total joy on the wedding day: *For as a young man marries a virgin. . . , and as a bridegroom rejoices over the bride, so shall your God rejoice over you* (Is 62:5); the drama of the break-up: *Plead with your mother, plead—for she is not my wife, and I am not her husband—. . . I will slay her with thirst* (Hos 2:4 ff.); and finally, full of hope, the re-birth of the ancient bond: *Therefore, behold, I will allure her, and bring her into the wildnerness, and speak tenderly to her* (Hos 2:16). *For a moment I hid my face from you but with everlasting love I will have compassion on you* (Is 54:8).

Nuptial love is fundamentally a love of desire. If it is true therefore that man desires God and, moreover, that the desire for God is what is deepest, most essential and greatest in the human being, the contrary, that God desires man, is also mysteriously true. Jealousy is a characteristic trait of nuptial love and in fact the Bible often affirms that God is a "jealous God" (cf. Ex 20:5; Dt 4:24; Ezek 8:3-5). In man jealousy is a sign of weakness. A jealous person fears for himself lest someone else stronger than he is should win the loved one's heart. God doesn't fear for himself but for his creature; he doesn't fear his own weakness but the weakness of his creature. He knows that in giving himself into the arms of idols, the creature is giving himself up to untruth and nothingness. In all its forms, idolatry is God's terrible rival throughout the Bible; the idols are the false lovers (cf. Hos 2:7 ff.; Jer 2:4; Ezek 16). God's jealousy is a sign of love and zeal and not of imperfection.

In revealing his love God reveals his *humility* at the same time. It is God in fact who seeks man, who gives in and pardons and he is always ready to start again from the beginning. To love is always an act of humility. When a young man kneels to ask a girl's hand in marriage, as used to happen in the past, he makes the deepest act of humility of his life. He becomes a mendicant. It's as if he were saying to the girl: "Give me your being because mine is not sufficient; alone, I am not enough to myself!" But why does God love and humble himself? Does he too, perhaps, have needs? No, his love is pure gratuitousness; he doesn't love to be completed but to complete, to be fulfilled but to fulfill. He loves because "goodness loves to spread itself." This quality is what makes God's love unique and unrepeatable. In loving, God does not even seek his glory; or rather, he does seek his glory but this glory is nothing other than that of loving man gratuitously. St. Irenaeus said that "God's glory is living man!" (*Adv.Haer.* IV, 20,7). The same saint wrote a page about the gratuitousness of God's love which the Church still meditates on today (it was inserted as a reading into the Liturgy of the Hours): "God—he says—didn't procure Abraham's friendship because he needed it but because, being good, he wanted to grant Abraham eternal life . . . because God's friendship procures incorruptibility and eternal life. Thus, in the beginning, God didn't create Adam because he needed man but to have someone on whom to pour his blessings. He blesses those who serve him simply because they serve him and those who follow him because they follow him but he doesn't receive any benefit from them because he is perfect and doesn't need anything. . . He prepared his prophets to accustom man on earth to having his Spirit and to being in union with him. He who needs nothing offered his communion to those who needed him" (*Adv.Haer.* IV,13,4-14,2). God loves because he is love; his love is a gratuitous necessity and a necessary gratuity.

Considering the unfathomable mystery of God's love we can understand the wonder of the psalmist who asked himself: "What is man that thou art mindful of him, and the son of man that thou dost care for him" (cf. Ps 8:5).

The contemplation of God's love throughout the Bible is also the best school for learning to love in our turn. If human love is a *symbol* of God's love, God's love is a *model* for human love. Considering what God's love *is* like, strong, tender, constant, gratuitous, we can discover what human love *should be* like; how a father and a mother should love, how a married couple should love, how we should love God and our neighbour.

What we have seen so far are just flashes of the great revelation of God's love in the prophets. It is not always God who speaks directly and in the first person in the prophets; more often than not it is the prophet himself who judges, orders and threatens, even if he does so in God's name. But when God's love is in question, the words nearly always come from the living voice of God; they are direct words. The "I" of the prophet is eclipsed to make room for the eternal "I" of God: "I generated sons. . ."; "I loved you with a lasting love. . ."; "I shall make you my spouse for ever. . . ." God does not talk to us of his love by means of a third person! What the prophets experienced in those moments of such sublime revelation is an impenetrable mystery to us. The prophetic vocation is realized to the full; in fact, at the height of his inspiration, the true prophet when speaking . . . is silent. He is silent because it is no longer he who is speaking; a much more powerful voice has taken over from him and he himself listens in mysterious silence. He is the first to accept the incredible revelations of God's love: "*I* love you . . ."; "*You* are precious in my eyes and I love you" (Is 43:4). And what a shock to realize that that "you" was also him, the prophet! To feel thus addressed by God in person!

2. "God's love has been poured into our hearts"

After listening again to the great revelation of God's love in the prophets, we are once more faced with the old question: what did the Lord bring us that was new when he came among us?, and once again the answer is what St. Irenaeus gave: "Know that he brought us every newness by bringing us himself!" (*Adv.Haer.* IV, 34,1). God, he said, sent the prophets ahead of him to accustom man on earth to having his Spirit and to being in communion with God; now all of this has been accomplished. At the beginning of chapter five in the Letter to the Romans, St. Paul wrote: *Therefore, since we are justified by faith, we have peace with God through our Lord Jesus Christ. Through him we have obtained access to this grace in which we stand, and we rejoice in our hope of sharing the glory of God. More than this we rejoice in our sufferings, knowing that suffering produces endurance, and endurance produces character, and character produces hope, and hope does not disappoint us, because God's love has been poured into our hearts through the Holy Spirit who has been given to us* (Rom 5:1-5). This is the wonderful and full news the Apostle anticipated in his opening greeting. The three words of the greeting are used again here: "love," "peace" and "grace," and this time he indicates the source of all this: justification by faith in Christ. Here too, more than just giving us theological ideas, the Apostle wants to communicate a state of soul, to make us conscious of the "state of grace" we find ourselves in. It is once again an elevated way of talking.

However, a leap in quality takes place. Now we are no longer told that we are God's beloved but that God's love has actually been "poured into our hearts." The expression "God's beloved" in the greeting was not referring only to the past; it is not just a title the Church inherited from Israel; it refers to recent events and talks of a new and relevant reality.

Jesus Christ is the origin of this new reality but for the moment we shall not go into the origin and development of this love. Even the fact that it was given to us "by means of the Holy Spirit" is not the most important thing at this point; the Apostle talks of the Holy Spirit further on in Chapter Eight. Now it is simply a question of accepting the new, overwhelming revelation that God's love has come among us permanently; now it is in our hearts! Two walls of separation existed between us and God's love which prevented full communion with God: the wall of *nature* (God is "Spirit" and we are "flesh") and the wall of *sin*. Through his incarnation Jesus defeated the obstacle of nature and through his death on the cross he defeated the obstacle of sin and so the pouring out of his Spirit and love was no longer impeded by anything. God has become "the life of my soul, the life of my life; my life itself" (cf. St. Augustine, *Conf.* III,6).

A wonderful new sentiment, the sentiment of *possession*, grows in us where God's love is concerned; we possess God's love or, better still, we are possessed by it. It's like when a man who has sought for years and years to get hold of a certain object he particularly likes or a work of art he greatly admires and who has often thought he had completely lost the chance of having it, can, unexpectedly, one evening take it home and lock it in the house. Even if for some reason he cannot unwrap it for months or years and contemplate it directly, it doesn't really matter as now he knows it is "his" and no one can take it away from him. "You shall be my people and I will be your God," God said through the prophets announcing these times (cf. Ezek 36:28). Now all this has been fulfilled; God has become "our" God in a new way. We possess God through grace. This is the supreme richness of a creature and the highest title of glory which, I dare to say, not even God possesses. God is God and this is certainly infinitely greater, but God has no God to rejoice over, to be proud of, to admire . . . Man has God! We could say that the difference between God and us can be reduced to the difference between being and having. What possession can be compared to this? Everything else we possess we shall have to leave behind us but not this one. It is ours forever. Truly speaking, God also has a God in whom he can rejoice and take delight because God is also triune: the Father "has" the Son and the Son "has" the Father and both "have" the Holy Spirit; but in the Trinity this has a completely different meaning than it does for us.

To estimate the difference that exists between this state and the one before Christ came, we would need to have experienced both; we would need to have lived first under the Old Testament and then under the New Testament. But St. Paul, who lived this unique experience assures us of the incomparable difference. He says that what once had splendour has come to have no splendour at all because of "the splendour that surpasses it" (cf. 2 Cor 3:10). Wanting to convince us of his love once and for all, God made a kind of external picture of it in the images he unrolled before our eyes of the life of Jesus to the culminating image of the cross to then grant us, through his Spirit, what we had "seen with our own eyes, contemplated and touched with our own hands." Jesus is the incarnation of God's love. An old Christian writing, paraphrasing John 1:14 says that "love (of the Father) became incarnate in him" (*Evangelium Veritatis,* from the Nag Hammadi scrolls).

What is this love that was poured into our hearts at baptism? Is it just a sentiment God has for us? Is it just a benevolent disposition towards us? An inclination? That is, something *intentional*? It is much more than all this, it is something *real*. It is literally the love *of* God, that is the love that is in God, the very flame that burns in the Trinity and which we partake of in the form of "indwelling." *My father will love him, and we will come to him and make our home with him* (Jn 14:23). We become "partakers of the divine nature" (2 Pet 1:4), that is partakers of divine love because God "is" love; love is, so to say, his nature. We find ourselves mysteriously caught up in the vortex of the work of the Trinity. We are involved in the incessant motion of reciprocal giving and receiving between the Father and the Son from which jubilant embrace the Holy Spirit springs who then brings down to us a spark of this fire of love. Someone who, through grace, experienced this said: "One night I felt the great tenderness of the Father enveloping me in a sweet and gentle embrace. Beside myself, I knelt down huddled in the dark. My heart was pounding and I abandoned myself completely to his will. And the Holy Spirit introduced me to the love of the Trinity. Also through me the ecstatic exchange of giving and receiving was taking place between Christ, with whom I was united, and the Father, and between the Father and the Son. But how can the inexpressible be expressed? I saw nothing but it was much more than seeing and there are no words to explain this jubilating exchange which was responding, soaring, receiving and giving. And from that exchange an intense life flowed from One to the Other like the warm milk coming from a mother's breast to her child. And I was that child and so was all creation that partakes of life, of the kingdom, of the glory as it had been regenerated by Christ. Opening the Bible I read: *For thy immortal Spirit is in all things* (Wis 12:1). O Holy and living Trinity! I was beside myself for a few days and that experience is still strongly impressed in my mind today."

The depth of meaning underlying Paul's words "God's love has been poured into our hearts" can only be understood in the light of the words Jesus exclaimed: *that the love with which thou hast loved me may be in them* (Jn 17:26). The love that was poured into our hearts is the same love with which the Father has always loved the Son. It is not a different love. It is the divine love of the Trinity overflowing into us. God communicates to souls "the same love that he communicates to his Son even if this takes place through union and not by nature as in the Son's case. . . Souls partake of God and with him fulfill the work of the Holy Trinity" (St. John of the Cross, *Spir.Cant.* V, 38). This is now, as it will be one day in eternal life, the greatest source of our beatitude. What gives greater joy and security to a child than the fact that his parents love each other? On an unconcious level this counts more for the child than the fact that they love him. A father and mother may each one of them love their child as much as they wish but if they don't love one another (and this is not uncommon), nothing will prevent the child from being unhappy and insecure deep down. A child doesn't want to be loved apart and with a different love but he wants to partake in the love which unites his parents knowing that this has been the source of his life. And this is the great revelation: the persons of the Trinity love each other with an infinite love and they allow us to partake in this love! They admit us to the banquet of life; the children of men "feast on the abundance of his house," he gives them to drink "from the river of his delights" (cf. Ps 36:9). The theological principle that "grace is the beginning of glory" (cf. St. Thomas Aquinas, *S.Th.* II-IIae, q. 24, art. 3, ad 2) means exactly that we already possess by faith and as "first fruits" what we will one day possess, visibly and fully, in eternal life and that is, God's love!

In the Old Testament God formed the prophets to infuse in the people a longing for these things to come about; now, in the Church, he has formed the saints to cultivate the memory of these same things. The saints and particularly mystics have the special role of talking to us of God's love and of helping us to glimpse something of the reality still hidden from our eyes. The mystics too are subject to the phenomenon of secularization. They occupy the minds of philosophers, psychologists, historians of religion and literature. Even from a cultural point of view they are too singular and fascinating to be ignored. All of this, however, contributes to removing them more and more from the ambit of the faith which is their true ambit, placing them beyond the reach of multitudes of believers. It is necessary to give back to the Church these privileged witnesses of God's love and it is a reason for hope to note that this is taking place in part. They are called "mystics" simply because they have had a particularly vivid experience of the christian "mystery." They are our safest guides in helping us to look into the reality and beyond the reality. They are our true mystagogues!

No one could better convince us that we are created for love than St. Catherine of Siena in her passionate prayer to the Trinity: "O Eternal Father, how then did you create this creature? I am greatly overwhelmed by this. In fact as you show me, I see that you didn't do this for any other reason if not because in your light you were forced to give us being by the fire of your charity in spite of all the iniquity we were to commit against you, O Eternal Father! It was fire therefore that forced you to do so. O ineffable love, even if in your light you saw all the iniquities your creature was to commit against your infinite goodness, you pretended almost not to see but fixed your eyes on the beauty of your creature whom you, intoxicated with love, loved and through love you drew her to yourself and formed her in your own image and likeness. You, eternal truth, communicated your truth to me, and that is that it was love that forced you to create her. . . ." I don't need therefore to look outside myself for proof that God loves me; I, myself, am the proof; my being is, in itself, a gift. Looking at ourselves in the light of faith we can say, I exist, therefore I am loved! It is true that for a christian "being is being loved" (G. Marcel).

Not everyone of course interprets creation in this way. *We were born by mere chance,* was already said at the time of the Bible (Wis 2:2). In ancient times there were those who saw the world as the work of a rival of God's or of an inferior God (the Demiurge), or as the result of a necessity or some accident which occurred in the divine world. God created the world because of an excess of energy (not of love!), almost as an excipient of his power which could not be contained in himself. Today there are those who hold the existence of man and of things to be the result of cosmic laws. There are even those who see it as a condemnation, almost as if we had been "thrown into existence." The discovery of existence which in St. Catherine of Siena generated wonder and exultation, generates only "nausea" in this latter perspective of atheistic existentialism.

To another of these mystics, a contemporary of St. Catherine's, God one day showed in a vision "a little thing, the size of a hazel-nut, on the palm of her hand" and it was revealed to her that it was all that was made. While she marvelled that it continued to exist though it was so small she received this answer from God: "It exists, both now and for ever, because God loves it" (Julian of Norwich, *Revelations,* Chap. 5). The same mystic received the revelation of another somewhat neglected but true aspect of the biblical doctrine of divine love and that is, the fact that God first rejoices in loving us: "In this way—she wrote—I saw that God was rejoicing to be our Father; rejoicing too to be our Mother; and rejoicing yet again to be our true Husband, with our soul his beloved Wife. And Christ rejoices to be our Brother, and our Saviour too" (Ch. 52). As regards the "motherhood" of God she said that "the fine and lovely word 'mother' is so sweet and so much its own that it cannot properly be used by any but him."

To another great Christian mystic, Bl. Angela of Foligno, God spoke these celebrated words: "I didn't love you as a joke! I didn't love you while remaining distant! You are me and I am you. You are made to my liking; you are very elevated in my majesty." She confesses that at times she felt as if she were "resting in the midst of the Trinity" (*The Book of Bl. Angela da Foligno,* Quaracchi 1985, passim).

We must convince ourselves that God didn't produce these souls just to make us envious, almost making us perceive what, deep down, each one of us yearns for more than anything else, to then tell us that all of this is not for us. God loves each one of us in this way and not just one or two persons in every epoch. In every epoch, to one or two persons chosen and purified for this by him, he entrusts the task of reminding others of it. But what is the difference of degree, of time or manner, between us and the saints in comparison with the main reality we share with them that we are all objects of the incredible design of God's love? What unites us to them is far greater than what separates us from them. We have seen that at the beginning of his Letter, St. Paul calls all christians "Holy" and not just some of them. If we knew at what price these souls acquired the light they transmit to us and what abysses they had to go through we would not set them aside so easily aside as if they were the prerogative of the erudite who sometimes discuss them without even believing in God. Just as the existence of false prophets has never caused the true prophets to be set to one side, so the existence of false mystics must not induce us to refuse the true mystics. It must only encourage us to await (and not to anticipate) the judgement of the Church and follow those approved by the Church and who have given long proof of their soundness in christian spirituality.

The words of love uttered to the Saints (such as: "I didn't love you as a joke!") are what would appear most similar to God's expressions in the prophets ("I have loved you with a lasting love. . ."); it is the continuation of this same revelation, even if in a "private" and not a public form. There has been a change in culture. People now have an individual conscience which at the time of the prophets wasn't felt or was just beginning to be felt. But also these words of fire uttered to the saints in the

Church are addressed to all God's people and, in a different way, they too are public. If this weren't the case, God would not have arranged, often miraculously, for these writings to be preserved from fire and destruction and oblivion and reach us intact, in spite of the humility of their authors. Today, endless books are written to answer the question, "Does God exist?," and often the question remains unanswered even at the end of these books. But, on opening a book by these men or women one discovers after only a few pages that God not only exists but that he is indeed "a consuming fire."

For the christian people, the mystics are like those who spied out the promised land and then came back to relate what they had seen ("a land which flows with milk and honey"), to encourage the people to cross the Jordan (cf. Num 14:6 ff.). Through them the first flashes of eternal life reach us in this life. As I have already said, their role closely recalls that of the prophets. It is true that the prophets recalled God's past love but they didn't stop at this, as the "historical" books of the Bible did; they also announced a future fulfillment, resolutely urging man to look ahead. They moved the barycentre of Israel's faith from the past to the future. They moved forward towards the fullness of the times. . . The mystics do the same in the midst of christians; they draw us towards the future and the consummation of God's love; they give us a glimmer of what is to come without, however, forgetting anything of what is past. Mystical matrimony, so often the conclusion of their vertiginous spiritual ascent, is not a suspicious experience to be analysed by psychoanalysts; it is simply the realization of the nuptial love of God sung by Hosea and other prophets. Their message can be summarized in St. Paul's words, who was one of them: "No eye has seen nor ear heard, nor the heart of man conceived, what God has prepared for those who love him" (cf. 1 Cor 2:9).

3. "Nothing can separate us from the love of God!"

The third expression that Paul uses about God's love in his Epistle to the Romans is existential. It takes us back to *this* life and to suffering which is its most striking aspect. The tone of the discourse is once again inspired and filled with deep emotion. *In all these things* (he is talking of tribulation, distress, persecution, famine, nakedness, peril, the sword) *we are more than conquerors through him who loved us. For I am sure that neither death, not life, nor angels, nor principalities, nor things present, nor things to come, nor powers, nor height, nor depth, nor anything else in all creation, will be able to separate us from the love of God in Christ Jesus, our Lord* (Rom 8:37-39).

Here St. Paul teaches us how to apply the light of God's love contemplated so far to our everyday life. The perils and enemies against God's love that he has listed are those he actually experienced himself in his own life: distress, persecution, the sword (cf. 2 Cor 11:23 ff.). He mentally reviews them and acknowledges that none of them is sufficiently powerful to withstand the thought of God's love. What seemed unsurmountable appears to be a trifle in this light. He implicitly invites us to do the same, to review our life as it is, to let the fears lurking in us surface, the sadness, threats, complexes, the physical or moral defect that prevents us from a serene acceptance of ourselves and expose all of this to the thought that God loves me. He is inviting me to ask myself what there is in my life that is trying to overcome me?

In the second part of the text the Apostle passes from his own personal life to a consideration of the world surrounding him. Here again he observes his world with the powers that threatened it at the time: death and its mystery, life as it was then with all its allurements, the astral powers and the infernal ones which struck such terror in ancient man. . . We too are invited to do the same: to look at our surrounding and frightening world with the new eyes given us by the revelation of God's love. What Paul calls the "height" and the "depth" are to us, in the growing knowledge we now have of the world's dimensions, what is infinitely great in height and what is infinitely small in depth and that is the universe and the atom. Everything is ready to crush us. Man is small and alone in a universe much greater than him and which has become more threatening since his scientific discoveries. But none of this can separate us from God's love. The God who loves me created all these things and he holds them firmly in his hand! *God is our refuge and our strength, a very present help in trouble. Therefore we will not fear though the earth should change, though the mountains shake in the heart of the sea* (Ps 46). How different is this view to the one which, ignorant of God, speaks of the world as "an ant-hill crumbling to pieces" and of man as "a useless passion" and as "a wave on the seashore which the next wave washes away"!

When St. Paul speaks of the love of God and Jesus Christ, he always appears to be "moved"; of Christ he says: *He loved me and gave himself for me* (Gal 2:20). He is showing us what the first and most natural reaction to grow in us should be after listening to the revelation of God's love and that is we should be deeply moved. When emotion is sincere and heartfelt, it is the most meaningful and worthy response that man can have before the revelation of a great love or a great sorrow. At any rate it is most beneficial to the receiver. Not a word, nor a gesture, nor a gift can substitute this because, it is in itself the most beautiful gift. It is the opening of one's own being to another. That's why we are reserved in showing our feelings as with the most intimate and holy things in which a person realizes that he no longer belongs entirely to himself but to another. We cannot conceal our deep feelings completely without depriving others of what is theirs by right because it exists in us for them. Jesus didn't hide his deep feelings: "he was deeply moved" before the widow of Naim and before the sisters of Lazarus (cf. Lk 7:13; Jn 11:33-35). It would be very helpful, especially for us, to feel moved as we set out on our spiritual journey to embrace God's word in a new way in our lives. It is in fact like the ploughing that precedes the sowing: it opens the heart and uncovers deep furrows so that the seed will not fall by the wayside. . . When God wants to give someone an important message for his life, he usually accompanies this with a certain emotion to help the person embrace his word and this deep feeling is, in its turn, the sign that it is God who is speaking to the soul. Let us therefore ask the Holy Spirit to help us feel deeply moved; let us ask him to grant us feeling that is not superficial. I shall always remember when it was also granted to me to experience a similar feeling for an instant. It was at a prayer meeting and I had just been listening to the Gospel passage where

Jesus says to his disciples: *No longer do I call you servants. . .but I have called you friends* (Jn 15:15). The word "friends" moved me deeply; it touched something deep down inside of me, so much so that for the remainder of the day I went about full of amazement and incredulity repeating to myself: He called me his friend! Jesus of Nazareth, the Lord, my God! He called me his friend! I am his friend! And I felt that I could fly over the roofs of the city and go through fire with such a certainty in my heart.

I have tried to be like the messenger who hastens home to give his vital news. I wanted to tell you first of all that God loves us so that this thought will ring loud and clear for us throughout our whole spiritual journey and at every moment as a sort of "precomprehension." When God's word becomes severe for us too and reprimands us for our sins, or when our own hearts start reprimanding us, we must continue to hear repeated within us "But God loves me! Nothing can separate me from God's love, not even my sins!"

Psalm 136 will now assist us to conclude, in prayer, this meditation on God's love by thanking him from the bottom of our hearts. It is called the "great hallel" and was also recited by Jesus during the last Supper. It is a long litany of titles and deeds by God in favour of his people and each time the people are invited to answer: *For his steadfast love endures for ever!* We could continue this psalm adding new blessings to the memory of God's ancient blessings: "He sent his Son among us; he gave us his Spirit; he called us to be believers; he called us his friends . . ." and each time let us answer: *For his steadfast love endures for ever!*

II. All Have Sinned

The mystery of impiety

This chapter deals with the first part of the Epistle to the Romans (Rom 1:18-3:20) which the Apostle sums up at the end in this well-known affirmation: *All have sinned and fall short of the glory of God!* (Rom 3:23). St. Paul is not so interested in telling us directly *what sin is* as, rather, in telling us that *there is sin*, that "we are all under the power of sin" (Rom 3:9) without exception. However, indirectly he also talks about what sin is and it is precisely on this point that we are now going to concentrate.

"What is sin?" asks a verse of a psalm in the Vulgate on which generations of Christians have meditated: "Delicta quis intellegit?" (Ps 19:13). One thing we know for certain and that is that only divine revelation really knows what sin is and neither human ethics nor philosophy can tell us anything about it. No man can say by himself what sin is for the simple reason that he himself is in sin. All that he says about sin can, in the end, only be a palliative, a minimization of sin. "To have a weak understanding of sin is part of our being sinners" (S. Kierkegaard). And Scripture says: *Transgression speaks to the wicked deep in his heart. . . for he flatters himself in his own eyes that his iniquity cannot be found out and hated* (Ps 36:2-3). Sin also "speaks" just as God does; it too delivers oracles and its place of teaching is man's heart. Sin speaks in man's heart and that's why it's absurd to expect man to speak *against* it. Although I am here writing about sin, I too am a sinner and I should therefore tell you not to rely too much on me and on what I write! But you can be certain that sin is a much more serious thing—infinitely more serious—than I shall ever be able to make you understand. At the most man can reach an understanding of sin against himself or against other men but not sin against God; the violation of human rights but not the violation of divine rights. In fact, if we take a close look around us we can see that this is what is happening in present-day culture.

Therefore only divine revelation knows what sin is. Jesus explains all this more closely by saying that only the Holy Spirit can "convince the world of sin" (cf. Jn 16:8). Only he can carry out the role of God's and Christ's advocate in the trial against the world as John Paul II reminded us in his encyclical on the Holy Spirit "Dominum et Vivificantem." Therefore God must be the one to talk to us of sin. If today's world has lost the sense of sin and no longer accepts the recall of the Church, perhaps it's because it thinks that in saying that "the Holy Spirit convinces the world of sin," the Church wants to identify itself immediately with the subject of the sentence and not with the object, placing itself on the side of the accuser and others on the side of the accused whereas, in fact, this is not the case. For if in one way, in virtue of the mandate it has received, the Church is with the "Spirit" who convinces of sin, in another way she knows that she is with the "world" too which is convinced of sin.

I have mentioned that God must be the one to talk to us of sin. When, in fact, God and not man talks against sin it is not easy to remain impassive; his voice is like thunder that "crushes the cedars of Lebanon" (cf. Ps 29:5). Our meditation will have fulfilled its aim if it manages even to touch our unshakable basic self-assurance and make us feel a wholesome fear in front of the terrible danger that not only sin but the very possibility of sinning holds for us. Such a fear would then become our greatest ally in the struggle against sin: *In your struggle against sin you have not yet resisted to the point of shedding your blood* (Heb 12:4).

1. Sin, a refusal to acknowledge God

Let us now listen to St. Paul revealing to us God's viewpoint on sin: *The wrath of God is revealed from heaven against all ungodliness and wickedness of men who by their wickedness suppress the truth. Ever since the creation of the world his invisible nature, namely his eternal power and deity, has been clearly perceived in the things that have been made. So they are without excuse; for although they knew God they did not honour him as God or give thanks to him, but became futile in their thinking and their senseless minds were darkened. Claiming to be wise, they became fools and exchanged the glory of the immortal God for images resembling mortal man or birds or animals or reptiles* (Rom 1:18-23).

The basic sin and primary object of God's wrath has been singled out by St. Paul as *asebeia*, that is impiety. He immediately explains what this impiety exactly consists of, saying that it is the refusal to glorify (*doxazein*) and thank (*eucharisten*) God. In other words in the refusal to acknowledge God as God and in not rendering him the respect that is his. It consists, we could say, in "ignoring" God, not however so much in the sense of "not knowing he exists" as in the sense of "behaving as if he didn't exist." In the Old Testament Moses shouts to the people, "Know that the Lord your God is God!" (cf. Dt 7:9) and a psalmist takes up the same cry: *Know that the Lord is God! It is he that made us, and we are his* (Ps 100:3). Sin is basically the denial of this "acknowledgement"; it is the attempt, on the part of the creature to cancel out on his own initiative and almost with arrogance, the infinite difference that exists between him and God. Thus sin infects the very root of things; it is "a stifling of truth," an attempt to keep truth the prisoner of injustice. It is something much more sinister and terrible than can be imagined or expressed. If the world knew what sin really is, it would die of terror.

This refusal took shape in idolatry in which the creature is worshipped rather than the Creator (cf. Rom 1:25). In idolatry man doesn't "accept" God but rather "makes" a god; it is he who decides about God and not God about him. The parts are inverted; man becomes the potter and God the clay which man moulds to his pleasure (cf. Rom 9:20 ff.).

So far St. Paul has shown us the withdrawal that took place in man's heart, his fundamental choice against God. Now he goes on to show the moral fruits of this withdrawal. All of this gave rise to a general dissolution in behaviour, a real and true "torrent of perdition" dragging humanity unconsciously to ruin. At this point St. Paul outlines the appalling picture of the vices of the pagan society: male and female homosexuality, injustice, wickedness, covetousness, envy, deceit, malignity, haughtiness, arrogance, disobedience to parents, faithlessness. . . The list of vices is taken from the pagan moralists but the whole picture that results from it is that of the "wicked one" so often spoken of in the Bible.

The disconcerting thing at a first glance is that St. Paul sees all this disorder as a consequence of divine wrath. In fact, he affirms this unequivocally three times: *God gave them up to impurity. . . For this reason God gave them up to dishonourable passions. . . And since they did not see fit to acknowledge God, God gave them up to a base mind* (Rom 1:24, 26, 28). God certainly doesn't "want" these things but he "permits" them to make man understand where his refusal of God leads him. St. Augustine wrote that "these things, although they are punishment, are also sins because the punishment for iniquity is that of being, itself, iniquity; God intervenes to punish evil and from his punishment other sins come" (*De nat.et grat.* 22,24; CSEL 60,250). Sin is the punishment of sin. In fact Scripture says: *One is punished by the very things by which he sins* (Wis 11:16). God is "obliged" to abandon people to themselves so as not to have to uphold their injustice and in the hope that they will retrace their steps.

2. "The mystery of wickedness is already at work"

So far, St. Paul has condemned the sin of the pagan society of his times, the impiety which manifested itself in idolatry, the consequence of which was moral disorder. If we want to follow his example and take advantage of his teaching, we cannot stop at this point and just simply condemn the idolatry of the Greek-Roman society of the Apostle's times; we must do what he did and look at our own society, as he looked at his, and discover the form impiety has taken in it. The Apostle unmasked the pagans and revealed that behind all their pride in themselves, their noble discourses on good and evil and on ethical ideals, was, in actual fact, hidden man's self-glorification and self-affirmation, that is, impiety and falsity. We must now let the Word of God act and we shall see first how it unmasks today's world in general and then each one of us in particular.

Let us therefore look first at today's world: let us bring the Word of God up-to-date and try to understand if and to what extent it applies also to our modern society and culture. St. Paul identified the root of sin in the refusal to glorify and thank God, in irreligiousness, for which he uses the Biblical term, impiety. In other words, in the refusal of God as creator and ourselves as creatures. Now, we know that this refusal has taken on, in modern times, a conscious and open form it certainly didn't have in the Apostle's time and maybe not in any other epoch in history. We must therefore admit that "the mystery of wickedness is already at work" (cf. 2 Thess. 2:7); it is not just a simple historical re-evocation or metaphysical speculation but a living reality.

I am insisting on sin against God—on impiety—not because sin against man doesn't exist in our world too, nor because this is any less serious, but because this is acknowledged and denounced nowadays on many sides, while sin against God which is the root of all this, is no longer acknowledged or it is undervalued. Sin against man actually serves sometimes as a pretext to deny sin against God. "Sin—it has ironically been written against Christianity—is a failing in respect, a *crime of lese divine majesty* and nothing more!. . . If, on the other hand, sin causes disorder, if it causes a growing disaster which spreads and which, like a disease, grips and strangles one man after another—all of this leaves indifferent this Oriental avid for honour in his heavenly abode: sin is an offence against him, not against humanity" (F. Nietzsche, *The Gay Science,* nr.153). He who wrote these words obviously doesn't remember that it was this oriental God "avid for honour" who said in Isaiah that he doesn't know what to do with incense, prayers, feasts and sacrifices if the oppressed are not succoured and justice is not rendered to the poor, and that he doesn't want fasting if not that of seeking justice, correcting oppression, defending the fatherless and feeding the hungry (cf. Is 1:10 ff.). Of the ten commandments God gave to mankind, three only concern our duty towards him, while all the others concern our duties towards man.

But the reason I insist on the sin of impiety goes even deeper. In all this modern talk about sin against man the idea of sin itself is lost. Sin is no longer "what God sees wrong" (cf. Ps 51:6) but what man sees wrong. Man decides what sin is, what is right and what is wrong; he defines his own moral law as he progresses through history just as "a river forms its own bed as it flows on its course." And this is once again relapsing into impiety. Without realizing it, it's possible to end up defining sin in purely "egoistic" terms. Finally, when sin against man is contrasted with sin against God, as in the words quoted, it is not man as such that is meant but the man who identifies with my social class, my beliefs and my reasons, or whom I can make use of against my adversaries. What really matters is not "man," but "me." It is hardly ever the man against whom *I* sin but always the man against whom *others* sin. Thus, this "new moral code" from which God is excluded, more often than not ends up being "a splendid vice" like that of the pagans, a seductive garment under which human egoism tries to hide itself. It can even justify the taking of innocent life, as, in fact, happens in the widespread and legalized practice of abortion.

Sin is what it is and it reaches an infinite degree only when God is involved, when the sinner exists and acts in the sight of God, when, in other words, God is the gauge. Sin against man can also be of infinite relevance precisely because God is involved and thus it is also a sin against God. Let us therefore not allow ourselves to be misled but let us return to the task the Word of God assigns to us, which is to denounce the impiety of the world. There is a precise reason for doing this, so that we may realize that there is a war between two "kingdoms" going on around us, before which we cannot remain neutral and that we may thus no longer be a party to the superficiality and a certain ingenuous and unbiblical optimism about the "world." Let us listen to a few of those who expressed refusal of God in modern times keeping in mind, however, that we are judging the words and not the intentions or moral responsibility of the individuals which are known only to God and which might be very different to what they seem to us.

Carl Marx gave this reason for his refusal of the idea of a "creator": "A person—he wrote—is an independent being only in so far as he is his own master, and he is his own master only in so far as he is master of his existence. He who lives through the 'grace' of another sees himself as a dependent being. . . But I would live entirely for the sake of another if he had created me, if he were the source of my life and my life was not my own creation" (C. Marx, *Manuscript of 1844*). Man's conscience—he wrote in his youth—is "the highest divinity"; "the origin of man is man himself" (*Critic of Hegel's Philosophy of Law*). J.-P. Sartre made one of his characters say: "Today I accuse myself and only I, man, can absolve myself. If God exists man is nothing. . . God doesn't exist! Happiness, tears of joy! Alleluia! No longer heaven. No longer hell! Nothing else but the earth" (J.-P. Sartre, *The Devil and the Good God*).

But can we really say "No longer hell"? Men of today must realize from where this thought comes according to which man must place himself as the ultimate foundation of himself and his own inventor. . . It's the duty of those announcing God's Word to reveal it to them so that they might cease deceiving both themselves and the simple of heart and begin to "tremble." The New Testament often talks of the "rebirth" of man, variously described as a rebirth from "on high," "by the Spirit," "by the Word of God" . . . St. John describes it as a rebirth "not from human desire or human will but from God himself" (cf. Jn 1:13). Satan too, when God allows him to approach certain souls to tempt them, proposes a rebirth. This is in line with his habit of disguising the work of God. The evil one, therefore, proposes a rebirth to man, but a rebirth precisely, "of man's will," that is of himself, not of God. This rebirth consists in a clear-minded decision to give a new beginning to one's existence, freeing oneself of every sense of dependence and considering oneself absolute master of oneself. God's ways are mysterious and sometimes he allows the enemy to instill such thoughts even in souls dear to him, to purify their faith. Then something mysterious and tremendous takes place which some of these persons have described as a warning to us. Man's spirit lives for a moment as if it were testing (that is, without true consent or moral responsibility) the sinister excitement of satanic freedom. He feels an unlimited pride and power in himself; he has the sensation of being in another world of which he himself is the king. He feels that he can do anything. He understands the meaning of the expression used in the Gospel to describe the temptation of Jesus in the wilderness: "He led him to a height" (Lk 4:5). The soul feels, in fact, as if it were soaring above the world in a dimension that is purely interior but so vivid as to seem real and physical. It experiences a sort of ecstasy, though of a negative kind, that is not leading towards the light but towards darkness and the abyss. When the power of satanic suggestion ceases, the person, dumbfounded, asks himself: "What happened?" "What was it?" and in God's light discovers the deception; he understands that the evil one has once again lied and unmasked himself to his own damage. Rebirth of man's will is, in fact, a rebirth of man's fancy; it is, therefore, a fancy of rebirth, not a true rebirth. The creature, Satan included, may want this but he cannot put the wish into effect because no one can change the fact that his being comes from God even if he so wishes. So this fancy just increases Satan's desperation and the desperation of the one who, unfortunately, follows him in this. These words, in actual fact, reveal hell instead of eliminating it. The secret of hell is enclosed in these words which must be written somewhere in hell: "I exist and persist through the power of deception." His strength is in deception. He makes what is evil seem good, or he makes what is really evil seem of no importance, something inevitable that everyone does. He says, as he did to Eve: "You will not die, on the contrary. . . ," while he knows well that it is precisely death that will follow.

Another way of arrogantly eliminating the difference between Creator and creature, between God and the "self," is to . . . confuse them which is the form that impiety sometimes takes on today in Depth Psychology. What Paul reproached the "wise men" of his times with was not for studying nature and admiring its beauty, but for not going beyond this; in the same way the Word of God doesn't criticize certain trends in Depth Psychology for having discovered a new area of the human mind, the unconscious, and of trying to throw light on this, but of having yet again made of this discovery an occasion for getting rid of God. Thus, the Word of God renders a service to psychology purifying it of what threatens it, just as psychology in its turn, can be of use—and has effectively been so in many cases—in purifying our understanding of the Word of God.

The impiety harboured in some of the most recent trends of this science is the suppression of the distinction between good and evil. Following a procedure that closely recalls that of ancient heretical gnosis, the limits move dangerously: the limit of the divine lowers and the demonic limit rises to the point of meeting and even of being superimposed. Then, in evil, nothing else is seen except "the other side of reality" and in the devil nothing else but the "shadow of God." There are some who have even gone so far as to accuse Christianity of having introduced the "ill-omened opposition between good and evil" into the world. The following words of Isaiah could have been written today for just such a situation: *Woe to those who call what is bad, good, and what is good, bad, who substitute darkness for light and light for darkness* (Is 5:20). Depth psychologists don't give any importance to "saving the soul" (even considered ridiculous) and not even to "analysing the soul," but to "helping the soul fulfill itself," that is, to making it possible for the human soul—which is like saying natural man—to express itself in all ways, repressing nothing. Salvation lies in self-revelation, in man making himself and his psyche known for what they are; salvation lies in self-realization. More credibility and importance are given to dreams than to God's Word or to Church doctrine, to common sense or centuries of experience. Salvation—it is thought—is within, immanent in man. It doesn't come from history but from the archetype manifested in myth and symbol; in a certain sense, it comes from the unconscious. The unconscious, which at the beginning was considered to be the natural place of evil where neurosis and illusions are rooted (including the "illusion" of God) is now, through what would be a disconcerting evolution of any "science," seen as the seat of good, as a mine of hidden treasures for man. When the secular ideologies refuse, a priori, every revealed truth and every reference to God's Word, all they are doing is inconsistently wavering between an affirmation and its opposite, and thus, mixing error with truth they destroy what had been acquired. "Separating themselves from the truth—St. Irenaeus said of the ancient gnostics—they get themselves worked up about every error and allow themselves to be pushed about from pillar to post; depending on the occasion they have different ideas about the same topic, without ever having one fixed thought as they prefer to be sophists of the word rather than disciples of truth. They are not founded on the one rock, but on the sand" (St. Irenaeus, *Adv.Haer.* III, 24, 2). One day, after reading some works on Depth

Psychology which were full of the ideas just mentioned, shocked and quite terrified, I was wondering what God's judgement on all this could possibly be. Shortly after, as I was reading the Word of Jesus in John's Gospel, the answer struck me very clearly: *Though the light has come into the world people, have preferred darkness to the light* (Jn 3:19). The Holy Spirit has the power of convincing even the world of Depth Psychology of sin, a world so proud and neglectful of God, intoxicated as it is with its own novelty and success.

We have not yet, however, reached the bottom. The forms of impiety that have crept into philosophy and psychology are the most dangerous because every means of communication is used to spread them, supported in many places by political systems and are uncritically inculcated in schools and universities. They are dangerous because they touch the ideas and principles which are the crucial points in any culture and because they are enveloped with the prestige associated with the word "science" today, but they are not, in themselves, the most serious. There is much presumption in them and often they are totally ignorant of a true and genuine experience of faith. We are surrounded by something much more mysterious which is less disturbing simply because it remains hidden. Alongside the atheist's *intellectual* denial of God, who is convinced (sincerely or insincerely) that God doesn't exist, we have the *voluntary* denial of those who refuse God, even though they know that God exists and they challenge him openly saying: We will not submit! "Non serviam!" This extreme form of sin, which is hatred of God and blasphemy, is expressed in an open and threatening insult to God, in the loud proclamation, accompanied by abominable signs and gestures, of the superiority of evil over good, of darkness over light, of hatred over love, of Satan over God. This is all directly manoeuvred by Satan. Who else, in fact, would be able to harbour the thought that "good is a deviation of evil and, like all deviations, is of secondary importance and destined to disappear one day," or that "evil, in fact, is nothing but good ill-interpreted"? The most evident signs of this form of impiety are: the profanation of the Eucharist (the excessive and inhuman hatred towards the consecrated host is a terrible, negative proof of the "real presence" of Christ in the Eucharist for those who need it); the obscene and sarcastic parody of the stories and words of the Bible; the staging of the figure of Jesus in films and spectacles which are willfully blasphemous and offensive. The ultimate aim is the loss of souls and war against the Church. To send a soul to their infernal lord, these persons are capable of such constancy and use of means as only the holiest of missionaries would put into practice to lead a soul to Christ. I don't know what St. Paul was actually referring to when he wrote to the Ephesians: *For it is a shame even to speak of the things that they do in secret* (Ep 5:12); I know, however, that these words can be literally applied to the situation I'm describing.

On the other hand, this situation is not as remote as many christians might think; it is, rather, an open abyss only a stone's throw away from the indifference and "neutrality" in which they live. One starts with abandoning all religious practice and ends up, one sad day, among the openly declared enemies of God either by adhering to organizations whose aim (mostly kept secret at the beginning) is to make war against God and cause an upheaval in moral values, or through sexual aberrations or use of pornography, or following rash contacts with magicians, spiritists, esoteric societies or other such people. Magic is, in fact, another way and the most blatant, of succumbing to the old temptation of wanting to be "like God." "The hidden force which guides magic—as is written in one of their manuals—is the thirst for power. The magicians' aims are defined quite appropriately for the first time by the serpent in the garden of Eden. . . The eternal ambition of the follower of the black arts consists in gaining power over the whole universe and making a God of himself." The fact that in most cases we are dealing with charlatans and nothing more is of no importance. The irreverent intention behind its practice or with which one turns to it is sufficient to place one in Satan's power. Satan works through lies and bluffing but the effects are anything but imaginary. In the Bible God says: *There must never be anyone among you. . . who practises divination, who is soothsayer, augur or sorcerer, weaver of spells, consulter of ghosts or mediums, or necromancer. For anyone who does those things is detestable to the Lord your God* (Dt 18:10-12). In the prophet Isaiah we find this severe admonishment: The Lord will strike the country because it is "full of deviners from the east and of soothsayers" (cf. Is 2:6). Man has only the two licit means of nature and grace for gaining power over himself, over sickness, over events and business. *Nature* indicates intelligence, the sciences, medicine, technology and all the resources that man has received from God in creation to dominate the earth in obedience to him; *grace* indicates faith and prayer through which cures and miracles are sometimes obtained but always from God, because "power belongs to God" (Ps 62:12). When a third way is taken, that of the search of occult power, almost in secret from God, without needing his approval or indeed abusing his name and signs, then in one way or another the master and pioneer of this way comes on to the scene, he who one day said all the power of the earth had been handed over to him, for him to give to anyone he chose if they would worship him (cf. Lk 4:6). In these cases ruin is assured. The fly has got caught in the web of the "big spider" and will not easily manage to get out alive. Exactly what Paul pointed out is happening in our technological and secularized society: *Claiming to be wise, they became fools* (Rom 1:22): they abandoned faith to embrace every kind of superstition, even the most childish.

Not even those who live in God's house, priests, religious, monks and nuns are safe from this extreme form of impiety, which is contempt for God. One starts by taking certain "liberties" which soon become sacrilege and ends up in a state of deaf rebellion and battle against God. St. Bernard defines it as the "liberty to sin" and the "habit of sinning" and he describes it thus in a monk: "Since, on account of God's terrible judgement moral insensitivity follows the first sins, it happens that once pleasure has been experienced it is repeated and, once repeated, its attractions become even greater, concupiscence is aroused and reason lulled. . . The monk now only does what he enjoys doing, not what is licit as if there were no difference whatsoever; he can no longer control his mind, his hands or his feet from thinking, doing or seeking what is forbidden. He manipulates everything that comes into his head, to his lips or with which he is dealing and he talks of it to everybody and he does it; evil, empty-headed, dishonest" (St. Bernard; *De grad.hum.et super.*, XXI, 51; PL 182, 969). A psalm says: *Why take pride in being wicked, you champion in villany?* (Ps 52:1). Having arrived at this point, the obstinate man boasts of evil and even manages to derive glory from this, making it pass for sincerity and a refusal of hypocrisy without realizing that the ostentation of sin is even more serious than hypocrisy (cf. Is 3:9). In fact, in hiding his sin the hypocrite shows that he is still aware of the superiority of good over evil, he renders homage to virtue, while he who vaunts his sin shows that he has gone beyond this last barrier. His speech holds a subtle vein of accusal against God because of his "impossible" commandments which are contrary to man's happiness. All moral precepts volatilize into subtle distinctions so as to justify every liberty. He gets to the point of openly defending sin and sin itself is blamed on God who withholds his grace! All of this goes on ambiguously, he says one thing and then goes back on what has been said so that it is always possible to retract and avoid compromising himself to the point of having to face his responsibilities and give up a state in which he has, meanwhile, created all he desires.

3. The wages of sin

But let us also examine the outcome of impiety so that not even the slightest shadow of doubt remains in our minds that anyone can prevail against God. In the prophet Jeremiah we read these words addressed to God: *All who abandon you will be put to shame* (Jr 17:13). The abandonment of God leads to personal confusion and the feeling of having gone astray; anyone who wants to save his life will lose it, said Jesus (cf. Mt 16:25). "Lost" and "gone astray" are the words most frequently used in the Bible when sin is spoken of: the lost sheep, the lost son. . . The very word to translate the biblical concept of sin in greek, *hamartia*, contains the idea of being lost and having failed. The same term was used when speaking of a river that flows away from its original course and is lost in the marshes and of an arrow which misses its aim and is lost. Sin is therefore radical failure. A man can fail in many ways: as a husband, as a father or as a business man. A woman can fail as a wife or as a mother; a priest can fail in his parish, as a superior or as a spiritual director. But these are all relative failures; there is always the possibility of compensation; one may fail in all these ways and still be a most respectable person, even a saint. But it is not so with sin; through sin one fails as a creature, that is fundamentally, in what one "is" and not in what one "does."

This is the only case where the words of Jesus about Judas apply to a person: "It would have been better for that man if he had never been born" (Mt 26:24). Man, in sinning, believes he is offending God, whereas, in fact, he is "offending" and mortifying only himself, to his own shame: *Is it really me they spite*—God says—*is it not in fact themselves, to their own confusion?* (Jer 7:19). By refusing to glorify God, man himself becomes "deprived of the glory of God." Sin offends God, that is, it saddens him greatly, but only in so far as it brings death to man whom he loves; it wounds his love.

But let us try to take a closer look at the existential consequences of sin. St. Paul affirms that *the wages of sin is death* (Rm 6:23). Sin leads to death; not so much to the *act* of dying—which lasts only a moment—as to the *state* of death, that is precisely to what has been called "mortal illness," a state of chronic death. In this state the creature desperately tends to return to being nothing but without succeeding and lives therefore as if in an eternal agony. From this state comes damnation and the pains of hell; the creature is obliged by One stronger than himself to be what he doesn't accept to be, that is dependent on God, and his eternal torment is that he cannot get rid of either God or of himself (cf. S. Kierkegaard, *The Sickness unto Death*). Satan embodies this state. In him sin has run its entire course and is shown in its extreme consequences. He is the prototype of those "who do know God (and how he knew him!) but do not give him the glory and thanks that belong to God." It is not necessary to fall back on the imagination or on who knows what theological speculation to learn Satan's feelings on this point because, as I have already said, he himself shouts them into the hearts of those whom God still allows him to tempt today, as Jesus was tempted in the wilderness: "We are not free" he shouts, "we are not free! Even if you kill yourself, your soul lives on, you cannot kill it, we cannot say no. We are obliged to exist forever. It's all deceit! It's not true that God created us free!" Such thoughts make us shudder as it would seem that we are directly listening to some of the remarks of the eternal argument between Satan and God. He, in fact, would wish to be left free to return to nothingness. Does this perhaps mean that Satan wouldn't want to exist but to cancel himself out as God's antagonist thereby doing God and all those who love God a great favour? This is certainly not the case. It's true that he doesn't want to be what he is and would wish to be different; but not in the sense that he'd want to be good rather than bad (if this were the case, we'd be facing Satan's conversion, which, through God's infinite mercy, would immediately make him again an angel of light), but in the sense that he'd want to be independent of God, with no one above him to thank for what he is. He'd want to exist, but not "through the grace of another." However, notwithstanding all his efforts this will never be possible because that Power above him is stronger than he is and obliges him to exist. And this is the way to pure desperation. Kierkegaard rightly said that "the formula for all desperation is to desperately want to free ourselves of ourselves" (*op.cit.*). In choosing absolute autonomy from God, the creature is aware of the unhappiness and darkness involved but he is willing to pay this price because, as St. Bernard said, "he prefers to be unhappy in his own sovereignty rather than be happy in submission" ("misere praesse quam feliciter subesse," *De Grad.hum.* X, 36), thus proving that the much talked about eternity of hell doesn't depend on God, who is always ready to forgive, but on the person who doesn't want to be forgiven and would accuse God of lacking respect for his freedom if God did this.

We have, today, the chance of actually verifying through our own experience the results of sin by observing what is happening in our present society after the extreme consequences the refusal of God has led to in certain places. Nietzsche, for whom sin was nothing other than an ignoble "Jewish invention" and good and evil just simple "prejudices of God" (once again we are judging words and not intentions) said: "We have killed him; we are God's assassins!" But then, having perceived or personally experienced the evil results of this, the philosopher added: "What have we done by unlinking this earth of ours from the chain that links it to its sun? Where is it going now? Where are we going? Isn't ours an eternal descent? Backwards, sidewards, forward, from all sides? Aren't we perhaps wandering as if through an infinite nothingness?" (F. Nietzsche, *The Gay Science,* nr. 125). "To kill God is really the most horrific suicide." Death is really the wages of sin and the proof lies in present-day nihilism.

At the end of this journey into the world of impiety, the words of a psalm come to my mind which I now want to repeat, making them my own:

> I say to the boastful, "Do not boast,"
> And to the wicked, "Do not lift up your hand;
> Do not lift up your horn on high,
> Or speak with insolent neck . . ."
> For in the hand of the Lord there is a cup,
> With foaming wine well mixed;
> And he will pour a draught from it,
> And all the wicked of the earth
> Shall drain it down to the dregs (Ps 75:5-9)

4. "You are the man!"

What part do we believers play in this tremendous tirade we have just read? From what has been said so far, it would seem that we are in fact accusers. But let us listen carefully to what follows. I have already said that the Apostle's words would unmask not only the world in general but also each one of us personally and it is now time to see how the Word of God fulfills this second and most difficult undertaking.

The Bible narrates this story. King David had committed adultery and to cover it up he had had the woman's husband killed in war so that, to make this woman his wife could even have seemed an act of generosity on the king's part towards the man who had died fighting for him. A real chain of sins. The Lord then sent the prophet Nathan to him who told him a parable, although the king didn't know it was a parable. There were, he said, two men in a certain city, one rich and the other poor. The rich man had very many flocks and herds and the poor man had nothing but one little ewe lamb and it grew up with him and used to lie in his bosom...Now there came a traveller to the rich man, and instead of taking one of his own flock or herd he took the poor man's lamb and prepared it for the man who had come to him. On hearing this story David's anger was greatly kindled against the man and he said to

Nathan: "The man who has done this deserves to die!" Then Nathan said to David: "You are the man!" (cf. 2 Sam 12:1 ff.).

This is what the Apostle Paul is doing with us. After making us feel a righteous indignation and horror for the impiety of the world, as we pass from the first to the second chapter of his Letter, as if he were suddenly addressing us, he repeats: "You are the man!" *Therefore you have no excuse, O man, whoever you are, when you judge another; for in passing judgement upon him you condemn yourself, because you, the judge, are doing the very same things. We know that the judgement of God rightly falls upon those who do such things. Do you suppose, O man, that when you judge those who do such things and yet do them yourself, you will escape the judgement of God?* (Rom 2:1-3). The recurrence, at this point, of the word "inexcusable" (*anapologetos*), which was used earlier for the pagans, leaves us in no doubt as to St. Paul's intentions. While you were judging others, he says, you were bringing about your own condemnation. It is time now to turn the horror you feel for sin against yourself.

The "person judging" in the second chapter, turns out to be a Jew who, however, is here seen as a kind of stereotype. The "Jew" is a non-Greek, or a non-pagan (cf. Rom 2:9-10); he is the pious believer who, with his strong principles and revealed morality, judges the rest of the world and feels safe in doing so. In this sense each one of us is the "Jew." Origen actually said that in the Church the Apostle's words were intended for Bishops, Presbyters and Deacons, that is, for the guides and teachers (cf. Origen, *Comm.in ep.Rom.* II, 2; PG 14,873). Paul himself experienced it when, from being a pharisee he became a christian and can therefore confidently indicate to believers the way to abandon phariseeism. He unmasks the strange and frequent illusions of pious and religious people who consider themselves safe from God's anger just because they can clearly distinguish between good and evil, they know the law and, when necessary, they know how to apply it to others whereas, as far as they themselves are concerned, they think that the privilege of being on God's side or, at least, God's goodness and patience with which they are very familiar, makes an exception for them. It's like a father scolding one of his sons for something he has done, while another son, who has done the same thing, wanting to get himself into his father's good graces starts shouting at his brother. His father had been hoping that he would learn from his brother's mistake and his father's kindness and patience and rush to throw himself at his feet confessing that he too was guilty of the same thing, promising never to do it again. *Or do you presume*—says the Apostle to us—*upon the riches of his kindness and forbearance and patience? Do you not know that God's kindness is meant to lead you to repentance? But by your hard and impenitent heart you are storing up wrath for yourself on the day of wrath when God's righteous judgement will be revealed* (Rom 2:4-5). "Do you not know that God's kindness is meant to lead you to repentance? But by your hard and impenitent heart you are storing up wrath for yourself. . . !" What a shock it will be the day when you realize that this word of God is actually directed at you and that you are really the "you" mentioned! It's like a jurist who is totally concentrated in analyzing a past sentence which is standard. On taking a closer look he suddenly realizes that the sentence also applies to himself and is still effective. His state of mind undergoes a sudden change and he ceases to be so sure of himself. The Word of God is here engaged in a real and true *tour de force*. It must reverse the situation of the person dealing with it. There's no escape. It's necessary to "give way" and repeat with David: *I have sinned!* (2 Sam 12:13), before the heart is hardened again and impenitence reinforced.

The specific accusation the Apostle makes against the "pious" is that "they themselves are doing the exact same things" they judge others for. But in what sense? Is it that they materially do the exact same things? This is also sometimes true (cf. Rom 2:21-24); but he is especially talking about the essence which is impiety and idolatry. There is a masked form of idolatry at work in our present world. If it is idolatry "to bow down to the work of our hands" (cf. Is 2:8; Hos 14:4), if it is idolatry "to put the creature in the place of the Creator," then I am idolatrous whenever I put the creature—*my* creature, the work of *my* hands—in the Creator's place. My creature could be the home or the Church I have built, the family I have formed, the child I have given life to (how many mothers, even christian mothers, unconsciously make a God out of their children, especially out of an only child!); it could be the work I do, the school I direct, the book I write. . . Then there is my "self," the prince of idols. In fact, idolatry is always based on autolatry, self-worship, self-love, placing oneself first at the centre of the world sacrificing everything else to this. The "substance" is always impiety, the non-glorification of God, but always and only one's self. It is even making use of God for our own success and personal affirmation. If it is true, in fact, that often those who defend man's rights are actually defending their own rights, it is no less true that often those who defend God's rights and the rights of the Church are really defending themselves and their own interests. This is why even today "the name of God is blasphemed among the Gentiles" (cf. Rom 2:24). The sin St. Paul denounced in the "Jews" throughout the whole Letter was that they sought self-justice and self-glory and they did this even in their observance of God's law.

Perhaps, deep within myself, I am ready at this point to acknowledge the truth, to admit that so far I have lived "for myself," that I am also involved in the mystery of impiety. The Holy Spirit has "convinced me of sin." The ever new miracle of conversion is beginning for me. What should I do in such a delicate situation? Let us open the Bible and intone the "De Profundis": *Out of the depths I cry to thee, O Lord* (Ps 130). The "De Profundis" wasn't written for the dead but for the living: the "depths" from which the psalmist cries is not a reference to Purgatory but to sin: *If thou, O Lord, shouldst mark iniquities, Lord who could stand?* It is written that Christ "in the Spirit went and preached to the spirits in prison" (cf. 1 Pt 3:19) and commenting on this one of the Fathers of the Church said: "When you hear that Christ, going down to the Hades, freed the souls who were prisoners there, do not think that these things are far removed from what is being done now. Believe me, the heart is a tomb (Macarius of Egypt, *De lib. ment.* 116; PG 34,936): We are now spiritually in the position of the "spirits in prison" who awaited in the Hades the coming of the Saviour and who the traditional icon of the Resurrection shows desperately outstretching their hands to grasp the right hand of Christ who is coming with his cross to snatch them from prison. Let us also raise a cry from the deep prison of our sinful "self" in which we are kept prisoners. The psalm we are saying is full of confident trust and expectation: *In his word I hope . . . My soul waits for the Lord more than watchmen for the morning . . . He will redeem Israel from all his iniquities.* We already know that help exists, that there is a remedy for our ills because "God loves us." So while we are shaken by God's Word, let us remain calm and confidently say to God: *For thou dost not give me up to sheol, or let thy godly one see the pit* (Ps 16:10).

III. The Righteousness of God Has Been Manifested!

Justification by faith

A writer, who was also a believer and a poet, told in the third person of the greatest act of faith of his life. A man, he said, had three children and one sad day all three fell ill. His wife was so worried that she became closed in herself and was unable to do anything. She no longer even spoke. But he was different. He was a man and he wasn't afraid to talk. He had realized that the situation could no longer go on as it was. So he acted on a stroke of genius. Looking back he was even full of praise for himself. It really had been a bold stroke of genius. Just as one would pick up three children and put them into their mother's or their nurse's arms who, delighted, would exclaim that there were too many of them to hold all at once, so he, taking his courage into his hands, had trustingly placed, in prayer, his three sick children in the arms of her who holds all the sufferings of the world. "Here, he said, take them and I'm going to turn and go away so that you can't give them back to me. You can well see that I no longer want them!" How pleased he was with himself that he had had that stroke of genius! From that day on all went well because it was the Blessed Virgin who was looking after the children. It's strange that not all christians behave in the same way. It's so simple really but we never seem to think of the simple things. We may as well admit at once that we are quite silly (cf. Ch. Péguy, *Le porche*, pp. 557 ff.).

I have started with this story because in this chapter we too are invited by God's Word to act on a similar stroke of genius in faith.

1. God Has Acted

St. Paul describes man under the law of sin. In reading the first two and a half chapters of the Letter to the Romans one has the impression of walking under a gloomy and threatening sky. But later on, at a certain point, at precisely verse 21 of chapter three, there is an unexpected change in tone, introduced by the adversative and temporal expression: *But now. . .* The atmosphere changes. It's as if the clouds have suddenly lifted and the sun has broken forth again. *The righteousness of God has been manifested!* (Rom 3:21): this is the sun that has appeared to illuminate the darkness of sin, this is what is new. It's not that men have suddenly changed their way of life and started doing good; no, the new thing is that God has acted and his action has fulfilled the times: *When the time had fully come, God sent forth his Son* (Gal 4:4) and when God sent his Son, the fullness of time came! It's not the time that determines God's action; it is God, through his action, who determines the time. The new fact is, therefore, that God has acted; he has broken his silence and is the first to stretch out his hand to sinful man. This "action" of God is a mystery that fills heaven and earth with joy and wonder each time it takes place: *Sing, O heavens, for the Lord has done it; shout O depths of the earth!* (Is 44:23). God had declared these things of old. All the prophets spoke of them; he suddenly did them and they came to pass (cf. Is 48:3).

But what does this "action" of God consist of? Let us listen to what the Apostle says: *Since all have sinned and fall short of the Glory of God, they are justified by his grace as a gift, through the redemption which is in Jesus Christ, whom God put forward as an expiation by his blood to be received by faith. This was to show God's righteousness, because in his divine forbearance he had passed over former sins; it was to prove at the present time that he himself is righteous and that he justifies him who has faith in Jesus* (Rom 3:23-26). God shows his righteousness while showing mercy! This is the great revelation, God's "revenge" on sinful man. The Apostle says that God is "just and justifying," that is, he is just with himself when he justifies man. In fact, God is love and mercy and that's why he is just with himself, showing himself as he really is, when he is merciful.

But none of this would mean a thing to us if we didn't understand what the expression "God's justice" means exactly. There's a risk that a person on hearing God's justice being spoken of but not knowing its exact significance, might feel dismayed rather than encouraged and think to himself: "It's what was to be expected. After God's wrath, now his justice is revealed, that is, his just punishment!" It was Luther who discovered or better still, rediscovered, that the expression "God's justice" doesn't indicate, in this context, his punishment or, worse still, his revenge against man but that on the contrary it indicates the act by which God makes man just. (Luther really said "declares" just and not "makes" just because he was thinking of an extrinsic and forensic justification, but not many agree with him today, even among protestants). Later he wrote: "When I discovered this I felt a new man and it seemed that the doors of paradise were opened wide to me" (*Pref. Latin Works*, Weimar Ed., 54, p. 186).

The "gospel," that is the good news St. Paul carries to the christians of Rome is, therefore, this: now God's benevolence has been manifested to men, that is, his good will towards man, his forgiveness; in a word, his grace. It is Scripture itself which thus explains the concept of "God's justice": *When the goodness and loving kindness of God our Saviour appeared, he saved us, not because of deeds done by us in righteousness, but in virtue of his own mercy* (Tit 3:4-5). To say "the righteousness of God has appeared" is like saying: the goodness and loving kindness of God has appeared.

2. Justification and Conversion

We should now be capable of discovering Paul's source on this point, of discovering another voice behind his, another kerygma or cry of which his is only a faithful echo. He says that "the Gospel is the power of God to everyone who has faith" (Rom 1:16). He talks of the "time" of divine patience which has been "fulfilled" (Rom 3:25 f.), of God's righteousness that has appeared. . . What and who do these words remind us of? They remind us of Jesus who, at the beginning of his ministry, went about proclaiming: *The time is fulfilled and the kingdom of God is at hand; repent and believe in the Gospel* (Mk 1:15). Paul transmits the teaching of Jesus in its purest form, the same terms and the same concepts: the time, the Gospel, faith. What Jesus encloses in the expression "God's kingdom" and, that is, God's saving initiative, his free action of salvation in favour of man, St. Paul calls "God's justice" but he is dealing with the same fundamental reality, the same action of God. "God's kingdom" and "God's righteousness" are brought together by Jesus himself when he says: *Seek first the kingdom of God and his righteousness* (Mt 6:33).

When Jesus said: "Repent and believe in the Gospel," he was already teaching justification through faith. Before Jesus, repentance always meant "going back," as the term used in Hebrew, *shub,* for the same action indicates. It signified going back to the broken covenant through a renewed observance of the law. In the prophet Zechariah the Lord says: "Return from your evil ways and your evil deeds" (Zech 1:3-4; cf. also Jer 8:4-5). Consequently, repentance mainly has an ascetic, moral and penitential significance and is achieved above all by changing one's way of life. Repentance is seen as a condition for salvation: repent and you will be saved, repent and salvation will be yours. This is the predominant significance of the word repentance even on the lips of John the Baptist (cf. Lk 3:4-6). But on the lips of Jesus this moral significance becomes of secondary importance (at least at the beginning of his ministry) with respect to a new, hereto unknown significance. With the coming of the Messiah, God's promise has been fulfilled: *Remember not the former things, nor consider the things of old. Behold, I am doing a new thing; now it springs forth, do you not perceive it?* (Is 43:18-19). Only on the lips of Jesus could the word repentance take on a new meaning addressed more to the future than to the past; only with him, in fact, did the barycentre of history move so that the most important thing is no longer in the past but ahead of man.

There are people today who believe that, where the Jews are concerned, we shouldn't talk of conversion as it is not necessary for the

Jews who become believers to renounce anything of their past history but to take a step forward. For the same reason they believe we shouldn't talk of "conversion" where St. Paul is concerned. But this is a misunderstanding of the meaning of conversion. Conversion, in the evangelical sense (for example in Mk 1:15), not only doesn't exclude the Jews but is directly addressed to them because in this context conversion doesn't mean to abandon something but, rather, to enter the Kingdom, to believe in Jesus and pass to the new covenant without abandoning the old one. It means exactly, therefore, to take a step forward. In fact, in the text "convert and believe in the Gospel" it is to the Jews and not to the pagans that Jesus is talking. In the preaching to the pagans after Easter, conversion will come to mean "turning to God from idols, to serve a living and true God" (cf. 1 Thess 1:9), or "to turn from the power of Satan to God" (cf. Acts 26:18). It is true that in this sense the concept of conversion doesn't apply to the Jews and to Paul, but it does apply in the primitive meaning the word had on the lips of Jesus, that is, in its true evangelical sense.

To be converted doesn't therefore mean to go back to the old covenant and the observance of the law; it means to take a step forward and enter the new covenant, to accept this Kingdom that has appeared and enter into it by faith. "Convert and believe" are not two different things succeeding one another; they are the same action: repent, that is, believe; convert believing! Conversion and salvation have changed places. It's no longer: *sin - conversion - salvation* ("convert and you will be saved; convert and salvation will be yours"), but: *sin - salvation - conversion* ("convert because you are saved; because salvation is yours"). We have God's action first and then man's answer, not vice versa. It was exactly on this point that the Scribes and the Pharisees, who were the adversaries of the preaching of Jesus, stumbled: *For, being ignorant of the righteousness that comes from God, and seeking to establish their own, they did not submit to God's righteousness* (Rom 10:3). God himself took the initiative in salvation: he made his Kingdom come; man has only to accept, in faith, God's offer and then live as is required of him. It's as if a king opens the doors of his palace where a sumptuous banquet has been prepared and, standing on the threshold, he invites those passing by to enter saying: "Come in, everything is ready!"

"Convert and believe" therefore means to pass from the old covenant based on the law to the new covenant based on faith. The Apostle says the same thing in his doctrine on justification by faith. The only difference is due to what had come about in the meantime between the preaching of Jesus and that of Paul: Christ had been rejected and put to death for man's sins. Faith "in the Gospel" ("believe in the Gospel"), now appears as faith "in Jesus Christ," "in his blood" (Rom 3: 25).

Faith, therefore, is the first fundamental conversion. Through it we enter into the Kingdom. If you had been told: the door to the Kingdom is innocence, the door is the strict observance of the commandments, the door is this or that virtue, you could have found excuses and said: It's not for me! I'm not innocent, I haven't got that virtue. But you are being told: the door is faith. Believe! This is not something above or beyond you, it is not so far removed from you. On the contrary, *the word is near you, on your lips and in your heart, that is, the word of faith which we preach; because, if you confess with your lips that Jesus is Lord and believe in your heart that God raised him from the dead, you will be saved* (Rom 10:8-9).

However, St. Paul strongly insists on one thing: all this comes about "gratuitously" (*doreàn*), through grace, as a gift; he comes back to this point numerous times using different terms. And we wonder why God is so determined on this point! It's because he wants to exclude from the new creation the canker that ruined the first creation: man's boasting. *Then what becomes of our boasting? It is excluded . . . For we hold a man is justified by faith apart from works of law* (Rom 3:27-28). Again Paul says that we have been saved by grace through faith; this is not by our own doing, it is the gift of God, not because of works, *lest any man should boast* (Eph 2:8-9). Man hides in his heart the innate tendency to "pay God his price." But "no man can ransom himself or give to God the price of his life" (Ps 49:8). To want to pay God his price through our own merits is another form of the never ending effort to be autonomous and independent of God, and not just autonomous and independent but actually God's creditors because "to one who works, his wages are not reckoned as a gift but as his due" (Rom 4:4). But *who has given a gift to him that he might be repaid?* (Rom 11:35).

What the Apostle expresses through the adverb "gratuitously," Jesus expressed in another way through the image of a child and so once again we see the perfect consonance that exists between the two proclamations of Jesus and of Paul. Jesus said we must receive the Kingdom "like a child" (cf. Mk 10:15). To receive the Kingdom like a child means to receive it gratuitously, as a free gift and not through merit. One day when the disciples were discussing about "who was the greatest in the Kingdom of heaven," that is about which of them could claim the most rights to occupy the highest place, Jesus called a child to him, put him in the midst of them and said that unless they turned and became like children, they would never enter the kingdom of heaven (cf. Mt 18:1-3). Children instinctively know the difference between merit and privilege and they would never renounce their privilege of being children for the merit. They certainly ask their parents for what they need: bread, a book, a toy, not because they have brought home a salary or think they have earned it, but simply because they know they are loved. They take advantage of, and sometimes even speculate on the fact that they are children and therefore heirs to everything. This doesn't cancel out the idea of merit or reward or even that of virtue or commitment or mortification and all the rest that is clearly indicated in the Gospel. It's a question of placing it in the right order not as the cause of salvation but as the effect of salvation, as something that must spring from faith. The merits are like coins a parent might secretly place in a child's pocket so that he will be able to buy a little present for his father on Father's day. The Council of Trent stated that "such was God's mercy towards man as to consider merits of ours what, in fact, are gifts of his" (DS, 1548).

Let us therefore leave the preoccupation of our merits to God while, nevertheless, doing all the good we can. Scripture says that God casts all our sins behind his back (cf. Is 38:17). Let us cast all our merits behind our backs. God casts all our sins behind his back and keeps, instead, all our good actions in front of him including that of a glass of water given to the poor (cf. Tob 12:12; Acts 10:4). Let us cast all our good actions behind our backs and keep our sins in front of us. The more we keep our sins in front of us the more God casts them behind him; the more we cast our good works behind us, the more God keeps them in front of him.

From where did St. Paul obtain his Gospel of "the free gift" of justification "through faith" which is so much in harmony with that of Jesus? He didn't obtain it from the book of the Gospel (it hadn't yet been written) but probably from the spoken tradition of the preaching of Jesus and especially from his own personal experience, that is, from how God had acted in his life. He himself affirms this saying that he didn't learn of the Gospel he was preaching (the Gospel of justification in faith!) from men but by revelation of Jesus Christ and he relates this revelation to the event of his own conversion (cf. Gal 1:11 f.). It could be said that in his Letter to the Romans, the Apostle doesn't do other than state in general terms applicable to all, the drama of his own conversion. Writing to the Philippians, he presents his conversion as a passing from "his own righteousness based on the law" to "a righteousness from God that depends on faith" (Phil 3:9). When reading the description St. Paul gives of his conversion in this text, I see the image of a man walking through a wood at night lit by the faint light of a candle. He is very careful not to let the candle go out because he depends on it to see his way. But as he goes on walking, dawn breaks. The sun appears on the horizon and his little light becomes fainter and fainter until he no longer realizes he is carrying it and throws it away. This is what happened to Paul. His little candle was his own justice, a miserable burnt out wick despite his high-sounding attributes: circumcised on the eighth day, of the people of Israel, a Hebrew, a Pharisee and blameless in his observance of the law. . . (cf. Phil 3:5-6). One fine day the sun also appeared on the horizon of Saul's life—the "Sun of righteousness," which, in this text, he calls with boundless devotion "Jesus Christ my Lord." From then on he saw his own righteousness as "loss," as "refuse" and no longer wanted "to be found with a righteousness of his own" but with that which depends on faith. God first made him dramatically experience what he was calling him to reveal to the Church.

3. Faith as Appropriation

As I have said, the key to everything is faith. But there are different
kinds of faith: there is faith as assent of the intellect, faith as confidence
and faith as stability, as Isaiah calls it (7:9). Which type of faith is involved where justification "in faith" is concerned? It's a special kind of
faith: faith as appropriation, the kind that makes the "stroke of genius"
possible. On this point St. Bernard says: "What I can't obtain by myself,
I appropriate to myself (*usurpo!*) with confidence from the pierced side
of the Lord because he is full of mercy. The mercy of God is, therefore,
my merit. So if great is the mercy of the Lord (Ps 119:156), I too will
abound in merit. And what about *my* righteousness? O Lord, I shall
remember only *your* righteousness. It is also mine because you are God's
righteousness for me" (*In Cant.* 61, 4-5; PL 183, 1072). In fact, it is written that God made Jesus Christ "our wisdom, our righteousness and
sanctification and redemption" (1 Cor 1:30). God himself urges us to
"profit" by his Son's passion. To a person, regretfully thinking of her
past life and saying: "Father, these are my empty hands!," the infinitely
tender voice of the Father answered within her: "Stretch out your hands
beneath the Cross and they will be filled with the most precious blood of
Christ!"

It is true that "we never think of the simplest things"! This is the
simplest and clearest thing of the New Testament but how hard it is to
discover it! It's usually discovered at the end and not at the beginning of
the spiritual life. It's like the discovery of certain laws in physics: experiments upon experiments are required to reach a conclusion on a certain principle which, in the end, turns out to be the simplest and most
elementary of all. After all, it's a question of simply saying "yes!" to
God. God had created man free so that man could freely accept life and
grace and accept himself as the beneficiary of God's grace and love. God
was only waiting for man's "yes"; instead he received a "no." Now God
offers man a second chance, like a second creation; he presents Christ as
expiation and asks man: "Will you live in his grace, in him?" To believe
means to answer: "Yes, I will!" And immediately you are a new crea-

tion, richer than the first; you are "created in Christ Jesus" (cf. Eph 2:10).

This is the stroke of genius I mentioned earlier on and it's really amazing to see how few people are prepared to make use of it. Its reward is "eternal life" and the way to gain it is "to believe." St. Cyril of Jerusalem, one of the Fathers of the Church, thus expressed this stroke of luck in faith: "O the wonderful goodness of God towards men! The just men of the Old Testament were acceptable to God for the fatigue of many years; but what they managed to obtain through a long and heroic service acceptable to God, is granted to you by Jesus in a brief space of time. For, if you believe that Jesus Christ is Lord and that God raised him from the dead, you will be saved and led into Paradise by him who led the good thief there" (*Cat.* 5, 10; PG 33, 517). Other Fathers tell us to imagine there has been an important wrestling match in a stadium. A brave man has fought against a cruel tyrant and with tremendous effort and suffering has defeated him. You didn't have to fight, you neither struggled nor got wounded. But if you admire the brave man, if you rejoice in his victory, if you make garlands for him, provoke and excite the crowd for him, joyfully bow to the victor and shake his hand—if, all told, you become so delirious as to consider his triumph yours, you will surely participate in the victor's reward. Moreover, let us suppose the victor doesn't need the prize he has won but longs to see his friend honoured and considers the crowning of his friend to be his prize, will that man not receive the crown without having fought or been wounded? Certainly he will! Well then, that's what takes place between Christ and us. Even though we haven't yet struggled or fought, even if no merit is ours yet, nevertheless, through faith we extol Christ's battle, praise his victory, honour his trophy which is the cross and show deep and ineffable love for him; we make his wounds and death ours (cf. St. John Cris., *De Coemet.*; PG 49, 396 and N. Cabasilas, *Life in Christ*, I,5; PG 150, 517).).

But what is this faith to which such great things are promised? In the Letter to the Hebrews there is a whole chapter dedicated to praising the faith of the ancient Fathers who, *through faith conquered kingdoms, en-*

forced justice, received promises, stopped the mouths of lions, quenched raging fire. . . , won strength out of weakness (Heb 11:33 f.). But it ends telling us that *God had foreseen something better for us* (11:40); something even greater to give us in exchange for our faith: himself! There would no longer be transitory things or earthly "kingdoms" but the kingdom of God and his righteousness! Faith is truly one of the most beautiful inventions of God's wisdom. Through it the finite reaches the infinite, the creature reaches God. By faith the Jews "crossed the Red Sea as if on dry land" (Heb 11:29); but what was this first exodus in comparison to the exodus carried out through faith in Christ? By it we pass from the kingdom of darkness to that of light, from the visible to the invisible. God created freedom thinking of faith, that is to make faith possible. Only in faith, when man believes, is freedom fully exercised. Only God knows the value of a creature's free act of faith because only God knows what he himself is worth. Scripture says the same of faith as it does of God himself, namely that it is omnipotent. *With God nothing will be impossible* (Lk 1:37) and again *All things are possible to him who believes* (Mk 9:23). We can therefore realize why God ran the risk of sin to make faith possible.

The divine nature of faith is revealed by the fact that it is practically endless. We can never go far enough in believing: it's always possible to believe still more. All God's grace is at work in leading man to an ever deeper and purer faith, to lead him "through faith for faith" (Rom 1:17), that is from one degree of faith to a more perfect degree, from a faith with signs to a faith without signs. As soon as a believer has overcome some obstacle in faith, God wastes no time in placing a greater obstacle in front of him, and then a still greater one, knowing what reward he is preparing for him with his other hand, until he asks of man what is (humanly speaking) impossible: a leap in the dark. The same thing happens with faith as with the high jump in athletics: at every successful jump, the pole is raised a little higher and so the previous record is continuously beaten even though the final record can still not be foreseen. This wonderful invention of faith by God never fails to amaze us. The glory of heaven, for example, that of Mary, is like a majestic tree rich in branches and fruit but it has grown from a small seed cultivated in the earth and this seed is faith. Imagine what we would do if one day an expert in this field were to give us a little box containing a small seed assuring us that it was the only one of its kind in the world which would produce a very rare tree that would make the owner very rich! How we would protect it and shelter it from the wind . . . That's what we must do with our faith; it is a seed that produces "the fruit of eternal life"!

4. "Behold, now is the acceptable time!"

St. Paul's teaching on justification by faith begins with an adverb of time: *"now."* The adverb "now" has three different levels of meaning: historic, sacramental and moral. It refers, in fact, first of all to the time when Christ died on the cross for us, that is, to the historic event when our redemption was accomplished; secondly, it refers to the moment of Baptism when the christian was "washed, sanctified and justified" (cf. 1 Cor 6:11); finally, it refers to the present moment, to this day of our existence. This latter significance is the one the Apostle is emphasizing when he exclaims to the Corinthians: *Behold, now is the acceptable time; behold, now is the day of salvation* (2 Cor 6:2). At this level "now" literally means now, the moment we are living.

Therefore, concerning justification by faith, there is something that must be done now, at once; something that I, and not another in my place, must do and without which all the best and deepest considerations on this problem would be left hanging in the air. Justification by faith is the beginning of the supernatural life but it is not a beginning quickly succeeded by other things following one after the other. It is a beginning that is always relevant and that must constantly be confronted and re-established. It is always God who "loves us first" and who justifies us first (not just once, at the beginning), so it must always be man who believes and who allows himself to be justified as a free gift. But in this continuity there can be more or less intense moments corresponding to moments of reawakening of man's faith and gratitude. We are here at this present moment not only to understand *a posteriori* what took place in us one day through Baptism but to relive it, so that our faith may become deeper in meaning.

A Father of the 4th century wrote these extraordinarily up-to-date "existential" words: "For every man the beginning of life is the moment when Christ was immolated for him. But Christ is immolated for him at the moment he acknowledges grace and becomes conscious of the life obtained for him by means of that immolation" (*Easter Homily* from the Early Church, *S.Ch. 36, p. 59 f.*). Therefore, all of this, the death of Christ and Baptism, becomes real and true for us the moment we become conscious of it, confirm it and rejoice and give thanks for it. It could be now, at this very moment, if we so wish. One day the tax collector went up into the temple to pray and during his short prayer something happened for which he "went down to his house justified" (cf. Lk 18:14). All he had to do was to say in all sincerity of heart: *God, be merciful to me a sinner!* We too can return home justified after a moment of intense prayer or after making a confession in which we have managed to say with deep conviction the same words: "God, be merciful to me a sinner!" It's a question of not doing as the Pharisee did, of not thinking that everything is all right and that our conscience is clear on this point. Luther remarked that: "There are those who take these words concerning grace lightly and rashly say: Who doesn't know that there is nothing good in us without grace? And they believe they really understand these things. Worse still, when asked if they consider their own righteousness to be a trifle, they immediately exclaim: Of course, I'm sure of it! It's a pitiful and serious blindness that they rate their level of perfection so highly, whereas they really haven't got the slightest understanding of perfection and do not savour it. How could a man be more full of pride than he who dares to claim he is free from all pride and evil inclinations?" (*The Seven Penitential Psalms*, Ps 143; Weimar edit., 1, p. 219f.).

Therefore, I can return home with the greatest reward that exists: justified by faith, that is made just, forgiven, saved, made a new creature. God's word, which cannot be false, assures me of this. I could have such a stroke of genius that I'd be able to be pleased with myself for ever. I can again place my sins in the arms of Christ on the cross just like the man who placed his three sick children in the arms of the Blessed Virgin and then ran straight away for fear of having to take them back. So I can present myself to the Father and say: "Now look upon me Father, look upon me because I am your Jesus! His justice is upon me; 'He has clothed me with the robe of righteousness' (Is 61:10). As Christ 'has put on my iniquity,' I have put on his sanctity, I have put on Christ!" (Gal 3:27). May God rejoice again in his creatures, *laetetur Dominus in operibus suis!*

God looks upon his creation and sees that it is "very good" again, thanks to the sacrifice of Christ, his Son. Man's boasting "has been excluded," yet there is something man can boast of: he can boast of the Lord: *Let him who boasts, boast of the Lord* (1 Cor 1:31). To be able to boast of the Lord! What boast can be greater than this? Who can be so foolish as to want to exchange this reason for boasting with his own righteousness? O yes, we shall boast of you, Lord. For ever!

IV. He Was Put to Death for Our Trespasses

A meditation on the passion of Christ

The fourth chapter of the Letter to the Romans is devoted to illustrating the case of Abraham which St. Paul considered to be the most exemplary case, before Christ, of justification through faith. The Letter ends with a solemn profession of faith in the Lord Jesus *who was put to death for our trespasses and raised for our justification* (Rom 4:25). This is one of the most "classical" texts on the *kerygma* to be found in the whole of the New Testament. The same original nucleus of faith is to be found, with slight variations, in several parts of the Letter, like an underlying rock that emerges here and there on the surface of the earth: in chapter six, where Baptism is spoken of (Rom 6:3 ff.); in chapter eight where it is said that "it is Christ, who died, yes, who was raised from the dead, who is at the right hand of God" (Rom 8:34) and again towards the end of the Letter where we read that "for to this end Christ died and lived again, that he might be Lord both of the dead and of the living" (Rom 14:9). It is the earliest content of tradition which the Apostle says he himself received from others (cf. 1 Cor 15:3) and which therefore takes us back to the very first years of the Church.

This is really the "gospel" the Apostle was referring to at the beginning of the Letter when, stating the theme of the whole Letter, he says: *I am not ashamed of the gospel: it is the power of God for salvation to every one who has faith* (Rom 1:16). In fact, to Paul the Gospel is essentially the news of salvation which centres on the cross and resurrection of Christ. There exists an almost perfect correspondence in meaning between the beginning of the Letter to the Romans and that of the Letter to the Corinthians: *For the word of the cross is folly to those who are perishing, but to us who are being saved it is the power of God* (1 Cor 1:18). The word "Gospel" used in Romans corresponds here to "the word of the cross," "ashamed" corresponds to "folly" and "everyone who has faith" to "who are being saved," while the expression "power of God" remains the same in both texts.

We have therefore reached a crucial point in our journey of re-evangelization. So far the Apostle has shown us *how* from the state of sin and privation of the glory of God in which we find ourselves, we can be saved, that is gratuitously, by faith; but he has not yet explicitly talked to us about salvation itself and the event that made salvation possible. We now know that justification comes from faith but where does faith come from? Where can we find the necessary strength to make that bold "stroke" of genius mentioned in the last chapter? And can he who realizes he has not yet made it still hope to do so? The chapters that follow in the Letter to the Romans help us to find the answers to these questions. Their aim is "to develop this message of justification by faith obtained for us by Christ's work of salvation. . . , explaining the *event* of justification by faith with reference to the gifts it offers" (H. Schlier, *op.cit.*). (These gifts, as we shall see, are essentially two: the negative one of freedom from sin and the positive one of the gift of the Holy Spirit).

We must now follow the Apostle along this decisive stretch of our journey. If we really want to evangelize or re-evangelize ourselves, now is the time to do so, opening ourselves to the central message of the Gospel in all its newness and power and that is to the death and resurrection of Christ. It is not, as we know, a synthesis of the whole Gospel which would be the result of a continual summing up of events; it is the original seed from which all the rest springs. At the beginning there was the *kerygma* as we find it in those short expressions that were absorbed here and there into the apostolic writings. The Gospels, as we know them, didn't exist yet. They were compiled later on to "support" this essential news and illustrate its historic background made up of the words and earthly works of Jesus.

In this spirit let us set about meditating first of all the death of Christ and then his resurrection. Just as the neophytes, on the week after Easter, joyfully returned all dressed in white to their Bishop to listen to his mystagogic catechesis, that is to the explanation of the great mysteries of the faith, so let us return to the Church, not a week but perhaps years after our Baptism, so that we too may be initiated into the great mysteries. It was on talking to the neophytes, on a similar occasion to this that the author of Peter's first Letter exclaimed those words which still hold for us: *Like newborn babes, long for the spiritual milk, that by it you may grow up to salvation* (1 Pet 2:2).

1. The Passion of Christ's Soul

It is written that "no one comprehends the thoughts of God except the Spirit of God" (cf. 1 Cor 2:11). Now, the Passion of Christ is a secret of God's and one of the most unfathomable of his secrets known only to the Spirit that was "in him" and to no one else either in heaven or on earth. If anyone else claimed to understand it, one might say: "Are you the one who suffered?" When suffering is just in the telling it is already no longer suffering. Let us therefore entrust ourselves to the Holy Spirit and humbly ask him to grant us some insights into the person of Christ and savour at least a small part of it.

The proclamation of Christ's death, given briefly at the end of chapter four of the Letter, is taken up again and developed immediately after in chapter five with the words: *While we were yet helpless, at the right time Christ died for the ungodly. Why, one will hardly die for a righteous man—though perhaps for a good man one will dare even to die. But God shows his love for us in that while we were yet sinners Christ died for us* (Rom 5:6-8). How does the Apostle speak of the Passion in this text and in general in his Letter to the Romans? At a first glance he would seem to be talking about it in a purely objective way, almost as an outsider considering it as a given fact which is summed up in a few words that have become more or less conventional, such as, "cross," "death," "blood." We—the Apostle says—are now justified "by his *blood*," reconciled "by the *death* of his Son" (Rom 5:9 ff.), in peace "by the *blood* of his cross" (Col 1:20). Christ "died for the ungodly," "for us," the Apostle states concisely (Rom 5:6-8), without dwelling upon how and in what circumstance he died or upon the price of such a death to his humanity. But such a detached way of speaking about the passion is so only in appearance due to the bare style of the *kerygma* which the Apostle closely keeps to when talking of the passion. In the matter of fact, it is precisely St. Paul who begins to open the "hard shell" of the facts and events and lays stress on the more subjective and dramatic aspects of Christ's passion. A little further on he affirms that God *condemned sin in the flesh* (meaning Christ's flesh) (Rom 8:3), thus immediately showing the real protagonists and terms of the passion: God, sin and, in-between, Jesus! Jesus appears as the "cursed one": *For our sake he made him to be sin who knew no sin* (2 Cor 5:21); Christ himself became "a curse for us" (Gal 3:13).

Such affirmations unexpectedly give us a different view of things. They open new and unfathomable horizons on the passion based on the words and deeds of Christ's life on earth which, as such, later become part of the gospel story of the passion even if, at Paul's time, these still circulated only in the spoken form. There exists a passion of Christ's soul which is . . . the soul of passion, that is, what gives the passion its unique and transcendent value. Others suffered the afflictions of the body that Christ suffered and maybe even worse. At any rate there's no doubt that, from the physical point of view, if we put together all the pain suffered by all men throughout the centuries, it would be greater than the pain Jesus took on to himself, whereas from the moral point of view all the suffering and sorrows together of all men will never equal the passion of the Redeemer's soul, of which they are themselves but a small part. In fact, he *has borne our griefs and carried our sorrows* (Is 53:4). On a physical level the difference between our suffering and that of Christ is only quantitative but where the soul is concerned, the difference is qualitative. We are dealing with a different type of suffering, that of the man-God, even if it is true that the physical suffering, suffered as it was by the person of the Word, was of infinite value.

In the past, christian piety dwelt much more on the bodily suffering than on the spiritual suffering of Christ. This was due to certain precise factors which conditioned the development of faith and devotion right from the start. Against the heresy of Docetism the Fathers of the Church had to insist energetically on the reality and possibility of the body of Christ. On the other hand, in fighting the Arian heresy which denied the divinity of Christ, they had to be careful not to place too much emphasis on the sufferings of Christ's soul (ignorance of the parousia, distress and fear) as this seemed to compromise the full divinity of the Word considered to be closely bound to the soul and at times even constitutive itself of Christ's soul. It was as if a veil was drawn over the most disturbing aspects of the passion. To explain these aspects recourse was made to the idea of "concession" (*dispensatio*) or divine pedagogy, according to which Christ was mainly preoccupied with teaching us how we ourselves should act in similar circumstances. In the East, where the consequences of Arianism were stronger, this initial approach was very rarely overcome and consideration of the glory of the resurrection always prevailed over the shame of the passion which was avoided even in the representations of Christ on the cross.

Today we can read the New Testament free from these preoccupations and thus understand something more concerning the "word of the cross." Certain aspects of modern thinking can also be of help to us, such as the stress that is placed today on the idea of subject and of existence. In fact suffering is more a part of the person than of nature, it has more to do with existence than with essence. Depth psychology can also indirectly be a help to us as it provides a more adequate means of analysis of the passion of the Saviour's soul than do metaphysics, physics or medicine. This new science is at least capable of attempting to see into that hidden part of the person that the Bible calls "the point of division of soul and spirit," of "joint and marrow" of the being (Heb 4:12).

We are not however the first to do this. Saints and mystics, especially from the West, have done so before us. By living Christ's passion in themselves they understood, through experience more than through study, the real dimension of the Saviour's passion and are therefore our safest guides to discovering God's love. They help us to realize that if God's love is "a never-ending ocean, bottomless and shoreless," so too is God's sorrow.

It is written that in Jerusalem there was a miraculous pool and that, when its water was stirred up, the first to dive into it was healed (cf. Jn 5,6). We must now throw ourselves, in spirit, into the pool, or ocean, of Christ's passion. In Baptism we were "baptized into his death," "buried with him" (cf. Rom 6:3 ff.); what once took place symbolically must now take place in fact. We must immerse ourselves in the passion so as to be renewed, fortified and transformed by it. "I buried myself in Christ's passion—wrote one of the above mentioned mystics—and I was given hope that there I would find my liberation" (Bl. Angela of Foligno, *op. cit.*, p. 148). All we have to do is be careful not to deceive ourselves. It's easy to remain on a human and superficial level while believing we have understood the passion in depth. In other words, there is a danger of seeing the passage from the symbolic and ritual level of Baptism to the existential level as a painless process in which the "existential level" merely consists of a strong idea or intense imagination of being buried with Christ in death. This would still be an idea of experiencing death with Christ and not a real experience of it. It's like standing beside a sheet of frozen water in winter and shivering just at the thought of falling into it. To become "like Jesus in his death" (Phil 3:10), we too must take up our cross and follow him. Like certain infections which pass only from wound to wound and not from a wounded body to a healthy one, the suffering of Christ can only be participated in by one who suffers.

Let us therefore start our "Via Crucis" through the passion of Christ's soul, making three "stations," three pauses: one in Gethsemane, another at the praetorium and another on Calvary. We shall complete the concise enunciations found in the Letter to the Romans with the more detailed accounts supplied by the gospels. We will retrace again the first steps of the faith and the catechesis of the Church, knowing as we now do that the Gospel accounts of the passion were written precisely to show what lay behind the simple enunciations of the apostolic *kerygma*: "He suffered under Pontius Pilate, died and was buried."

2. Jesus in Gethsemane

The agony of Jesus in the garden of Gethsemane is an attested fact in the Gospels by all four of the evangelists. In fact, even John speaks of it in his own way when he attributes to Jesus the words: *Now is my soul troubled* (which recall the synoptics expression "my soul is troubled") and the words: *Father, save me from this hour* (which recall "remove this cup from me" of the synoptics) (Jn 12:27). There is also an echo of this in the Letter to the Hebrews where it is said that Christ, *in the days of his flesh offered up prayers and supplications, with loud cries and tears, to him who was able to save him from death* (Heb 5:7). It's quite extraordinary that this not very "apologetic" fact should have been given so much importance in tradition. The emphasis placed on this moment in Christ's life can only be explained by a very strongly attested historical event.

In Gethsemane the apostles found themselves in front of an unrecognizable Jesus. He, at whose beck the winds ceased, who drove out devils, healed the infirm, to whom the crowds listened, is now a pitiful sight asking them for help. Jesus—it is written—*began to be greatly distressed and troubled. And he said to them, "My soul is very sorrowful, even to death; remain here, and watch"* (Mk 14: 33 ff.). The verbs used (*ademonein* and *ekthambeisthai*) suggest the idea of a man who is a prey to deep bewilderment, to a sort of solitary terror, as if he feels he is being dragged away from humankind. Jesus is completely alone, like one who finds himself suspended in some remote point of the universe, where every cry falls on deaf ears and where there is nothing anywhere, neither above nor below, to the right or to the left, to hold on to. His gestures are those of a person struggling in mortal anguish; he "fell on the ground," got up to go to his disciples, went back to kneel down, then he got up again . . . From his lips came the cry: *Abba, Father, all things are possible to thee; remove this cup from me* (Mk 14:36).

In the Bible the image of the cup almost always evokes the idea of God's wrath against sin. The "cup of staggering," Isaiah calls it (Is 51:22); it is said of it that the wicked "shall drain it down to the dregs" (Ps 75:9). Also the Apocalypse talks of "the wine of God's wrath, poured unmixed into the cup of his anger" (Rev 14:10). At the beginning of his Letter to the Romans, St. Paul establishes a universal principle: *The wrath of God is revealed from heaven against all ungodliness and wickedness* (Rom 1:18). Wherever sin exists, God's judgement cannot but be focussed on it, otherwise God would reach a compromise with sin and the very distinction itself between good and evil would no longer exist. Now, Jesus in Gethsemane is impiety, all the impiety of the world. He is man "made sin." Christ, it is written, died "for sinners"; he died in their place and not only in their favour. He accepted to answer for all men; he is, therefore, "responsible" for all, the guilty one before God! It is against him that God's wrath "is revealed" and that is what "drinking the cup" means. A correct understanding of Christ's passion is hindered by an extrinsic view of things according to which we have, on one side, man and his sin and on the other side, Jesus suffering and expiating those sins, though he remains detached and untouched by sin. Whereas the relation of Jesus to sin is not distant or indirect, or even simply juridic, but real and close. Sin, in other words, was in him, he bore it, because he had freely "taken it on to himself": *He himself bore our sins in his body* (1 Pt 2:24). He felt he was in some way the sin of the world. For once, let us give a name to the reality of sin so that it will not remain something abstract to us. Jesus bore all human pride, all rebellion against God, all lust, all hypocrisy, all injustice, all violence, all untruth, and all hatred, which is such a terrible thing. (Let he who has ever been the victim of this dreadful sentiment and experienced its effects on himself, think of that moment and he will understand).

Jesus enters into the "dark night of the spirit" which consists in simultaneously and unbearably experiencing the proximity of sin and, because of it, the absence of God. We have two objective means for looking at this abyss the Saviour now finds himself in: one is the words of Scripture, especially the Psalms, which prophetically describe the sufferings of the righteous one and which, according to what the Apostles and Jesus himself said, refer to him, and the second one is the experience of the saints, especially of the mystics, who received the grace to painfully experience Christ's passion. The first is knowledge of the prophecies and the second is knowledge of "the fruits."

In Jesus, in Gethsemane, the words of Isaiah are completely fulfilled: *Bruised for our iniquities, upon him was the chastisement that made us whole* (Is 53:5). Now the mysterious words of many psalms will come true, like those in psalm 88: *Thy wrath lies heavy upon me, and thou dost overwhelm me with all thy waves . . . Thy wrath has swept over me; thy dread assaults destroy me.* These words suggest the image of an island left desolate and bare by a hurricane. What would happen if the whole physical universe with its billions and billions of celestial bodies rested on only one point like an immense overturned pyramid? What pressure that point would have to bear! Well then, the whole moral universe of sin, not any less boundless than the physical universe, weighed at that moment on the soul of Jesus. The Lord has *laid* on him the iniquity of us all (Is 53:6); he is the Lamb of God who takes "away," or "upon himself" the sins of the world (Jn 1:29). Sin was the real cross that Jesus took upon his shoulders and which he carried all the way to Calvary and to which he was eventually nailed!

Because Jesus bears sin in himself, God is absent; God is the cause of his greatest torment, not in the sense that he is responsible, but in the sense that by simply existing he brings sin to light and makes it unbearable. The infinite attraction between the Father and the Son is now thwarted by an equally infinite repulsion. God's supreme holiness clashes with the supreme evil of sin, causing an indescribable upheaval in the Redeemer's soul, like when in the Alps a mass of cold air approaching from the north clashes with a mass of hot air coming from the south and the atmosphere is so disturbed by thunder and lightning that even the mountains shake. How can we then wonder at the cry that came from the lips of Jesus: "My soul is very sorrowful, even to death!" and at his sweat of blood? Jesus lived what we call today a "limit-situation," but the limit he reached was not a relative one, but the absolute limit of any possible human experience.

I have said that God was not the cause of this suffering, nor was he responsible for it, but in a certain sense (we shall see this later when talking of the Father) he was, and this is the deepest aspect of the passion. Blessed Angela of Foligno, she who "buried herself in the passion," wrote: "Christ's suffering was indescribable, manifold and mysterious, the greatest suffering that can be imagined, reserved for him by the divine wisdom. In fact, God's will, which the human mind cannot define and which is eternally united to Christ, reserved the greatest of all suffering for him. Just as much as the divine will surpasses everything else in wonder so Christ's suffering surpassed all intensity and depth. It was an agonizing, inexpressible suffering given by the divine will, so intense that it cannot be comprehended by the human mind. The will of God was the source and origin of all the sufferings that fell to Jesus; they came from this will and were fulfilled in it" (B. Angela da Foligno, *op.cit.*, p. 442 ff.). Suffering too reaches an infinite level when its cause and measure is God, when God is involved, and that's what happened in the passion.

3. Jesus in the Praetorium

Let us now move from Gethsemane to Pilate's praetorium. It was a short interval between the time Jesus was condemned and executed and as such, easily goes unnoticed in the reading of the passion, whereas it is full of significance. The Gospels narrate that after Jesus had been delivered into their hands to be crucified, the soldiers led him inside the palace and called together the whole battalion to watch the spectacle: *And they clothed him in a purple cloak, and plaiting a crown of thorns they put it on him. And they began to salute him, "Hail, king of the Jews!" And they struck his head with a reed, and spat upon him and they knelt down in homage to him* (Mk 15:6-19). And when they had done this, they stripped him of the purple cloak and put his own clothes on him. And they led him out to crucify him.

There's a painting by J. Mostaert, a sixteenth century Flemish artist, which always makes a tremendous impression on me especially because it simply puts together the information given to us by the four evangelists about this particular moment of the passion making it possible for us to visualize and observe the scene. On his head Jesus is wearing a crown of thorns that have just been gathered, as can be seen from the green leaves still hanging on the twigs. Drops of blood fall from his head and mingle with the tears falling from his eyes. His weeping is bitter; but looking at him one immediately realizes that he is not weeping for himself but for whoever is looking at him; he is weeping over me who doesn't understand yet. After all, he himself said to the women: *Do not weep for me* (Lk 23:28). His mouth is slightly open like one who is finding it difficult to breathe and is caught in a state of mortal anguish. On his shoulders he is wearing a heavy, threadbare cloak which looks more like metal than material. Lower down in the picture you can see his wrists tied together, several times over, with a rough cord; in one hand he is holding a reed and in the other a bunch of rods, symbols of mockery of his regality. It is the hands above all that make you shudder when you look at them; Jesus can no longer move even a finger; he is totally helpless and immobilized. Whenever I pause to contemplate this image, especially when I am going out to preach the Word of God, my soul is filled with shame because I realize the great distance that lies between him and me; I, the servant, am free to go and do as I please; he, the Lord, is bound and imprisoned. The Word in chains and the messenger in liberty!

Jesus in the praetorium is the image of man who has "given God's power back to him." He expiated all the abuse we have made and continue to make of our freedom; this freedom we want no one to touch and which is nothing other than slavery to ourselves. We must impress this episode of Jesus in the praetorium well in our hearts, because the day will come when we will also find ourselves in this state either due to man or to age and then only Jesus will be able to help us understand and sing, amid tears, our new found freedom. There's an intimacy with Jesus that can only be obtained by staying close to him, cheek to cheek, in the hour of his and our ignominy, we too bearing "his abuse" (cf. Heb 13:13). Many people have been condemned by illness or a disability to a helplessness similar to Christ's in the praetorium and have to spend their lives in wheelchairs, or in bed. Jesus reveals the secret greatness hidden in these lives if lived in union with him.

4. Jesus on the Cross

Let us now make our third station in this via crucis through the passion of the Saviour's soul. Let us take ourselves in spirit to Calvary. Here too there is a visible passion—the nails, the thirst, the vinegar, the piercing with a lance—which we must never lose sight of, and there's an invisible and much deeper passion, which takes place in Christ's inner self. Guided by God's word let us now try to take a look at this.

When writing to the Galatians, St. Paul says "he publicly portrayed before their eyes Jesus Christ as crucified" (cf. Gal 3:3). Immediately after, in the same chapter of the Letter to the Galatians he tells us what the crucified one whom he placed before the eyes and impressed on the hearts of believers of the communities he founded was like. *Christ*—St. Paul says—*redeemed us from the curse of the law, having become a curse for us—for it is written, "cursed be every one who hangs on a tree"* (Gal 3:13). Paul didn't "confuse the cross with roses!" The word "curse" (*katàra*) is synonymous, in the Bible, with abandonment, emptiness, solitude, separation from God and of being excluded by the people. It was a sort of total excommunication. At a certain point in the Letter to the Romans when speaking of his Hebrew kinsmen, St. Paul formulates the chilling hypothesis of he himself becoming "accursed and cut off from Christ for the sake of his brothers" (cf. Rom 9:3). What he conceived, as being the greatest of sufferings, although he didn't have to endure it, was really lived by Jesus on the cross to the bitter end. Jesus really became accursed and cut off from God for the sake of the brothers! On the cross, he cried out: *My God, my God, why hast thou forsaken me?* (Mt 27:46).

The experience of God's silence which modern man feels so keenly, helps in understanding something new of Christ's passion, so long as it is kept in mind that God's silence didn't have the same meaning for biblical man as it does for man today. If God doesn't speak to biblical man, he becomes "like those who go down to the Pit" (Ps 28:1); he dies because he lives from God's Word. To be alive is, by definition in the Bible, to be spoken to by God. God's silence is measured by the intensity with which one believes in him and invokes him. It means almost nothing to him who doesn't believe in God or, believing, turns to God in a lukewarm way. The greater the trust placed in God and the more passionate the entreaty, the more painful is God's silence. We can sense from this what God's silence must have been like for Jesus. His enemies beneath the cross do nothing but intensify his sufferings taking God's silence as proof that God was not with him and saying among themselves so that he could hear: *He trusts in God; let God deliver him now, if he desires him* (Mt 27:43). Also Mary beneath the cross knew what God's silence was like. No one has more right than she had to make hers a cry made by one of the Fathers of the Church when thinking over a moment of fierce persecution of the Church: "How hard it was, o God, to bear your silence that day!"

On the cross Jesus experienced to the end the greatest consequence of sin which is the loss of God. He has become the godless one, the atheist—an atheism of loss, not of sin—and he has done this to expiate all the culpable atheism that exists in the world and in each one of us under the form of rebellion against God and of indifference to God. Truly, *upon him was the chastisement that made us whole* (Is 53:5). Certain doctors of the Church and certain mystics say that Jesus experienced in himself the suffering of the damned which consists in being deprived of God and in unexpectedly realizing that God is all things and that without him you can neither live nor die and that you have lost him for all time. A saint who experienced this suffering said that in this state you cannot even turn to God "because you know you are in a place of justice and not of mercy." She went on to say that "all suffering is nothing compared to this. It suffices to say that these souls are deprived of God. Hell is nothing other than the loss of the Supreme Good" (St. Veronica Giuliani, *Diary*, 16.7.1697).

We can at least learn in part what Jesus felt at being nailed to a cross and in the hours that followed from those whom he allowed to bear his stigmata impressed in their flesh or in their hearts. We easily think of the stigmata that some saints received as signs of God's special benevolence, as a distinctive privilege or sort of glorious trophy, as they indeed are; but those who receive them experience them as they were, in fact, for Christ, when he received them on Calvary, as a sign of God's terrible judgement against sin, like being literally "pierced" for our sins. I shall always remember the impression I got on reading, in the choir at San Giovanni Rotondo where it is exposed in a little frame, the description Padre Pio of Pietrelcina made to his spiritual director of his stigmata which he actually received there. He ended with these words of the psalm: *O Lord, rebuke me not in thy anger, nor chasten me in thy wrath!* (Ps 3:2). And you can sense with what spirit he must have recited the rest of the psalm where it says: *Thy arrows have sunk into me, and thy hand has come down on me. There is no soundness in my flesh because of thy indignation . . . I am utterly spent and crushed; I groan because of the tumult in my heart . . .* On reading this description it is possible to understand something of the drama of Calvary. We go beyond a superficial view of it and we see what lies behind the psalmist's words: *Thy wrath has swept over me* (Ps 88:16).

All of this was necessary "so that the body of sin might be destroyed" (Rom 6:6) and so that instead of a curse, a blessing might come upon us (cf. Gal 3:13). Since ancient times the Fathers of the Church have applied to Christ on the cross the biblical figure of the "bitter" water of Marah which becomes sweet when Moses threw the tree into it (cf. Ex 15:23 ff.). On the tree of the cross Christ himself drank the bitter water of sin and changed it into the sweet water of grace. He transformed man's immense "No" to God into "Yes," into an even greater "Amen," so much so that it is now through him that "we utter the Amen to the glory of God" (cf. 2 Cor 1:20). But no one will ever know or be able to describe what all of this meant to the human soul of the Saviour. No one knows the passion of the Son except the Father . . . .

Let us now pause a little beneath the cross to get an overall view of the whole passion of Christ's soul and see what new things have been fulfilled in the world because of it. Through his passion, Jesus fulfilled the great "mystery of piety" (cf. 1 Tim 3:16); through his *eusebeia* or piety, he transformed the *asebeia* or impiety, thus creating man's new state before God which we call salvation.

After sin, the greatness of a creature before God lies in bearing in himself the least possible *guilt* of sin and the most *pain* for sin. In other words, in being a "lamb," that is, a victim and in being "without blemish," that is, innocent. It doesn't lie so much in either one or the other of these things taken separately—that is in innocence or in suffering—as in the sum of both being present simultaneously in the same person. The supreme value is, therefore, the suffering of the innocent. At the top of this new scale of greatness we find Jesus of Nazareth whom the Scripture justly calls "the lamb without blemish" (cf. 1 Pet 1:19). In fact, although he committed *no* sin, he bore *all* the guilt of sin. *He committed no sin . . . , but he bore our sins* (1 Pet 2:22-24); God made him to be sin who knew no sin (cf. 2 Cor 5:21).

To say that Jesus himself bore the *pain* of sin does not mean that he bore only the *punishment* but also the dreadful *imputation* of sin. He took sin on to himself without having committed sin. In order to grasp something of this new order of greatness before God, it is necessary not to dwell on the words or images used to express it but to try, instead, to reconstruct interiorly the experience it presupposes. Man is created for innocence; guilt revolts him more than anything else does, even more than suffering itself. No one wants to be guilty. If at times, a person takes pride in his misdeeds, it is because, in fact, he has himself previously inverted the values or found some other justifications, so that what others might consider to be wrong, he sees as merit. We have all had the bitter experience of being blamed for something, perhaps in the eyes of a person whose regard and affection we most value and we know the state this created in our hearts. Every day we see how difficult it is for us to openly take the blame for something, however small and deserved, without trying to defend ourselves. We can then understand the abyss hidden behind the fact that in the eyes of the Father Jesus was "guilty" for all the sins existing in the world. Jesus experienced the most tremendous deep-rooted and universal source of human suffering which is "the sense of guilt." This is, therefore, also redeemed radically and it is possible for certain souls called to a particular union with the divine Spouse to be inwardly consumed together with him, for years and years, by this sort of martyrdom which makes them feel guilty of everything until the day in which, freed by God's power, they feel celestial and angelic, no longer having any relation whatsoever with sin. They become free and innocent, sharing in the same innocence of God's Son.

The greatest thing in the world is, therefore, not a just suffering but an "unjust suffering" as it is called in Peter's first Letter (cf. 1 Pet 2:19). It is so great and precious because it is the only type of suffering that is close to God's way of suffering. Only God alone, if he suffers, does so unjustly, as one who is innocent. All men, when they suffer, must say, like the good thief on the cross, "We are suffering justly"; only of Jesus can it be said in absolute, what the good thief said: "This man has done no wrong" (cf. Lk 23:41).

This is also the main difference that the Letter to the Hebrews sees between Christ's sacrifice and that of every other priest: *He has no need . . . to offer sacrifices, first for his own sins and then for those of the people* (Heb 7:27). When the person suffering hasn't any sins of his own to expiate, his suffering becomes a pure power of expiation; not having in himself the sad sign of sin, the level of his suffering is purer and his voice "more eloquent." The voice of Abel's blood was like that once, but it was only a weak resemblance (cf. Gen 4:10; Heb 12:24). The suffering of the innocent which is the biggest and most insuperable scandal in the eyes of the world is, before God, the greatest wisdom and justice. It is a mystery but that's the way it is and on this point God seems to repeat to us what Jesus said one day in the Gospel: "He who has ears to hear, let him hear!" (cf. Mt 19,12).

5. "For our sake"

Meditation on the passion cannot be limited to an objective and historical reconstruction of the event however much interiorized, as we have tried to do so far. It would be like stopping half-way. The *kerygma,* or proclamation, of the passion is always made up of two factors even in the shortest texts: the fact, he "suffered" and "died" and the motivation of the fact, "for our sake," "for our sins." He was put to death, the Apostle says, "for our trespasses" (Rom 4:25); he died for "the ungodly," he died "for our sake" (Rom 5:6,8). It is always the same. This second point has also constantly emerged in the considerations we have made so far but only incidentally. It is now time for us to see it in a fuller light and concentrate our attention on it. The passion will inevitably remain extraneous to us until we go into it through the very narrow door of the "for our sake" because only he who acknowledges that the passion is his fault truly knows the passion. Everything else is a digression.

If Christ died "for me" and "for my sins," this means that *I* killed Jesus of Nazareth, that *my* sins crushed him. That's what Peter strongly proclaimed on the day of Pentecost to the three thousand people listening to him: "You killed Jesus of Nazareth!," "You denied the holy and righteous one!" (cf. Acts 2:23; 3:14). St. Peter must have known that the three thousand and others he was addressing these words to weren't all really present on Calvary hammering in the nails and neither were they all there before Pilate asking him to crucify Jesus. Yet he repeated these tremendous words three times and those listening, inspired by the Holy Spirit, acknowledged that what Peter said was true of them also because it is written that *they were cut to the heart and said to Peter and to the rest of the Apostles, "Brethren what shall we do?"* (Acts 2:37).

This throws new light on what we have meditated on so far. My sin was also present in Gethsemane, the sin I committed, and it weighed on the heart of Jesus; in the praetorium there was also the abuse I made of my freedom which kept Jesus bound; on the cross Jesus was expiating also my atheism. Jesus knew this, at least he knew it as God, and perhaps at that moment, someone was placing this fact before his eyes in the desperate effort to stop him and make him desist. It is written that after ending every temptation in the desert, the devil departed from Jesus until an opportune time (cf. Lk 4:12) and we know that, for the evangelist, this "opportune time" is the time of the passion, the "hour of darkness" as Jesus himself calls it when he was being arrested (cf. Lk 22:53). *The ruler of this world is coming,* Jesus said as he left the cenacle to go forward towards his passion (cf. Jn 14:30 ff.). In the wilderness the tempter showed him all the kingdoms of the earth, here he is showing him all generations throughout history, including ours, and he shouts within to his heart: "Look at them, look at who you are suffering for! See what they will do with all your suffering! They will go on sinning as before and will not give it much thought. It's all in vain!" And, unfortunately, it is certain that I am also one of that crowd that doesn't give much thought to what happened. I, who am even able to write these things about the passion while remaining impassive, whereas it should only be written about in tears. The words and notes full of faith of a negro spiritual re-echo in my ears: "Were you there, were you there when they crucified my Lord?," and in my inner self I have to answer each time: Yes, I was there when they crucified the Lord! What the rest of the song says is also true: "Sometimes it causes me to tremble, tremble, tremble."

It is necessary for an earthquake to take place in the life of every man and that he should feel in his heart something of what took place in nature as a warning, at the moment of the death of Jesus when the curtain of the temple was torn in two, the stones broke and the tombs opened. It is necessary that a holy fear of God should shatter once and for all our proud hearts so sure of themselves in spite of everything. All the holy people who were assembled at the Passion are examples of this and encourage us to do just this; the good thief crying out "Remember me!," the centurion praising God, the multitudes beating their breasts (cf. Lk 23:39 ff.). There have been souls in the Church who experienced this spiritual earthquake and they can help us understand what it consists of. "In a flash I saw myself completely immersed in blood while my spirit knew that it was the blood of the Son of God, for which I myself was to blame for all the sins I saw before me in that moment and I knew that this precious blood had flowed for my salvation. If God's goodness hadn't upheld me, I think I would have died of terror so dreadful and terrifying was the sight of sin, no matter how small. Human words cannot express it. To see God, infinite goodness and pureness, offended by a mere worm of the earth surpasses every horror . . . And besides this, seeing that you are personally responsible for what happened and that if you had been the only one to sin, the Son of God would still have done what he did for all men, destroys and humbles the soul" (Bl. Mary of the Incarnation, *Autobiographical Relation of the Year* 1654).

St. Peter too had a similar experience and if he was able to shout out those tremendous words to the multitudes it was because he had first shouted them to himself: "You have denied the Holy and Righteous One!" At a certain point in the story of the passion we read: *And the Lord turned and looked at Peter and Peter went out and wept bitterly* (Lk 22:62). The look that Jesus gave Peter pierced right through him and changed him. Think of two prisoners in a concentration camp. Imagine you are one of them and you have tried to escape knowing that the punishment for this would be death. A companion is blamed in your presence but he doesn't inform on you; he is tortured in your presence and he still doesn't say anything. Finally, while they are taking him to the place of execution, he turns and silently looks at you for a split second without a shadow of reproach. When you manage to get back home, could you ever be the same person again? Would you ever be able to forget that look? Such was the look Peter received from Jesus. How often, on hearing the passion of Christ being spoken of, or speaking of it myself, or on looking at that image of Jesus in the praetorium mentioned earlier, have I repeated to myself the well-known verse of Dante Alighieri: "What do you weep at, if you do not weep at this?"

The mistake is that we unconsciously think of the passion as something that happened two thousand years ago and which belongs to the past. How can we be moved and weep over something that took place two thousand years ago? Suffering touches us when we see it, not when we remember it. We can only contemplate Christ's suffering as contemporaries and we have it from reliable sources that "Christ's passion is prolonged to the end of time" (S. Leo the Great, *Sermons* 70,5; PL 54, 383) and that "Jesus will be in agony even to the end of the world" (B. Pascal, *Pensées* n.552 Br.). Countless souls feel, even today, that Jesus is still suffering, that he will be on the cross as long as sin exists in the world and, in actual fact, Scripture itself says that those who sin "*crucify* the Son of God on their own account and hold him up to contempt" (Heb 6:6). One day when I was all intent on reflecting on the resurrected Christ, trying to understand what he is like now in *reality* and that is beyond the categories and concepts by which we represent him, I was given a crucifix that was horribly desecrated and disfigured and I heard a voice within me saying: "This is how I am *in reality!*" which left me speechless.

All of this is not just simply a way of talking, it corresponds to the truth. In spirit Jesus is also now in Gethsemane, in the praetorium, on the cross and not just in his mystical body, that is in the suffering, the imprisoned or those who have been killed, but also inexplicably in his very person. This is true not *in spite* of the resurrection but *because* of the resurrection which made Jesus crucified "living for all time." The Apocalypse presents the Lamb in heaven "standing," that is resurrected and living, but "as though he had been slain" (cf. Rev 5:6).

Thanks to his Spirit which he gave us, we have become contemporaries of Christ; his passion is taking place "today" (*hodie*) as the liturgy tells us. When we contemplate the passion we are in a similar situation to a son whose father had been condemned, deported far away and subjected to every sort of ill-treatment through his son's fault. One day, unexpectedly, he sees his father reappear before him in silence, the signs of all his sufferings visible on his body. It's true that it is all over now, his father is back home and suffering no longer has any hold over him. But that doesn't mean that the son will be able to remain unmoved at the sight of his father. Rather, he will burst into bitter tears and throw himself at his father's feet now that he can finally see with his own eyes what he has done. In St. John's Gospel we can read: *They shall look on him whom they have pierced* (Jn 19:37), and the prophecy he is quoting goes on to say: *They shall mourn as one mourns for an only child, and weep bitterly over him as one weeps over a first born* (Zech 12:10). Every meditation on the passion which enriched the history of the Church and made numerous saints is based on this; it is the fulfillment of this prophecy. Has it ever been realized in my life or is it still awaiting fulfillment? Have I ever looked at the One I pierced?

It is time that "being baptized in Christ's death" be realized in our lives. It is time that something of the old self be discarded and buried for ever in Christ's passion. The old self with its carnal desires must be "crucified with Christ." A stronger idea has now taken over scaring the old man to death and persuading him to forsake all his "fixed ideas" and vanities. St. Paul gives an account of this experience when he says: *I have been crucified with Christ; it is no longer I who live, but Christ who lives in me* (Gal 2,20). It is no longer I who live, that is, my "self" no longer lives. Was it perhaps that Paul no longer felt the impulses and temptations of the old self? Was he already in possession of the eschatological peace and free from all struggle? This wasn't the case because he himself confesses his interior battle between the laws of the flesh and that of the Spirit (cf. Rom 7:14 ff.). But something irreversible had happened which made it possible for him to say that his "self" no longer lived. Now the case of "self" is a lost one. St. Paul freely accepted to lose his "self," to deny himself and if his "self" lives as well and makes itself felt at times, it is however subjugated. What counts for God here is the will because the question concerns the will. This is what we must do too if we want to be "crucified with Christ."

The fruit of the meditation on the passion is therefore to kill the old self and give birth to the new self which lives according to God. This is what the baptismal burial symbolized. St. Basil wrote that "rebirth is the beginning of a new life but to begin a new life, the old one must first come to an end. It's like a double race in a stadium where the runners are allowed a rest before taking up the race again on the opposite track, so it would seem that in changing life, a death must come between the two lives to end what had gone before and start the new life" (*De Spir.S.*,XV,35; PG 32,129).

6. "But far be it from me to glory"

After passing through this new understanding of our Baptism, we see the death of Christ in a completely new light, transformed from being an accusation and a reason for fear and sadness into a reason for joy and confidence. St. Paul exclaims: *There is therefore no condemnation for those who are in Christ Jesus* (Rom 8:1). Condemnation has ended its course in him and given way to benevolence and pardon.

The cross now appears as a "boast" and as a "glory," which in St. Paul's language means a confident jubilation together with a heartfelt gratitude to which man raises himself in faith and expresses in praise and thanksgiving: *But far be it from me to glory except in the cross of Our Lord Jesus Christ* (Gal 6:14). How can we glory in something that is not ours? The reason is that now the passion has become "ours." The "for me" which first meant "through my fault" (*dia, propter*) now, after a humble acknowledgement of fault and confession, means "in my favour" (*hyper, pro*). It is written that for our sake God made him to be sin who knew no sin, so that in him we might become *the righteous of God* (2 Cor 5:21). This is the righteousness St. Paul was talking about when he said, *the righteousness of God has been manifested* (Rom 3:21). This is what made and continues to make that "stroke of genius" possible. When, in fact, on our part we add faith to Christ's passion, we truly become the righteous of God, the holy and the beloved. God becomes for us what he had foretold, *The Lord-Our-Righteousness* (Jer 23:6).

Now we can fearlessly open ourselves to that joyful and spiritual dimension in which the cross no longer appears as "foolishness and scandal" but, on the contrary, as "God's power and God's wisdom." We can make it the reason of our unshakable certainty, the supreme proof of God's love for us, the endless theme of our preaching and we can say with the Apostle: *Far be it from me to glory except in the cross of Our Lord Jesus Christ!*

V. He Was Raised for Our Justification

Christ's resurrection, the source of our hope

The Angel who appeared to the women on Easter morning said to them: *Do not be amazed; you seek Jesus of Nazareth, who was crucified. He has risen!* (Mk 16:6). The closer we come, even today, to this original and simple way of announcing the resurrection and the more it is a message of faith and life rather than of proof and doctrine, the more powerful the message is and the more deeply it touches the heart. The most beloved of Russian saints, Seraphin of Sarov, after spending about ten years in a wood without speaking a word even to the brother who occasionally brought him some food, was later sent back among men by God. He would approach those who sought him at his monastery in ever increasing numbers saying with great enthusiasm: "My joy, Christ has risen!" These simple words were sufficient to change the heart of whoever he was addressing and the world around him. The timbre of his voice was like that of the Angel's. In the words of the Saint, I too wish to tell those of you who have come so far on this spiritual journey and have gone through the dark night of the passion: "My joy, Christ has risen!" The Easter liturgy invites us to greet Mary in a similar way; she, who more than any other awaited the resurrection and rejoiced in it and who can guide us on this Easter journey: "Queen of Heaven, rejoice, alleluia! for he whom you were made worthy to bear, alleluia! has risen as he said, alleluia!"

In the world of the spirit the resurrection of Christ is what according to recent discoveries, the first "big bang" was for the universe when a small superdense mass was transformed into energy by a cataclysmic explosion thus starting off the whole movement of expansion of the universe and which is still going on after billions of years. In fact everything that exists and moves in the Church—the sacraments, doctrine, institutions—draws its strength from Christ's resurrection. It was the moment in which death became life and history became eschatology. It is the new creation as the liturgy inculcates by choosing the story of creation in Genesis 1 as the first reading for the Easter vigil. It is the new "fiat lux!," let there be light! said by God. Thomas touched with his finger this source of all spiritual energy when he touched the body of the risen Lord and he received such a "shock" that all his doubts immediately disappeared and full of certainty he exclaimed: *My Lord and my God!* Jesus himself then told Thomas that there is a more blessed way of touching him and that is through faith: *Blessed are those who have not seen and yet believe* (Jn 20:29). The "finger" with which we too can touch the risen Christ is therefore faith and it is this finger we must now stretch out with the ardent desire to receive light and strength from this contact.

1. "If you believe in your heart"

The resurrection of Christ can be approached from two different ways: that of interpretation (or, as scholars say, hermeneutics) and that of faith. The first way is based on the principle of *understanding to believe* while the second one is based on the principle of *believing to understand*. These are not two irreconcilable ways but the difference remains considerable and in certain extreme cases one may exclude the other. Much of what has been written in recent years on the resurrection since the advent of the theory of demythologization belongs to interpretation. It tries to throw light on the significance of the terms "he has risen" or "he appeared"; on whether these are historical or mythological or eschatological affirmations and on whether Christ has risen in history or in the *kerygma* and whether what is living now in the Church is the *person* of the risen Christ or just his *cause*. Kept within certain limits this work is very precious and, in fact, helps us to overcome certain rough representations of the resurrection which are unacceptable to man today. It therefore fosters a purification of faith itself.

But there is the great risk involved in this that the next step, a leap in faith, will never be taken. If we want to understand to believe, and as the resurrection can never be completely understood—being as it is the mysterious work of divine omnipotence and not man's—the problem is continually postponed and we never reach belief. "Faith wants to state the Absolute whereas reason wants to continue reflection" (S. Kierkegaard). And this explains a lot about the actual situation of theological discussion on Christ's resurrection. As long as he is seeking truth, it is man who is the protagonist, it is man who is in control of the situation; on these conditions the rationalist accepts to spend even his whole life talking about God. But when truth has been acknowledged it is truth that reigns and man must be ready to bow down before it. But very few are willing to do this.

The safest and most profitable way is that of believing and then understanding . . . But understand what? That we can't understand! At the end of John's Gospel immediately after the account of the resurrection we can read: *These things are written that you may believe* (Jn 20:31). It doesn't say so that you may interpret them but so that you may believe. We cannot therefore absurdly continue to hold that if you show a personal faith while dealing with the Bible and in particular with the resurrection of Christ, it would be a "defilement" of the scientific character of your argument, because the Bible was written precisely to be believed. We are therefore immediately opting for the way of faith as is proposed by the Apostle in his Letter. This was the way the announcement of Christ's resurrection converted people at the beginning, changed the world and gave birth to the Church—not through scientific proof and demonstration but because it was proclaimed "in Spirit and power." And this is an incontrovertible fact which is never given enough importance.

The statement: *He was raised for our justification* (Rom 4:25) is again taken up and developed by St. Paul especially in chapter ten of his Letter where he writes: *If you confess with your lips that Jesus is Lord and believe in your heart that God raised him from the dead, you will be saved* (Rom 10:9). Salvation therefore depends on faith in the resurrection. Elsewhere the Apostle says that man is also raised "through faith in the working of God who raised Jesus from the dead" (cf. Col 2:12). "Through the passion—says St. Augustine—the Lord passed from death to life thus opening the way for those who believe in his resurrection so that they too may pass from death to life." The celebration of Easter, that is to pass from death to life, signifies believing in the resurrection. The saint goes on to say that "there is nothing special in believing that Jesus died; even pagans and the Jews and reprobates believe this; everyone believes it. The great thing is to believe that he rose from the dead. The faith of Christians is the resurrection of Christ" (St. Augustine, *Enarr.* Ps. 120,6; CC 40, p. 1791). Christ's death is not in itself sufficient testimony of the truth of this cause, but only of the fact that he believed in its truth. Men have died for a wrong or even an unjust cause believing, wrongly but in good faith, that the cause was good. Christ's death is the supreme testimony of his charity (as "there is no greater love than this, to lay down one's life for the loved one"), but not of his truth. This is adequately testified only by the resurrection. And, in fact, before the Areopagus, Paul says that God gave "assurance" to all men by raising him from the dead (Acts 17:31); God literally "vouches" for Jesus, he guarantees for him. The resurrection is like a divine seal which the Father places on the life and death, the words and actions of Jesus. It is his "Amen," his "yes." Dying, Jesus said "yes" to the Father obeying him to death; raising him, the Father said "yes" to the Son making him Lord.

2. "Faith comes from what is heard"

If faith in the resurrection is so important that everything in Christianity depends on it, the immediate question is how and where to obtain this faith. St. Paul's answer is crystal clear: from hearing it, *fides ex auditu*! (Rom 10:17). Faith in the resurrection blossoms in the presence of the word proclaiming it. This is something singular and unique. Art is born of inspiration, philosophy of reasoning, technology of calculation and experiment. Faith alone comes from listening. However man expresses himself thought precedes the word that expresses it but the opposite is true of what comes not from man but from God; the word comes first and then the thought through which man believes and produces theology. Therefore man cannot give himself faith; it depends basically on an event, a gift. It depends on the words "He has risen!," spoken and listened in a certain way.

But where does the power come from that causes the proclamation "He has risen" to generate faith and lead us into a new world, seen that it doesn't come from a historical demonstration or any other human proof? It comes from *the fact,* because what it proclaims really took place. History is at work in this in a far stronger and much more direct way than it is in the historical *demonstration* of the fact which is the work of man. What came about is present in it and in the words that narrate it, it becomes clear and impresses itself unaided in man's spirit. Its historicity— for those who have eyes to see and ears to hear—*shows* itself and doesn't need to be *demonstrated.*

It is like what happens in creation. St. Augustine says that God didn't make the world and then go away and leave it. By him it was created and in him it exists (cf. *Confessions,* IV, 12). This is why creatures talk of him, why "the heavens proclaim God's glory" and why "the earth is full of his glory." What took place with things in creation, took place with words in Scripture and, above all, it took place with the solemn words of the kerygma which proclaim the resurrection. The risen Christ did not give these words to the Church and then go away leaving us to search for him in the Church as in an empty tomb. No, he entered into it in his Spirit as he did, in a similar way, in the bread and wine of the Eucharist. Therefore the kerygma is full of Christ and generates him in hearts. The risen Christ is within the kerygma like a flame in a lantern, or even like the current in the copper wire that conducts it.

But if faith comes from hearing the Word, why is it then that not all who hear it believe? St. Paul himself sadly notes that *they have not all heeded the Gospel* (Rom 10:16). In noting the fact, he almost implicitly gives an explanation which lies precisely in obedience; not everyone is willing to obey and bow down before God. And so we get to the bottom of the problem which lies in the rough soil of human freedom which can accept or refuse God's sovereign action. There are different levels of responsibility involved in not obeying the Gospel; there are those who don't believe because they have never heard it announced or because whoever transmitted it to them distorted it or emptied it of meaning through his own lack of faith or coherence. In this case responsibility spreads out to a point that only God knows and judges. But let us interest ourselves in those to whom a "good" announcement has been made such as those who received it from the apostles in person. Why didn't all of them believe? St. Peter gives a revealing answer on this point. After proclaiming that the God of our fathers raised Jesus exalting him as Leader and Saviour, he adds: *And we are witnesses to these things* (meaning himself and the other apostles) *and so is the Holy Spirit whom God has given to those who obey him* (Acts 5:31; cf. also Jn 15:26 f). That's how the act of faith blossoms in the resurrection! There is above all an apostolic testimony, exterior and visible, which is transmitted horizontally, so to say, in the Church and there is an interior testimony, invisible and unrepeatable, which falls perpendicularly, so to say, on each one who hears it. Let us look at both these types of testimony.

The apostolic testimony constitutes on its own all that is necessary and sufficient to believe "reasonably," that is so that the act of faith will have a historical basis acceptable to man (as faith, like the sacraments, "is for man"). It is, in fact, a serious and credible testimony. Thinking it over well, the discrepancies about numbers, order and place of apparitions strengthen rather than weaken the impression of veracity because they show us that we are not dealing with something worked out to convince us at all costs. The apostles couldn't deceive themselves as they were anything but given to believing easily even during the Master's life and we have definite proof from the texts that they doubted to the end and resisted against believing that he was risen. Neither can we think they wanted to deceive others, even knowing how things had gone because it would have been against their own most vital interests and they themselves would have been the first to be deceived and to pay the price. Chrysostom notes: "How could it ever have entered the minds of twelve poor men, and uneducated at that, who had spent their lives on the lakes and rivers, to undertake a similar task? How could they, who had perhaps never set foot in a city or a square, think of facing the whole world? When Christ was arrested after carrying out numerous miracles, all the apostles ran away and their head denied him. How, therefore, can it be explained that while they had not been able to stand up against a few Jews when Christ was still alive, they, later on when he was dead and buried and—according to the incredulous—not risen and therefore not able to speak, received the courage from him to make them rank themselves against the whole world? Shouldn't they rather have said: And now, what shall we do? He wasn't able to save himself so how can he defend us? When he was alive he was not able to conquer even one nation and we, in just his name, must conquer the whole world? Wouldn't it be foolish to undertake such a task or even to simply think of it? It's obvious therefore that if they hadn't seen him risen and hadn't received indisputable proof of his power, they would never have exposed themselves to such a risk" (*In Ep 1 ad Cor* 4:4; PG 61,35 ff.).

First of all, then, there exists an external historic testimony as proof of the resurrection which is that given by the apostles who tirelessly repeat: *God raised him from the dead. To this we are witnesses* (Acts 3:15). But this testimony is not enough on its own. One might even admit that such testimony is worthy of faith and still not believe. Something of this kind happened to the disciples on Easter Sunday when they went to the tomb and "found it just as the women had said; but him they did not see" (cf. Lk 24:24). It is necessary to add the interior testimony of the Holy Spirit to the exterior testimony. And St. Peter tells us that God denies no one this testimony but grants it to all who "obey him" that is to all those whose heart is docile and are willing to obey God. In other words, faith presupposes a basic will to obey. Faith itself is obedience! (cf. Rom 1:16). It is a question of whether man is disposed to obey God who reveals himself and acknowledge his right as God. It is on this point that the "division of the spirit" takes place between believers and nonbelievers.

Therefore, there are those who don't believe in the resurrection because they have never heard of it or heard of it inadequately; but there are also those who don't believe in it through pride, because they do not want to make room for the Absolute or, through indolence, because they know that if they were to believe, they would have to change their way of living and they are not willing to do so. The unbeliever says: "I would renounce pleasure had I faith," but Pascal answers back: "You would soon have faith if you renounced pleasure" (*Pensées*, n. 240 Br.). To some scribes and pharisees of his time Jesus said one day: *How can you believe, who receive glory from one another*? Some scholars don't believe in the resurrection for the basic reason that they seek glory from one another; they want to say something original rather than repeat what is true. This is an admonition for everyone including myself as I am writing this.

What the Apostle says of those who do not believe in the creation (cf. Rom 1:18ff.) is true also in a certain sense of those who do not believe in the resurrection. These are "inexcusable" because what can be known of the resurrection (not all can be known!) is manifested to them; God himself manifested it to them. In fact, from the time of the resurrection on, the reality and the presence of Christ risen can be contemplated in the works he carries out in the Church.

Recapitulating, we can see how St. Paul, in chapter ten of his Letter to the Romans, gives a complete picture of the way of the Word. This way goes from the ears to the heart and from the heart to the lips. Faith, he says, comes from what is heard. The words, "He is risen!" reach the ears of man and penetrate his heart and here the ever new miracle of believing takes place, the mysterious meeting between grace and freedom, the nuptial embrace in which the spouse freedom gives itself to its Lord . . .The third stage follows; from the heart the Word rises and becomes, on the lips, a joyous profession of faith in the Lordship of Christ: *Because if you confess with your lips that Jesus is Lord and believe in your heart that God raised him from the dead, you will be saved. For a man believes with his heart and so is justified, and he confesses with his lips and so is saved* (Rom 10:9 f.).

3. The Resurrection, the Father's Work

So far we have contemplated the resurrection almost solely in relation to ourselves. But God's word presents us with another more intimate view from which the mystery of the resurrection draws its strength. We have seen that we come into contact with it through an act of faith; now we must open ourselves to its meaning and ask ourselves what the resurrection of Christ is in itself.

The resurrection of Christ is not only a question of apologetics destined to give us sure proof of Jesus; it is not principally a demonstration of truth and power; it is not only the beginning of the Church and a new world. All of this comes about afterwards as a consequence. The resurrection must not be reduced to a purely public exterior fact relevant to history or to the Church, almost as if God resurrected Jesus for others and not, instead, for Jesus himself. The resurrection is, above all, an act of infinite tenderness through which the Father, after the dreadful suffering of the Passion, gives life back, through the Holy Spirit, to the dead body of his Son and makes him Lord. It is therefore an act of the Trinity and this is how we want to contemplate it now. It constitutes the peak itself of God's action in history, his highest title of glory. God will be known from now on as "He who has raised Jesus Christ from the dead" (cf. 2 Cor 4:14; Gal 1:1; Col 2:12). Of this title—and much more than of the title "the God of Abraham, of Isaac and of Jacob,"—he now says: *This is my name for ever, and thus I am to be remembered throughout all generations* (Ex 3:15).

The resurrection is therefore, first of all, a gift of the Father to his beloved Son in whom he was pleased. It was his embrace after the atrocious separation of the cross, an act of infinite fatherly tenderness. "For a long time he had held his peace, kept still and refrained himself, but now he cries out" (cf. Is 42:14). The resurrection of Christ is the cry with which God breaks his "silence." Even in the development of the events the human witnesses intervene later on; the first fruits of the resurrection were all consumed between Jesus and the Father in the Holy Spirit, in the most absolute intimacy. No living creature was present at the moment of the resurrection but the Father was there. The first words the Church, guided by the Holy Spirit, places on the lips of the risen Christ in the introit to the Easter Mass, are a cry of joy which he addresses to his Father: "I am risen and I am still with you! *Resurrexi et adhuc tecum sum.* You have placed your hand upon me!" These words were taken from psalms 3 and 138 which from most ancient times (since St. Clement of Rome and St. Justin) have been attributed to the resurrection of Christ. The Father, on his part, cries to Jesus risen, as the same Scripture tells us: *Thou art my Son, today I have begotten thee* (Acts 13:33; Rom 1:4), almost as if the resurrection of Christ doubles his joy at the eternal generation of the Word.

This intimate and "fatherly" aspect of the resurrection is, I repeat, contained in Scripture and not only in the liturgy and piety; it is a reality and not the fruit of our imagination. God, Peter said on the day of Pentecost, raised Jesus up, "having loosed the pangs of death"; he applies the words of psalm 16 to Christ: *I keep the Lord always before me . . .* (Ps 16:8 ff.). The Apostle says that in fact it is also Jesus and not only David who is speaking in this psalm; he expresses his unshakeable hope that his Father will not abandon him in the tomb or in the pit, nor let him see corruption; it is Jesus who says to the Father: *Thou wilt make me full of gladness with thy presence* (cf. Acts 2:24 ff.). In the resurrection the Father solemnly said to the Son: *Sit at my right hand* (Acts 2:34); He "exalted him at his right hand" (cf. Acts 5:31) and granted him to sit "with him on his throne" (cf. Rev. 3:21).

The word the authors of the New Testament prefer to use to express the resurrection is the verb "reawaken" (*egeiro*). It is also used in Rom 4:25 which literally translated would be: "He was reawakened for our justification." To express ourselves in human terms, the Father drew near to Jesus in the tomb as one would delicately draw near to the cradle of a sleeping baby and he awakened him from the sleep of death. The Gospel narrates that one day Jesus drew near to the bier of a young man who was dead and cried: "Young man, I say to you arise!" and the dead man sat up. And he gave him to his mother (cf. Lk 7:14). Now it is the heavenly Father who draws near to the tomb of Jesus and cries: "Young man, my Son, I say to you arise!" and Jesus arose and was resurrected. In one of the psalms which irresistibly recalls Christ's resurrection, the worshipper thus describes his liberation:

> He reached from on high and took me,
> he drew me out of many waters
> he delivered me from my strong enemy . . .
> he brought me forth into a broad place,
> he delivered me because he delighted in me (Ps 18:16-19).

In another prophetic passage God says of Ephraim, "his darling child," that as often as he speaks against him, he remembers him still, that his heart yearns for him (cf. Jer 31:20). These words were already applied to the Messiah in late Judaism and, in fact, it was only in Christ at the moment of his resurrection, that they were completely fulfilled. It is written of the elect—who have come out of the great tribulation—that God will be with them "to wipe away every tear from their eyes" (cf. Rev. 7:14; 21:4). What must it have been like when Jesus came to the Father? He was really coming from "the great tribulation"!

Truly, as is sung in the Easter liturgy, this day of resurrection is "the day which the Lord has made, it is marvellous in our eyes" (Ps 118:22 f.). Jesus is the "living stone rejected by men but in God's sight chosen and precious" (cf. 1 Pet 2:4). The Father showed that he had accepted the Son's sacrifice and was pleased with his obedience. In this sense the resurrection is the crowning of the sacrifice of the cross. God's part in the resurrection is the source of the greatest hope for us because it tells us he will do the same for us one day.

4. According to the Holy Spirit

The "hand" the Father placed on Jesus was nothing else but the Holy Spirit. In fact, St. Paul says right at the beginning of his Letter to the Romans that Jesus, in the resurrection, was designated Son of God in power "according to the Spirit of holiness," that is, the Holy Spirit (Rom 1:4). The statement that Christ was raised from the dead "by the glory of the Father" (Rom 6:4), means the same thing. Elsewhere it is written that Jesus was "vindicated in the Spirit" (1 Tim 3:16), that is, he was declared just and glorified in the Spirit. In the first Letter of Peter it is written that Christ being put to death in the flesh was "made alive in the

Spirit" and "in the Spirit" he went and preached to the spirits in prison (cf. 1 Pet 3:18 f.).

In the Creed the Church proclaims: "I believe in the Holy Spirit, the Lord and giver of life": the resurrection of Christ is the supreme fulfilment of this prerogative, the action *par excellence* of the Spirit, the giver of life. We sometimes see the resurrection, as it is portrayed by certain artists, in a materialistic and superficial way: Jesus coming forth from the tomb with a sort of vexilium in his hand while the soldiers fall to the ground. But the true resurrection is a "spiritual" event. The Holy Spirit, who lived in fullness in Christ's humanity and who was never separated from his soul (even when his soul left his body), entered Christ's lifeless body as a sign of God's will, gave life to it and made it enter the new life which the New Testament calls life "according to the Spirit." Christ's resurrection came about as had been foreseen in the prophecy of the dried bones and which in this event has found a complete and exemplary fulfillment in him: *Behold, I will open your graves, and raise you from your graves, O my people . . . And I will put my Spirit within you and you shall live* (Ezek 37:12-14). The Father put his Spirit into Jesus and he returned to life and the tomb opened as it couldn't hold such life.

This action of the Holy Spirit in the resurrection is also a source of joy and hope for us because it tells us that this will come about for us too: *If the Spirit of him who raised Jesus from the dead dwells in you, he who raised Jesus Christ from the dead will give life to your mortal bodies also through his Spirit who dwells in you* (Rom 8:11). A great Eastern spiritual master said that "the resurrection of all people is carried out by the Holy Spirit. By this we do not mean only the resurrection of the body at the end of the world but also the spiritual rebirth and the resurrection of those souls that are dead and this occurs every day spiritually. This resurrection comes through the Holy Spirit from Christ who died once and is resurrected in all those who merit it" (St. Simeon the New Theologian, *Catechesis* VI; SCh. 104 p.44 f.).

5. "The power of the resurrection"

The resurrection is, therefore, the work of the Father who, through the Holy Spirit, raised Jesus from the dead and made him both Lord and Christ (Acts 2:36). The Lordship of Christ is the focal point where everything meets and which transforms the resurrection from an act into a state: *For to this end Christ died and lived again, that he might be Lord both of the dead and of the living* (Rom 14:9). The next step we must take after believing in our hearts that God raised him from the dead, is to confess openly *that Jesus is Lord* (Rom 10:9). Jesus, the Apostle says, "was designated Son of God in power" in the resurrection (Rom 1:4). These words open a new horizon of faith in the resurrection of Christ which belongs to those who, through grace, already believe in *the fact* of the resurrection. In his Letter to the Philippians, St. Paul says that he has suffered the loss of all things and counts them as refuse, *and this*—he adds—*in order that I may know him and the power of his resurrection* (Phil 3:10). Paul was well aware of the resurrection of Christ; he had strongly defended this in his discourse in the Areopagus and in his Letter to the Corinthians, and he had actually seen the risen Christ (cf. 1 Cor 15:8). What then was it that he didn't know and was yearning for so strongly? The interior power of the resurrection! he answers. "To know" in this context means "to experience" or "to possess." The Apostle was overwhelmed by the feeling of the power of resurrection of the Christ. In his Letter to the Ephesians he talks of "the unmeasurable greatness of his power and the working of his great might" which God accomplished in Christ when he raised him from the dead (cf. Eph. 1:18 f.). He unites in one phrase all the words the Greek language offered him to express might, greatness and power and he applies them to the event of the resurrection.

Where the resurrection of Christ is concerned therefore, it is necessary to go beyond a purely intellectual faith so as to make it a living experience: an undertaking that terminates only in heaven. One can have spent one's life reading or writing book after book about the resurrection of Christ and still not "know" it! It is in the Church that we shall learn this new and living knowledge of the resurrection! The Church was born of faith in the resurrection: it is literally "impregnated," full of it. To say "in the Church" means to say in the liturgy, in the doctrine, in art and in the experience of the saints. The Easter "Exultet," culminating in the cry: "O felix culpa!," almost contagiously communicates to us, especially if we listen to it being sung, the thrill of the resurrection. An Easter vigil prayer going back to the Gelasian Sacramentary says: "Let the whole world see and acknowledge that what was destroyed has been remade, what was old has been renewed and everything has been restored to its integrity."

But it is especially the Eastern Church that is rich in testimony and illuminating examples. Just as in the Trinitarian mystery it was given to the Eastern Church to experience at greater depth the Trinity of the persons and to the Western Church the unity of nature, and as in the mystery of redemption it was given to the Eastern Church to place greater value on the Incarnation and to the Western Church on the Paschal mystery, so within the paschal mystery itself it was given to the Eastern Church to give greater value to the resurrection and to the Western Church, the Passion. This took place to make us dependent on one another and to give rise to the appeal for ecumenical unity from the very depth of the mystery we celebrate together. For each great mystery it's as if God made two "keys" to be used together, giving one to the Eastern Church and the other to the Western Church so that neither one nor the other can open to or reach the fulness of truth without the other. As an ancient axiom said: "You cannot reach such a great mystery by one way only."

We see, for example, that the phenomenon of being like Christ Crucified through the stigmata is more typical of Latin holiness whereas the likeness to Christ resurrected is more typical of the Orthodox Church. We can see this in the lives of St. Simeon the New Theologian and in St. Seraphin of Sarov, two of the most beloved saints of Orthodox Christianity. At the height of Western sanctity we find St. Francis of Assisi who, on Mount Alvernia, is made to look even visibly like the Crucified Lord and at the height of Eastern holiness we find St. Seraphin of Sarov who, in winter in the open cold and snow, while talking to one of his disciples, was visibly transformed in the image of the risen Christ, thus giving us an idea of how Christ must have appeared to them after Easter (cf. St. Seraphin of Sarov, *Conversation with Motovilov*).

Faith in the resurrection of Christ is most deeply rooted in Russian sentiment. At Easter time they, like all the orthodox brethren, greet one another saying: "Christ is risen!" and the response is: "He is truly risen!" Once, at the beginning of the Bolshevik revolution, a debate on Christ's resurrection was organised and the pope, who was to speak in favour of the resurrection, went up on to the platform. He simply said, "Christ is risen!" and all those present answered, without thinking, in chorus as if with one voice: "He is truly risen!" and the pope left the platform in silence. When, one day, the trumpets of the "great Russian Easter" ring out, the Russian people will arouse themselves and shake off their atheism like the hero who on waking up shook off the dry leaves which had fallen on him during the night. As sure as dawn that day will come.

The clearest expression of the feeling in orthodox spirituality for the power of the resurrection is the icon of the resurrection. It shows Christ, radiating divine energy, going resolutely down into the Hades. He takes hold of Adam and Eve by the hand and he pulls them out of the infernals while behind the two first parents forms an unending queue of the just from the Old Testament who are following them towards the light. With those outstretched hands of Christ, the icon is silently affirming that we are facing a new universal exodus: God himself has come to free his people "with a mighty hand and outstretched arm." In contemplating this icon we are still filled with faith today. I must myself confess that I owe more to it than to all the books on the resurrection. It is a *kerygma* in colour; in it the resurrection is not demonstrated but shown. It withdraws the veil and puts us in contact with the invisible reality. In all other forms of representation it is man who looks at the image but in the icon it is the image that looks at man and completely dominates him.

6. "Born anew to a living hope through the resurrection of Jesus Christ"

Just as the proclamation of the death of Christ consists of two parts so does that of the resurrection: the fact itself "he has been raised" and the meaning the fact holds for us: "for our justification." The word "justification" closes the fourth chapter of the Letter to the Romans and opens the following one in a sort of anaphora. At the beginning of this chapter the Apostle shows how the three theological virtues of faith, hope and charity spring from the Paschal mystery of Christ: "Justified by *faith,* we have peace with God . . ." St. Paul says, "and we rejoice in our *hope* of sharing the glory . . . and hope does not disappoint us, because God's *love* has been poured into our hearts . . ." (Rom 5:1-5).

Of these three theological virtues, Peter's first Letter associates especially the resurrection with hope telling us that by the great mercy of God the Father *we have been born anew to a living hope through the resurrection of Jesus Christ* (1 Pet 1:3). By resurrecting Jesus, the Father didn't therefore just give us a "real proof" of him but he also gave us a "living hope"; the resurrection is not just a topic on which the truth of Christianity is based; it is also a power that nourishes hope from within.

Easter is the Christmas Day of christian hope. The word "hope" is missing in Christ's preaching. The Gospels report many of his sayings on faith and charity but nothing on hope. On the contrary, after Easter, we witness a literal explosion of the idea and sentiment of hope in the teachings of the Apostles. Hope takes its place beside faith and charity as one of the three components that make up the new christian life (cf. 1 Cor 13:13). God himself is called the "God of hope" (Rom 15:13). And the reason for this is understandable: Christ, in rising, broke the seal on the source of hope; he created the object of theological hope which is a life with God even beyond death. What in the Old Testament had been perceived and longed for in only a few of the psalms and that is "to be continually with God" (Ps 73:23), to find "the fullness of joy in his presence" (Ps 16:11), has now become a reality in Christ. He has opened a breach in the awful wall of death through which we can all follow him.

Nowadays, this relation between the resurrection and hope is deeply felt but it is sometimes seen the wrong way round; it is not the resurrection that gives hope but hope that gives the resurrection. In other words, the starting point is the hope in man's heart that he will not succumb completely to death, that he will not undergo injustice forever and thus he tries to justify and prove Christ's resurrection. In some extreme cases it happens that the "for us" or "for our hope" takes the place of the fact "he was resurrected." The meaning of the event is substituted for the event. There is no divine *event* from which our hope springs or which gives it meaning but it is our hope that solicits the idea of the resurrection. To affirm the resurrection means, therefore, to give a meaning to our hope and show its true value. The resurrection, from being a real and divine *event*, has been transformed into a human *postulate*; it is no longer based on God's authority and omnipotence but on the common or religious sense of man. This, however, goes against what the Apostle says and, that is, that if Christ has not been truly and really raised up, our hope, like our faith, is in "vain," that is, it is empty and without foundation (cf. 1 Cor 15:12 ff.), or at least without any other foundation but that of the human desire to give it one. It would be wishful thinking. Just as it's possible to empty the cross of Christ (cf. 1 Cor 1:17), there is also a way of emptying the resurrection of Christ, of secularizing it and this effort once again comes from placing interpretation above faith and in the place of faith. "We must therefore ask ourselves how God manifested his action and power in Jesus Christ and not just project our own personal or collective hopes on to the word 'resurrection' because in so doing we are in danger of sadly misunderstanding the great hope placed in the resurrection (C.M. Martini).

With the true perspective of faith re-established we can now open our hearts to the living hope that comes from the resurrection of Christ and let ourselves be invested by it as if by a renewing breath. On this point St. Peter talks of a regeneration (*anagennesis*), of being "born again." This is what actually happened to the Apostles. They experienced the power and sweetness of hope. It was hope in its nascent state that made them reunite again and joyfully cry out to one another: "He has risen, he is alive, he has appeared, we have seen him!" It was hope that made the disconsolate disciples of Emmaus retrace their steps back to Jerusalem.

The Church is born of hope and it is necessary to rekindle it today if we want to give a new impetus to faith and make it able to conquer the world again. Nothing can be done without hope. The poet who had the famous "stroke of genius" wrote a poem on theological hope. He says that the three theological virtues are like three sisters: two of them are grown and the other is instead a small child. They go forward together, hand in hand with the child hope in the middle. Looking at them it would seem that the bigger ones are pulling the child but it is the other way round; it is the child who is pulling the two bigger ones. It is hope that pulls faith and charity. Without hope everything would stop (cf. Ch. Péguy, *Le porche* pp. 538 ff.). We can see this in our everyday lives. When a person reaches the point of having no hope in anything, it's as if he were dead. Often people even kill themselves or allow themselves to die slowly. Just as a person about to faint is quickly given something strong to drink or smell to revive them, so to those on the point of giving up the struggle a reason to hope must be offered. They must be shown that they still have a chance so that they will take heart and start again. A miracle takes place each time a seed of hope blossoms in a person's heart; everything seems different even if nothing has actually changed. Even a community, a parish, a religious order revives and begins to attract new vocations if hope blossoms in them again. There is no form of propaganda that can do what hope manages to do. It is hope that animates the young. It's the same in a family. When hope is present one stays or returns home willingly. To give hope to someone is the most beautiful gift that can be offered. Just as once the faithful passed the holy water from hand to hand as they were leaving church, so Christians must pass divine hope from hand to hand, from father to son. Just as on the night of Easter the faithful light their candles from one another starting with the priest, who lights his from the Paschal candle, so we must pass theological hope to one another which is buried in the hearts of the christian people. Never before has eschatology been so much spoken of among christians and never has it been so little practised as in our day. Eschatology—that is openness to the future, to the last and eternal future—has been removed from life for fear that it might give rise to a lack of commitment and alienation and has been transferred to theology books. In certain cases it has become an ideology, dealing with a restricted future which is all contained in history.

The object of Christian hope, as I have said, is the resurrection from death: *He who raised the Lord Jesus will raise us also* (2 Cor 4:14). Christ was the "first fruits" (cf. 1 Cor 15:20) and the first fruits promise a full crop which must follow if the first fruits are to exist. But the resurrection of the body is not the only resurrection; there is also a resurrection of the heart and if the resurrection of the body will take place on the "last day," that of the heart takes place every day. And it is this resurrection that is of most interest to us because it practically depends on us right from now. St. Leo the Great said: "Let the signs of the future resurrection now appear in the holy city and that which must be accomplished in the body be now accomplished in hearts" (*Ser.* LXVI, 3; PL 54, 366). This is how a brother of ours in faith sings of the resurrection of the heart he experienced in his conversion:

> "My God, I am risen and I am still
> with You!
> I was sleeping and lying down like someone dead
> in the night.
> God said: Let there be light and I
> awoke like one about to cry!
> I arose and I awoke. I am standing,
> ready to start with the new day!
> My Father, you begot me before the dawn,
> I am standing in Your Presence.
> My heart is free and my mouth is clean,
> my body and spirit are fasting.
> All my sins have been absolved
> which I confessed one by one.
> The wedding ring is on my finger and my face
> is cleansed.
> I am like an innocent being in the grace

which you granted me."
(P. Claudel, *Cor. Ben. Anni Dei*)

In these pages we have undertaken a journey of spiritual renewal. To reach a conclusion we must let the child hope take us by the hand. We must hope that some change will take place in our lives too and that it's not true that everything will continue as inevitably as before and that there will never be anything new for us on this earth. To hope means to have faith that "this time" things will be different even if we've believed the same thing hundreds of times in vain. Perhaps in the past you've often decided to undertake the holy journey of conversion; one Easter maybe or during a retreat, or at an important meeting, you decided to make the move, and then saw your enthusiasm decrease and die away as you gradually approached it and each time you found yourself bitterly on the shores of Egypt. If, notwithstanding everything, you still hope, you will touch God's heart and he will help you. God is moved before the hope of his creatures. "The faith I prefer—he says—is hope. Faith doesn't surprise me. Charity doesn't surprise me. But hope, God says, is what fills me with wonder. That those poor creatures see how things are going and believe that tomorrow it will go better surprises me. And I am full of wonder myself. My grace must, indeed, be incredibly strong" (Péguy, *Le porche* p. 531 f.).

No effort, however useless it might seem, is worthless if it is sincere. God keeps account of all of them and one day his grace will be given in proportion to the times we have had the courage to start again from the beginning as if a hundred wasted efforts meant nothing. It is written that *they who wait for the Lord shall renew their strength, they shall mount up with wings like eagles, they shall run and not be weary, they shall walk and not faint* (Is 40:31). We must hope that there is no chain, no matter how strong, that cannot be broken. The Jesus who in Spirit went to visit those who were in the darkness and who "shattered the doors of bronze and cut in two the bars of iron (Ps 107:16) can free us from any state of spiritual bondage and death. He can cry out, as he is now crying out to me here and now, what he cried out to Lazarus in the tomb: "Come out!" (Jn 11:42).

Let us therefore take hold of the Saviour's outstretched hand as Adam and Eve do in the icon and let us also rise with Jesus. Let us repeat to one another when we meet and especially at Easter time, the words of the saint: "My joy, Christ, has risen!"

VI. God Did Not Spare His Own Son
The mystery of God's suffering

This chapter is dedicated to the Father. Jesus is always—or at least often—spoken of, as is the Holy Spirit in recent times. But what about the Father? Who ever talks of the Father? I feel how true what Jesus said is even today: *No one knows the Father* . . . (Mt 11:27) and I was impatient for the right moment to talk of the Father. It is such a great undertaking that I'm already sad at the thought of wasting this opportunity. In the attempt to say many things about the Father, the power of his name will surely be lost and I shall not keep to the living, simple and ineffable reality of what the Father is. That's why I wanted to pronounce his name at once, as if to put it safely in your hearts thus giving you the "whole," before dispersing it into as many fragments as the words themselves. This is the name "from whom every fatherhood in heaven and on earth is named" and before which St. Paul invites us to bow our knees together with him (cf. Eph 3:14). I wish I had at this moment the heart and lips of Jesus so as to speak properly of the Father. Every preacher has a special topic close to his heart which he never gets tired of talking about and through which he best expresses his ability. The theme of Jesus is the "Father"! When Jesus talks of the Father, the eyes of the disciples open wide, they become deeply nostalgic and Philip exclaims: *Show us the Father and we shall be satisfied!* (Jn 14:8). But the Father isn't just a "theme" for Jesus, he is his *Abbà,* his Father, he who gave him his glory and his name "before the world existed"; he to whom he is also infinitely attracted even as man. His whole mission on earth is to make the Father known to men and so he ends his preaching on the kingdom saying: *I made known to them thy name, and I will make it known, that the love with which thou has loved me may be in them, and I in thee.* (Jn 17:26). The passion itself must serve to make man know his love for the Father: "So that the world may know that I love the Father," he said as he went towards his passion, "rise, let us go hence!" (cf. Jn 14:31).

But let us see how a discourse on the Father can be relevant at this point in our journey. The central chapters of the Letter to the Romans (5-8) have as their basic theme the salvation brought about by Christ through his death and resurrection. But is our salvation exclusively the work of the Son only, or is it the work of the whole Trinity? Is it something that is entirely decided in history or does it go beyond history? We find an answer to these questions in the Letter to the Romans and precisely in chapter 5, the chapter we have now arrived at, which reveals a new trinitarian dimension of salvation and of the very passion of Christ itself. We have had the chance of stressing the Father's action when speaking of Christ's resurrection but given the importance and relevance of the topic, we now want to study it at greater depth.

1. The Father's Refusal

In Romans 5:6-11 and again at the end of the section in Romans 8:32, the Apostle talks to us of God the Father's love for us as the ultimate source from which redemption springs. Let us carefully heed what he says: *God* (the Father) *shows his love for us in that while we were yet sinners Christ died for us,* and again: *God did not spare his own son but gave him up for us all* (Rom 8:32). God the Father shows his love for us in causing his own Son to die! Humanly speaking this is an unbelievable thought, even scandalous really; the fact that Christ died doesn't show the Father's love, if anything it shows his cruelty or, at least, his strict justice. In fact, knowledge of the Father is almost impeded in our present day culture by numerous prejudices. It must be with sadness that Jesus repeats what he said one day: *O righteous Father, the world has not known you!* (Jn 17:25).

The difficulty that modern man finds in reconciling the Father's goodness with the agonizing death of Jesus on the cross has two main reasons. The first lies within the Church itself and consists in inadequate representations of the mystery (inadequate at least for modern feeling). I'm not talking of interpretations given by great masters of faith (such as St. Thomas) which are generally quite sober and respectful of the mystery, but of explanations divulged in manuals and of a certain type of preaching the passion which has ended up giving a deformed image of the drama of redemption. For example, this is how Bossuet presented the Father in a discourse held on Good Friday 1662 to the Royal Court in France: "The holy soul of my Saviour is oppressed by the horror a threatening God inculcates and while he feels drawn to throw himself into the arms of such a God to seek comfort and relief, he sees that God turns his face and rejects him; he abandons him leaving him completely in the grip of the Father's fury and his angry justice. O Jesus, you throw yourself into the Father's arms and you are rejected, you feel that he is persecuting you, striking you, abandoning you; it is he who is crushing you beneath the enormous and unbearable weight of his anger . . . The anger of an irritated God; Jesus prays and his angry Father doesn't hear him; it is the justice of a God vindicating the abuses he has received; Jesus suffers and the Father is not appeased!" (*Oeuvres*, IV, Paris, 1836, p. 365). If this is how one of the most famous and profound preachers that history recalls expressed himself, we can imagine what other preachers abandoned themselves to!

It's obvious that such a view based on the juridic concept of expiation couldn't but generate with time a secret repulsion for this "implacable" Father who impassibly awaits in heaven for the blood of ransom and of his own Son to be shed for him. This way of explaining things doesn't take sufficient account of a fundamental truth and that is of the divine union of wanting between the Father, the Son and the Holy Spirit in strength of which what the Father wants the Son wants in the same way. If therefore there was "cruelty" in God, this wasn't of the Father against the Son but of God against himself. God was cruel with himself for love of man.

The weak point of Scholastic theology and in part of Patristic theology on the Redemption is that it takes as concepts what were really only images in the Bible. The image, taken from what actually and practically happened in the ancient world when a slave was ransomed, becomes a juridic and abstract concept of "ransom" with obvious consequences. Images are part of the indirect language of symbols, whereas concepts are part of direct language. Images are more discreet than concepts; they give way to other images at the right moment which integrate and modify them; they are like the parables Jesus used; they serve to say something and then are easily left aside and in part even denied by the spiritual reality they must illustrate. Concepts, instead, once they are involved follow an inflexible logic; they resist and impose themselves; there is no stopping half way with concepts and this involves risks when a mystery is in question especially if it is not kept in mind that in this concepts are always analogical.

The second motivation for the refusal of the Father comes from outside the Church and theology; it comes from the prejudices and suspicions that have grown around the paternal figure. It wasn't difficult for modern psychology to emphasize all the distortions which make up the Father figure: paternalism, authoritarianism, masculinism. Psychoanalysis discovered with Freud the so-called Oedipus complex according to which every son more or less hides in his subconscious the desire to kill his own father. If these observations had been kept in the sphere of human pathology from which they were taken, they might have been useful and liberating; the difficulty arose when an attempt was made to give an absolute and universal value to these discoveries, applying them even to God and making use of them to explain or rather to deny the existence of a God Father.

But obviously it was not psychoanalysis that created all of these negative premises from nothing. Many of them have their roots in the person's life. It's possible to cultivate resentment towards a father in numerous ways and in the widest range of experiences; there are those who refuse their father because he was despotic and those who refuse him even if they have never known him. A young girl thus explained her refusal of God based on her own personal experience. She grew up fatherless and every time she did something wrong her mother would blame her saying: "If your father were alive, you wouldn't do such things!" She soon became very happy that her father was dead. The word father was synonymous with denial to her, with one who takes away freedom and not of one who gives freedom.

2. The Suffering of God

One of the reasons that turns human thought against the Father is the suffering of the innocent. People say they cannot accept a God who allows the suffering of so many innocent children! And if you try to explain to them that Jesus suffered too, they answer: It's really Jesus who's our main topic of discussion! Why did he too have to suffer? At least it's certain he was innocent! At the bottom of human resentment against God the Father there is, therefore, the suffering of the world, the fact that he, man, suffers and God doesn't; that the Son suffered while the Father remained impassible. It's on this point, therefore, that we want to be enlightened with the help of the Holy Spirit.

First of all we want to be enlightened *on the Father's attitude where suffering in general is concerned.* When the Bible came into contact with Greek philosophy, what was most shocking in it were God's "passions," the fact that the God of the Bible "suffered." In fact we read in the Old Testament that God "was grieved to his heart" (cf. Gen 6:6), that he was grieved in the desert" (cf. Ps 78:40). And it is not just a question of a few odd phrases. The whole Bible contains from beginning to end a sort of heartbroken lament by God expressed in the cry: "My people, my people . . . !" *O my people, what have I done to you? In what have I wearied you? Answer me!* (Mic 6:3). The deep reason for this lament is the love of a betrayed Father: *Sons have I reared and brought up, but they have rebelled against me* (Is 1:2). But God is not afflicted because of this for his own sake as if he were lacking something; he is afflicted for man's sake who is thus lost. He is therefore afflicted for pure love. The Bible doesn't fear to make obvious a certain "impotence" on God's part caused by his love for man. Men do all in their power to provoke God with their idols and rebellion; God should in his justice destroy them but this is where we witness a contrast, a certain drama in God himself, revealed in these words of Hosea: *How can I give you up, O Ephraim! How can I hand you over, O Israel!. . . My heart recoils within me, my compassion grows warm and tender. I will not execute my fierce anger* (Hos 11:8-9). Even when God is obliged to fall back on punishment to make his people see light and purify them from their iniquity as during the exile, it is written that *He does not willingly afflict or grieve the sons of men* (Lam 3:33). If man suffers, God suffers too because he is acting against his will. In a rabbinic comment on the destruction of the temple we can read that that day "the Holy One cried" and to Jeremiah he says: "Today I'm like a man whose only son has died on the day prepared for his wedding; don't you grieve for me and my son?" (*Midrash on the Lamentations*, in *Eka R. Petichta*). In the *Lamentations* it is God himself and not only the prophet who is lamenting. And yet it is well-known how sensitive Hebrew thought is to the theme of divine transcendence and glory.

I have mentioned the scandal of philosophers concerning this revelation about God. To them God was an idea, the idea of Good and not a living person; an idea doesn't suffer or "have passions." In fact it is said that their God "cannot mix with man" (Plato, *Symp.* 203a), that, at the most, he can be "loved" but never "loving": he "moves the world in so far as he is loved," as the final cause, Aristotle says (cf. *Metaph.* XII, 7, 1072b), and not in so far as he loves and loves first. He would disqualify himself if he did because he would be submitting to what is changeable and particular. God is the Unmoved Mover, that is he who moves everything while remaining, in himself, immobile and impassible. We can comprehend how intolerable biblical God's anger, suffering and all the other "passions" must have appeared to them. "God—one of these wrote—must not be subject to any temporal sentiment of hatred or love whatever and therefore he cannot feel either anger or mercy; he must not be perturbed by sorrow nor allow himself to be a prey to impatience but, free from all passion, he cannot be subject either to sorrow or to joy, neither can he unexpectedly wish for or not wish for a given thing" (Apuleius, *De Deo Socratis*, 12).

This was the dominating idea of God at the time when christian theology was at its beginning. For centuries there was a strong attempt by certain scholars (the gnostics) to eliminate all these things from the Bible and adapt the concept of God to that of philosophers to make the "God of Abraham, Isaac and Jacob" the "God of philosophers." But how did the faith of the Church react? Tertullian, one of the strictest and most courageous wrote: "To know who God is we don't approach the school of philosophers or Epicurus, but we go straight to the prophets and to Christ. We, who believe in a God who even came on earth wanting to share with us the lowness of the human state for our salvation, are very far from the idea of those who want a God who cares for nothing. From this follows the idea of the heretics which says: But if God can become angry, can raise his voice and grieve, then he can also be corrupted and die! In fact, Christians do believe that God died even if he lives forever and ever. How foolish they are! They judge divine things in the same way as what is human and, as in man these passions imply corruption, they think it is the same for God whereas if the corruptibility of human nature makes these passions signs of corruption in us, divine incorruptibility in God makes them free from all corruption" (*Adv. Marc.* II, 16; CCL I, p. 493).

Even those scholars who were fascinated by Greek philosophy remained faithful to the Bible on this point. Origen, the most famous of these, commenting on the Bible, reaches the point of affirming that in a certain sense in God the Passion preceded the Incarnation and that the earthly and historical passion of Christ is the manifestation and consequence of a preceding passion which the Father had suffered for us. In fact he wrote: "The Saviour came on earth out of pity for the human race. He suffered our passions even before suffering the cross, before he deigned to take on our flesh. If he had not undergone them first, he would not have come to participate in our human life. What was this passion which he suffered for us at the beginning? It was the passion of love. Doesn't the Father, God of the universe, full of forbearance, of mercy and pity suffer in some way, too? Or perhaps you disregard the fact that when he occupies himself with human things, he suffers a human passion? He suffers a passion of love" (Origen, *In Ez.hom.* 6,6; GCS, 1925, p. 384 f.; cf. *Tom in Mt.* 10,23; GCS, 1935, p.33).

Origen goes back to the real root of the problem which is to know whether we believe in a God of love or not. Pagan philosophers were well aware that if God loves man and is interested in what happens to him and in some way enters into their vortex, he is no longer "impassible and tranquil." For this reason they positively denied that he loved, saying that he can only "be loved," but he cannot "love." But Christians could not accept this conclusion without suddenly denying the whole Bible; thus they opened themselves to the mystery of a suffering God. St. Paul himself talks of the possibility of "grieving" the Holy Spirit, that is causing him to suffer (cf. Eph. 4:30). To a God who "is love," suffering and passion are certainly more fitting than their opposite which is the impassibility of God. God suffers "a passion of love," that is a passion that comes from the fact that he really loves. The word "passion" itself expresses in our language this mysterious bond between suffering and love: it is in fact used for a great overwhelming love as well as for a great suffering. What the *Imitation of Christ* (III,5) says is also true of God and that is that "there is no love without sorrow." "We are dealing with a decisive development in our view of God which is not in the first place 'absolute power' but absolute love and whose sovereignty is not manifested in keeping for himself what belongs to him but in abandoning it" (H.U. von Balthasar, *Mysterium Paschale*, I,4; *in Mysterium Salutis*, III, 2, Einsiedeln 1969).

Certainly, the words "passion" and "suffering" applied to God, have an analogical significance which differs from their meaning in the human sphere. It is a question of infinitely free suffering which doesn't depend on any necessity or fact and which doesn't destroy the other divine attributes but confirms them even if we can't see how. It is "the passion of the impassible" as one of Origen's disciples, St. Gregory Thaumaturgus says (*Ad Teopompum, in* Pitra, *Anal.Sacra*, IV, 1883, p. 363 ff.). On the contrary certain ancient Fathers pointed out that a basic incapacity to suffer would constitute a limitation for God and would be a sign of a lack of freedom. God can suffer if he so wishes and because he loves, he wants to suffer. God's passion is a sign of infinite sovereignty and power not less than his other perfections. The same must be said of God's famous "anger" which the Bible, including the New Testament, so often talks about. This is a pure manifestation of love because it is always anger against sin and never against the sinner: *Have I any pleasure in the death of the wicked, says the Lord God, and not rather that he should turn from his way and live* (Ezek 18:23). God strikes fear into the heart of the sinner simply to save him from sin; he strikes him in this world to save him for eternity even if this truth wasn't immediately understood from the beginning by those to whom revelation was destined for. In fact, he "is merciful to all and has loathing for none of the things he has made; he corrects little by little those who trespass so that they may be freed from wickedness and put their trust in him (cf. Wis 11:23; 12:2). Wrath in God is a manifestation of his transcendent holiness. "To the worshippers of the Old Testament this wrath in no way detracts from his figure but rather it is a natural indispensable expression of holiness itself. And rightly so! In fact this wrath is nothing but the same *tremendum* which in itself is completely irrational but is here expressed through an ingenuous analogy with the natural world and precisely with the passionate life of man. It is an extraordinarily life-like and impressive analogy which enhances its value and is necessary for us if we wish to give expression to religious sentiment" (R. Otto, *The Idea of the Holy*, 1923, chap. 4).

3. The Father's Compassion

Let us now look at the other aspect of the problem which started with Christianity following the revelation of the Trinity and the new "fatherhood" of God the Father, that is at the *Father's attitude towards the passion of his Son Jesus Christ.* Is it true that God the Father is only he who "causes" the suffering of the Son and sees him suffer? If it is written that "he afflicts the sons of men against his wish," what can we say of this Son who is the beloved Son and all love and obedience to the Father? St. Paul affirms that God "didn't spare his own Son but gave him for all of us." If we read this text in an edition of the Bible suitably annotated with references (for example, the so-called Jerusalem Bible) we find in the margin of the passage of the Epistle to the Romans a precise reference to Genesis 22:16. It is Abraham who is being spoken of. God says to Abraham: "Because you have done this and *have not withheld your son, your only son,* I will indeed bless you." "Let us compare these words— writes Origen—with those of the Apostle when he says of God: *He did not spare his own Son but gave him up for us all*" (*Hom. in Gen.* 8,12; GCS, 29, p. 84). Abraham, walking in silence towards Mount Moriah to offer his son Isaac as a burnt offering was, therefore, the figure of another father. The liturgy too appropriates this spiritual reading of the episode of Abraham when it puts together (2nd Sunday in Lent, Year B) the reading of Genesis 22 and that of Romans 8:32 ("God did not spare his own Son").

This helps us to form a more exact idea of the Father's attitude in the mystery of redemption. He was not absent, in heaven, while his Son went towards Calvary. On the contrary, he was with him. Jesus said to his disciples: *You will leave me alone; yet I am not alone for the Father is with me* (Jn 16:32). Who can describe Abraham's sentiments as he accompanied his son towards the place of immolation? Origen says that the moment of greatest temptation for Abraham was when, along the way, his son innocently turned to him and asked him where the victim for the burnt offering was and calling him "my father!" At the words "my father!" Abraham started as one at fault and answered: "Here am I, my son!" How could he say to his son: "You are the burnt offering!" This was indeed the voice of temptation for Abraham; all his innermost paternal feelings were shaken at the words "my father!" Who knows what passed in the heart of the heavenly Father when, in Gethsemane, Jesus turned to him with the same words: "My Father!": *Abbà, Father! All things are possible to thee, remove this cup from me* (Mk 14:36). Abraham would certainly have preferred to die a thousand times rather than kill his son. The Father and Son are, therefore, together in the passion and the moment in which Jesus feels the Father most distant and cries out: *Why have you abandoned me?* is, in fact, the moment in which the Father is closest to him and lovingly embraces him to himself even more closely if this were possible, because it is the moment when the human will of the Son is most closely united to the divine will.

Now we understand what St. Paul means when he says: "God did not spare his own Son but gave him for all of us"; he means that he did not spare him for himself, that is, he didn't keep him for himself "as a jealous treasure." The Father is not only the one who received the Son's sacrifice but he also makes the sacrifice of his Son; he made the great sacrifice of giving us his Son! St. Augustine exclaimed: "How great was your love for us, good Father, for you did not even spare your own Son, but gave him up to save us sinners! How great was your love for us!" (*Conf.* X,43).

The earliest theology of the Church spoke of God's suffering in Christ with the greatest simplicity and certainty. Tertullian reports the words of a witness of this archaic theology which flourished above all in Asia Minor: "If the Son suffered, the Father suffered with him," and again, "How could the Son have suffered without the Father suffering with him!" (Tertullian, *Adv.Prax.* 29, CCL 2, 1203).

Soon, however, these simple words inspired by the Bible were disturbed by heresy. (I do not think that the expressions just quoted were part of the heresy as Tertullian insinuates when reporting them). This heresy denied the distinction between Father and Son; in other words, it denied the Trinity. It held that as there is only one person in God, to say that the Son suffered is the same as saying that the Father suffered; the names change but the person is the same. This is why their adversaries called them "Patripassians," that is those who attribute the passion to the Father. This, however, was a very different idea to the orthodox one according to which the Father, while remaining the Father, participated in the Son's passion who remained the Son, that is, a distinct person. As usually happens in such cases, the rejection of this heresy brought with it a rejection of the truth that preceded it as if to leave the heresy without any claims. The theme of the compassion of the Father disappeared from the language and conscience of the Church; it was completely disregarded. It became the common thing to strictly distinguish between the passion as something *willed*, and this is common to the Father and to the Son, and the passion *suffered* which belongs to the Son only. The general and inexorable process of adaptation to the culture of the time caused the Biblical idea of God's suffering to be sacrificed to the Greek idea of God's impassibility. It was also influenced by the fact that the impassibility (*apatheia*) became, in certain monasteries, the highest ascetic ideal, the very peak of sanctity, causing it to be supremely attributed to God. "Thus ontological metaphysics was able to penetrate theology gradually and definitely supplanting the biblical way of thinking . . . The immediate consequence was that the image of God as defined by tradition took on, against the intentions of the Councils of Nicaea and Constantinople, the typically Greek features of an immobile and indifferent God" (W. Kasper, *Jesus der Christus,* III, 1,2, Mainz 1974).

Nevertheless it has remained a fixed starting point in the dogma of the Church from which to start again. Even amidst numerous contrasts the faith of the Church has always continued to profess *Theopaschism,* the doctrine of the suffering of God in Christ, holding strongly to the old affirmation that "God suffered" (cf. DS, 201, 222). The meaning of this dogmatic affirmation is that God suffered "in the flesh" but we know from theology that "who" suffered in the flesh—the subject—is the person of the Son, that is, God. "One member of the Trinity suffered" and if one suffered, because of the reciprocal interpenetration of the three divine persons the whole Trinity suffered. In the body of Christ which is the Church, "if one member suffers, all suffer together" (1 Cor 12:26): how could what holds for ecclesial communion not hold for Trinitarian communion which is its source and model? The Father's suffering was certainly different to that of the Son made man; it was a reflex suffering or a suffering of compassion. As the first theologians rightly said, "if the Son suffered because of his passion, the Father suffered because of his com-passion."

In our times after the long silence about God's suffering, a silence in which the strange idea of an "implacable" God found space, we are witnessing a reflourishing of this truth in the conscience of the Church (cf. K. Kitamori, *Theology of the Pain of God,* Richmond 1965). It is one of those unpredictable but providential surprises of the Holy Spirit, an authentic sign of the times. Certain theologians of different origins and tendencies have started to talk again of this mysterious fact. Some have affirmed that the act of "giving his own Son" causes God deeper suffering than any suffering in the created world and that the task of "Jesus Crucified" is exactly that of manifesting the Father's passion. K. Barth notes that our opinion, according to which God can be absolutely and nothing other than active in opposition to all suffering, proves itself false and pagan in the light of the fact that in Jesus Christ, he *is* and *does* just this (that is, he lowers himself, solidarizes with the world and suffers); it is not for us to be wiser than God and establish what can be reconciled or not with the divine nature but we must deduce it from what he does; his glory consists in the freedom of his love (cf. *Kirchliche Dogmatik,* IV/1, 303 ff.).

Recently, the International Theological Commission which works for the Congregation for the Doctrine of the Faith, examining this aspect of Trinitarian doctrine, considered this new insight as a good thing judging it to be in line with what the Scriptures and the Fathers of the Church say and, in particular, they acknowledged the Trinitarian dimension of the Cross of Christ and that all three persons, the Father, Son and Holy Spirit, were involved in different ways in Christ's passion. Pope John Paul II also welcomed this "rediscovery" of the true aspect of Biblical God. In his Encyclical on the Holy Spirit he wrote: "The concept of God as the necessarily most perfect being certainly excludes from God any pain deriving from deficiencies or wounds; but in the depths of God there is a Father's love that, faced with man's sin, in the language of the Bible reacts so deeply as to say: 'I am sorry that I have made him!'. . . The Sacred Book speaks to us of a Father who feels compassion for man, as though sharing his pain. In the end, this inscrutable and indescribable fatherly 'pain' will bring about above all the wonderful economy of redemptive love in Jesus Christ, so that through the *mysterium pietatis* love can reveal itself in the history of man as stronger than sin. . . In the humanity of Jesus the Redeemer, the 'suffering' of God is concretized" (Ency. *Dominum et Vivificantem,* 39).

Before the theologians there were simple believers who perceived in their hearts something like an echo of God's lament coming from afar and from that day on their whole lives changed to the point of not being able to speak of other than this (cf. Mother B. Schlink, *Who Hears God's Lament?* Darmstadt, 1983). These souls did not learn of God the Father's suffering from a study of theology as if it were a thing of the past; they learnt it directly because God the Father still suffers for men, for their refusal of his love . . . In the lives of certain saints we can read that the thought "love is not loved" almost drove them crazy and they used to repeat these words for whole nights, shouting them even to inanimate things so that they would join them in their crying. How can we therefore say again that "man suffers but God doesn't?" O thoughtless man, pause for a moment and consider if there is suffering like God's suffering!

4. Love and Obedience

We must now face the most delicate point from which the image of an "implacable" Father towards his Son Jesus Christ, comes. Why did the Father "give" him up to die and how can this be reconciled with his "compassion"? In St. John's Gospel Jesus says: *For this reason the Father loves me, because I lay down my life, that I may take it again. No one takes it from me, but I lay it down on my own accord. I have power to lay it down, and I have power to take it again; this charge I have received from my Father* (Jn 10:17-18). Jesus speaks of "power" to lay down his life and a "charge" to do so, of a free act and of obedience and the key to the mystery lies in this paradox. How and when did the Father give his Son the "charge" to freely lay down his life? St. Thomas tells us that the Father gave his Son to death "in so far as he inspired him with the will to die for us infusing him with love for us" (*S.Theol.* III, q. 47, a. 3). What a different image of the Father emerges from these words if compared to the image evoked at the beginning! The "charge" the Son received from the Father is therefore first of all, a charge to love us. In transmitting his nature, which is love, to his Son, the Father transmitted his "passion of love" and this passion of love took Jesus to the cross!

In the New Testament it is sometimes mentioned that Jesus gave himself up for us "because he loved us" (cf. Eph 5:2) and at other times that he gave himself up for us "to obey" the Father (cf. Phil 2:8). The two things, love and obedience, seem different to us and we prefer to believe that he died for love rather than for obedience. But God's Word and Church theology offer us an insight into a deeper point of view where both things converge. It is true that Jesus died for love of us but it was in this that his obedience to the Father lay! The offering and the need, love and obedience, are so interwoven that we cannot reach a full under-standing because they lose themselves in the mystery of the Trinity it-self, that is in the fact that God is, at the same time, one and triune. Love comes from the unity and obedience comes from the Trinity. (Love, in fact, is common to all three divine persons but obedience belonged only to the Son). St. Bernard threw light on a true aspect of the mystery, even if only partially, when he wrote that "God the Father did not *demand* his Son's blood but he accepted its *offer to him* ("Non requisivit Pater san-guinem Filii, sed tamen accepit oblatum") (*De err. Abael.* 8:21; PL 182, 1070). The most perfect obedience doesn't lie in carrying out to perfec-tion an order received but in making the will of the person commanding one's own will. That was what the Son's obedience was like; he actually shared the same will with the Father. Yet, the obedience of Jesus wasn't easy; on the contrary, it was the most difficult type of obedience imag-inable, so much that it cost him to sweat blood because the Son of God obeyed "according to human nature"; he had to carry out such a perfect act of obedience with a will like ours. He had to fulfill, as man, a divine obedience!

5. Confidence in the Father!

What does all we've said so far on God's suffering signify? Does it mean that perhaps God is impotent against evil? But let us not commit the error of distorting the Biblical image of the Father. He remains the "three times holy," the Almighty, he who is sovereign above everything else; all his suffering is a sign of "condescension" and not of weakness. The unique characteristic of the God of Jesus Christ is that while remain-ing God, the highest, he "who is in heaven," that is, above everything and who can do everything, is given to us as Father, (*Abbà*). "I believe in God the Father almighty," is the first article of our faith: a Father but the almighty; the almighty but a Father! A father however good but not strong and free and capable of instilling security would not be a real father and man couldn't have complete confidence in him. This is what the enemy tries to insinuate at times in the heart of man, that God him-self is unable to stop evil; but this is not true. The answer is that it is ac-tually in suffering that God shows the greatness of his power because—

as a prayer of the liturgy says—"he manifests his omnipotence especially when he forgives and shows mercy." "God manifests his power in impotence. His infinite power is also infinite suffering" (W. Kasper, *loc.cit.*). In his infinite wisdom, God decided to overcome evil by suffering it, taking it in some way upon himself. He wanted to overcome it, in accordance with his nature, not by force but out of love and thus he gave us the first example of how "we must overcome evil with good" (cf. Rom 12:21). We must, however, remember that the Father's "compassion" for the Son does not end with the cross but with the resurrection. He gave his Son the charge to lay down his life "so as to then take it up again." He never thought even for one minute of his Son's death without thinking of his resurrection. It's we who are not able to think of the two things at the same time. In the resurrection Jesus was "justified in the Spirit" (cf. 1 Tim 3:16), that is, the Father justified him according to the Spirit, thereby rendering justice also to himself and to his victorious love. St. Paul says that in raising Jesus from the dead, God the Father showed "the immeasurable greatness of his power and the working of his great might" (cf. Eph 1:19-20).

Therefore we can have confidence in the Father! This is the certainty we were looking for and which we need. God's fatherly love "is the only indestructible thing in this life, it's Archimedes' real principle" (Kierkegaard, *Journal* III, A 73). If a child is certain that his father loves him, he will grow up sure of himself and able to face life. A child out walking holding his father's hand or being swung around by his father with exclamations of joy or who talks to his father as man to man is the happiest and freest creature in the world. Once an acrobat did a trick on the top floor of a skyscraper; he leant out as far as he could possibly go supporting himself on the bare tips of his toes and holding his small child in his arms. When they came down someone asked the child if he'd been frightened and the child, surprised at the question, answered: "No, I wasn't, my father was holding me!" Faith gives us back a little of this confidence which can make us new and free creatures; it wants to lead us to the point where, convinced, we exclaim as St. Paul does in our text: "If God is for us, who is against us? Who shall bring any charge against us, who is to condemn, who shall separate us from the love of Christ?

We are more than conquerors through him who loved us!" (cf. Rom 8:31 ff.). And Jesus tells us therefore to free ourselves of all fear, of all cowardice, of all discouragement. Why do you fear? Your Father "knows" . . . Even the very hairs of your head are counted. You are worth more than many sparrows (cf. Mt 6:25-32).

The Apostle uses the solemn affirmation that "God did not spare his own Son" precisely to inculcate this confidence: "If God did not spare his own Son but gave him up for us all, *will he not also give us all things with him*?" (Rom 8:32): the first part of the sentence is there to make the second part credible.

St. Ireneus says that the Father has two arms; the two arms of the Father are the Son and the Holy Spirit (*Adv.Haer.* V,1,3). With these arms he sought us in the darkness of the world and now that he has found us, he holds us to himself. We are more closely united to the Father through Christ in the Holy Spirit than any son has ever been to his father or mother because we don't remain apart from him but are admitted to him. Jesus said, and he was certain that he would always be heard: *Father, I desire that they also, whom thou hast given me, may be with me where I am* (Jn 17:24), and where else can the Son be if not at the Father's side? That, therefore, is where our "prepared place" is, our "mansion." That is where we shall go and there we shall remain to contemplate his glory saying an eternal, amazed *Abbà*! Father!

Before this mystery of the heavenly Father's tenderness it comes spontaneously to us to turn to Jesus and say to him: "Jesus, you are our elder brother, tell us what we can do to show ourselves worthy of so much love and suffering on the Father's part!" And Jesus answers us through his Gospel and life. "There is, he says, something you can do, something I also did and which pleases the Father: have confidence in him, trust him and do him credit! Do this against everything, against everyone and against yourselves." Let us think of a man accused by the whole world; all the evidence is against him, so much so that not even his family believe in him any longer and, in fact, it would be madness to still want to defend him. But this man's son defends him against everyone stating that what was said cannot be true because he knows his father and he will never give in . . . Wouldn't the joy and courage this father receives from his son's unshakable trust in him, compensate for all the incomprehension of the rest of the world? Well, we can be such a son for our heavenly Father! When therefore we are in darkness or distress, when we can see nothing ahead of us but absurdness and we are on the point of giving in, let us pull ourselves together and cry out with faith: "Father, I no longer understand you but I place my trust in you!" Jesus too cried out like this in the garden of olives. He said: "Father, let this cup pass from me!" The cup didn't pass but Jesus didn't lose his confidence in the Father and he died exclaiming: "Father, into your hands I commend my spirit!" (Lk 23:46). And the Father heard him for his filial submission (cf. Heb 5:7). And how he was heard! He was heard more than if the cup had passed without him having to drink it because the Father raised him from the dead and made him, also as man, our Lord.

There exists a tragic "father complex" and the very people that introduced this idea have often been victims of such a complex without realizing it. It consists in the inability to accept oneself as "son" at a deeper and more general level than the physical one, that is as being generated by someone, as being dependent creature and, as a consequence, the inability to accept a Father who is the origin of one's existence and freedom and in whom the last meaning of things is placed. The refusal of the Father which exists in our day, and which psychoanalysis emphasizes, has the same basis mentioned by St. Paul when speaking of the refusal of God in general, and that is, impiety. This is man's will to be himself God, his own origin or at least to be able himself to build his own God to which he can submit himself, calling "god" the work of his own hands or his own "invention." In reading how certain psychologists, such as Freud, describe the Oedipus complex of their patients, a believer has the same painful feeling that the wife of a doctor unknowingly suffering from cancer might have on hearing her husband, who is still unaware of his illness, pitifully explain the terrible symptoms of this disease to a patient. Psychology cannot do much about helping man to get rid of the father complex if it doesn't get rid of it itself first. There is only one way to do this: through faith. In believing one takes that leap which carries one "completely into the arms of the invisible," in blessed dependence on truth and discovers that he has found in God what he had always been looking for with all his strength without ever having found it: a refuge and strength, a very pleasant help in trouble" (Ps 46:2).

6. A Feast for the Father

It's sad that in the whole of the liturgical year there is no feast for the Father; in the Missal there is not even a votive mass in his honour. It's rather strange if we think about it. There are numerous feasts for Jesus, for the Son; there's a feast for the Holy Spirit and many feasts for the Mother . . . But there is not even one for the Father, "the source and origin of all divinity." We could almost say that now it is the Father and no longer the Holy Spirit who is "the divine unknown." It's true that there is a feast for the most Holy Trinity which is, however, the feast of a mystery or a dogma and not of a person or, at any rate, not of one only divine person. On the other hand, the fact that there exists a feast for the Holy Family doesn't prevent the Church from celebrating the three persons of the Holy Family also individually. There is a feast, two in fact, for Jesus' foster father but there's not even one for the real Father. Might not this be the time to fill the gap? Many feasts were created to answer particular needs of an epoch: the feast of *Corpus Domini*, for example, was started as an answer of faith to the denial of the real presence by Berengar of Tours; the Church answered the threat of Jansenism with the feast and cult of the Sacred Heart and no one will ever know how many or what spiritual blessings this cult has been the source of. As I have already mentioned, today the threat is against the very core of the Christian faith and that is the revelation of God as Father, the "Father of our Lord Jesus Christ" as St. Paul always calls him, and therefore of the Trinity itself. If providence is today making us again aware of the mystery of God's suffering, this is not just by chance but because the Holy Spirit knows that this is a necessary remedy to cure the sick mind of modern man who has found, in suffering, the stumbling block that keeps him far from God.

In the pedagogy of the Church, feasts have always been a privileged means of getting a particular mystery, or event in the history of salvation, to penetrate the lives of the faithful. Our knowledge of the Holy Spirit and our familiarity with him would certainly be much weaker without the feast of Pentecost. Feasts are a living catechesis and today there is urgent need for a living catechesis on the Father. Besides the importance as a catechesis, a feast for the Father would have, like all feasts, an importance as *homologesis*, that is, it would be a public and joyful confession of faith. A feast is in fact the highest and most solemn way of proclaiming the faith because it unites praise, celebration and thanksgiving and because all the people participate chorally. Christians would undoubtedly give great joy to the heart of the risen Lord if they managed to realize this project "ecumenically" that is if all the Churches agreed to celebrate together a feast for the Father on the same day. It is not a question of introducing a new feast in the liturgical calendar, but rather of dedicating a Sunday of the year to the Father (for instance, the one in which the parable of the prodigal son is read) and naming it "the Sunday of the Father," as the Orthodox liturgy does when it names certain Sundays after the leading biblical character of the day.

While waiting for that day we can already celebrate the Father's feast within our hearts "in spirit and truth" encouraging perhaps little spiritual and local initiatives aimed at making the Father better known, honouring him and expressing our filial love to him in union with Jesus who constantly feasts his Father . . . This is already taking place and many people are experiencing the new and extraordinary impetus it gives to their faith and indeed to their whole spiritual lives.

Referring to man's state before Christ an author of the 2nd century said: "Ignorance about the Father was the cause of much distress and fear" (*Evang. Veritatis*). Hoping to have dispelled a little of this ignorance about the Father which unfortunately still exists in the world, let us now continue on our way of discovering salvation, keeping ourselves well anchored to God's word.

VII. Let Not Sin Reign in Your Mortal Bodies!

Freedom from sin

Chapter six of the Letter of the Romans continues to develop the theme of salvation but it does so from a different point of view. So far St. Paul has told us *how* to reach salvation (gratuitously, through faith); he has talked to us about the *author* of salvation and of the *event* that made it possible (Jesus Christ and his passion and in the background, the Father and his compassion). Now the Apostle goes on to tell us about the *content* of salvation, that is about the elements that constitute it. This content has a negative aspect which is freedom from sin and the law (Rom 6 and 7) and a positive aspect which is the gift of the Holy Spirit (Rom 8). That's how salvation was described by the prophets who had heralded the new and eternal covenant and that is how it was accomplished: *I will sprinkle clean water upon you and you shall be clean from all your uncleannesses and from all your idols I will cleanse you,* God says in Ezekiel and he immediately adds: *And a new heart I will give you and a new spirit I will put within you* (Ezek 36:25-26). Jesus fulfilled the first of these two actions through his death and resurrection and the second through Pentecost.

These two aspects are interdependent. Freedom is in fact the condition for the coming of the Spirit; freedom from the lordship of sin is the presupposition for entering the lordship of Christ which is done through the Spirit. In the Book of Wisdom it is written that *Wisdom does not enter a deceitful soul, not dwell in a body enslaved to sin* (Wis 1:4) and Jesus says that new wine is not put into old wineskins (cf. Mt 9:17). God does not put the new wine of his Spirit into the old wineskin of a heart still enslaved to sin. "Suppose that God wants to fill you with honey: if you are filled with vinegar where will you put the honey? It's necessary to empty the jar, rather, the jar must be cleaned out thoroughly and rinsed well to make it ready to receive the new substance" (St. Augustine, *In Ioh. Ep.* 4,6; PL 35, 2009). St. Peter said something concerning this to the people on Pentecost day and he made a promise that holds for us too: *Repent . . . and you shall receive the gift of the Holy Spirit* (Acts 2:38). We have reached the heart and crucial point of our journey. It is now in fact, through repentance and the gift of the Holy Spirit, that we must carry out the renewal and realization of Baptism which constitutes the most concrete fruit of all the work undertaken. What we are about to accomplish is a direct consequence of the *kerygma* we have just listened to. "Christ died for our sins": therefore, let us die to sin; "Christ rose for our justification": therefore, let us walk in the newness of life, let us walk according to the Spirit!

Chapter six is the passage from the Letter to the Romans that will guide us in the effort to free ourselves from sin and the following expressions are particularly useful: *Are we to continue in sin that grace may abound? By no means! . . . We know that our old self was crucified with him so that the sinful body might be destroyed and we might no longer be enslaved to sin . . . So you also must consider yourselves dead to sin . . . Let not sin therefore reign in your mortal bodies, to make you obey their passions. Do not yield your members to sin as instruments of wickedness* (Rom 6:1-13).

It is a true and real Paschal "exodus" we are talking about. To celebrate Easter means "to cleanse out the old leaven to be a new lump"; it means to pass from "the leaven of malice and evil to the unleavened bread of sincerity and truth" (cf. 1 Cor 5:7-8). The Fathers of the Church said it meant "to pass from sin to life, from guilt to grace, from being blemished to holiness" (St. Ambrose, *De Sacr.* 1,4,12; CSEL 73,20). Through the Apostle's words or through other words of the New Testament which talk of freedom from sin, we can distinguish the acts or steps we must take to fully carry out our "happy migration" from sin and with God's help fulfil it in ourselves—this very day, if possible. In fact it is written: *Today, when you hear his voice, do not harden your hearts* (Heb 4:7).

1. Acknowledge Your Sin

The first step is the acknowledgement of sin. Fundamentally, the Apostle made us take this step at the beginning of his Letter by telling us that "all have sinned," that "we have no excuse" before God and then, where Christ's passion is concerned, in telling us that he died "for our sins." Now, however, it's a question of extending this acknowledgement to our present sins and the different state of each one of us. It's a question of coming to the real point and passing from theory to practice. The world has lost the sense of sin. It treats it lightly as if it were the most innocent of things. It advertises its products and activities with the idea of sin to make them more attractive. It talks of sin, even of the most serious ones, in a caressing way: little sins, little vices, sweet sins . . . but it no longer fears it. It fears everything but sin; atmospheric pollution, incurable diseases, nuclear war but it doesn't fear war against God who is eternal, omnipotent and love whereas Jesus tells us to fear only the one who, after he has killed, has power to cast into hell (cf. Lk 12:4-5).

This "environmental" state exerts a tremendous influence even on believers who want to live according to the Gospel. It anaesthetizes their conscience into a sort of spiritual numbness. There is such a thing as a narcosis of sin. Christians no longer recognize their real enemy, the master who enslaves them, simply because it's a sweet slavery. Many people who talk about sin have a completely inadequate idea of it. Sin becomes depersonalized and projected only on the structures and in the end it is identified with the attitude of one's political or ideological adversaries. Some say that sin lies in being "right wing!" while others say sin lies in being "left wing." But what Christ says of the kingdom of God is valid for the kingdom of sin too (cf. Lk 17:21): When they tell you: sin is here or sin is there, don't believe them because sin is within you! An inquiry into what people think sin is would probably give very frightening results. Instead of concentrating on freeing ourselves from sin, every effort is made today to free us from the *remorse* of sin; instead of struggling against sin, we struggle against the *idea* of sin. We do what is considered the worst thing of all in every other field and that is we deny the problem rather than solve it; we push the evil back and bury it in the unconscious rather than get rid of it. It's like thinking we can eliminate death by eliminating the thought of death or like worrying about getting rid of a temperature without curing the actual illness of which the temperature is just a providentially revealing symptom. St. John tells us that if we say that we have not sinned, we deceive ourselves and make God a liar (cf. 1 Jn 1:8-10); God, in fact, says the opposite; he says we have sinned. Scripture says that Christ "died for our sins" (cf. 1 Cor 15:3). If you take away sin, you have rendered vain the very redemption of Christ and destroyed the significance of his death. Christ would have struggled against simple windmills; he would have shed his blood for nothing.

The type of acknowledgement of sin we have mentioned so far is what we could call a doctrinal acknowledgement in the sense that such acknowledgement is an acceptance of Biblical and Church doctrine on sin. But this is not enough; another type of acknowledgement is required of us which is not only theoretical and general but existential and individual too. This acknowledgement consists in the sudden awareness that sin—this monstrous and dreadful thing—is beside you and within you. It is an awareness that makes you shudder. Like someone getting up one morning who discovers that he has slept the whole night with a poisonous snake coiled up in a corner of his room. "Let yourself experience sin as a lump, realizing that it is yourself, but without defining it precisely. Then cry out in your heart this one word 'sin', 'sin'. God can teach you through experience far better than words can. For it is best when this word is wholly interior without a definite thought or actual sound. Yet, occasionally, you will be so satisfied with the meaning of sin that the sorrow and burden of it will flow over your body and soul and you may burst out with the word itself" (Anonymous, *The Cloud of Unknowing*, ch. 40).

The first step, therefore, in our exodus from sin is to acknowledge sin, acknowledge it in all its tremendous seriousness, awakening ourselves from the sleep we have been thrown into by the "exhalations" of the world.

2. Repent of Sin

The second step is repentance. The Acts of the Apostles tell us that when they heard the awful accusation mentioned earlier on: "You Crucified Jesus of Nazareth!," those present *were cut to the heart, and said to Peter and the rest of the Apostles, "Brethren, what shall we do?" And Peter said to them, "Repent!"* (Acts 2:37 ff.). A little further on in the same Acts of the Apostles, we find something to reflect on. Peter repeats the same kind of discourse before the Council. He says: *The God of our fathers raised Jesus whom you killed by hanging him on a tree.* But the reaction is very different this time: *When they heard this they were enraged and wanted to kill them* (Acts 5:31-33). What they couldn't do on that occasion to the Apostles, they did, instead, shortly after and for the same reason to Stephen (Acts 7:52-58). This comparison shows us that before God's Word reprimanding us for sin it is possible to follow two ways which are diametrically opposite: repentance or hardness of heart. It is said that the three thousand listening to Peter on the day of Pentecost "were contrite" (*katenugesan*), that they were cut to the heart. It is said that the members of the Council listening to Peter and Stephen were cut to the heart too, that they trembled (*dieprionto*) but with rage and not with repentance. It is here that sin against the Holy Spirit is placed which Jesus says will not be forgiven in this age or in the age to come (cf. Mt 12:31). It consists in fact in the refusal to accept the remission of sins which comes through repentance: "If Jesus says that blasphemy against the Holy Spirit cannot be forgiven either in this life or in the next, it is because this 'non-forgiveness' is linked, as to its cause, to 'non-repentance,' in other words to the radical refusal to be converted" (John Paul II, Ency. *Dominum et Vivificantem,* 49). We are dealing with the mystery of human freedom which can choose either God or oneself. As I have already said, this should fill us with fear and trembling; in fact the alternative exists also for us; we too can follow either one way or the other, either that of the multitude or that of the Council.

But what does repentance mean? The original word, *metanoein,* signifies a change of mind, of way of thinking, but it's not a question of changing our way of thinking for another way of thinking that is still ours, however different; it's not a question of substituting our old mentality with another mentality that is still ours or a judgement of ours for another judgement of ours. It's a question of substituting our way of thinking with God's way of thinking, our mentality with God's, our judgement with God's judgement. Yes, repentance means *accepting God's judgement*. God has his own judgement on us, on our spiritual state, on our behaviour. This is the only totally and absolutely true judgement. God alone can see into the depths of our hearts, our responsibility and the attenuating circumstances. God knows all about us. Repentance means accepting this judgement of God's saying: My God, I submit to your judgement: *Thou art justified in thy sentence and blameless in thy judgement* (Ps 51:4). All of this requires "compunction," that is a sort of piercing of the heart because in order to admit that God is right, you have to admit that you are wrong, you must die to yourself. This is the case also because when you accept God's judgement you can see what sin really is and it frightens you. As a psalm tells us, God's judgement "is like a great abyss" (cf. Ps 36:6).

When it is sincere, *sorrow* is an essential part of repentance. Man not only acknowledges that he has done wrong but he is sorrowful for having done so and he is sorrowful not only for the punishment he has deserved and must accept but more so for the sorrow he has caused God and for having betrayed God's great love. He is sorrowful for what sin caused Jesus to undergo on the cross. True sorrow grows only in the presence of love: "He loved me and gave himself for me" (Gal 2:20). Tears are often the visible sign of this sorrow that touches the heart and cleanses it. It's a good thing to ask to experience at least once this cleansing of water and fire. One day, while meditating on the agony of Jesus in Gethsemane, a man heard these words echoing within him: "Dost thou wish that it always cost me the blood of my humanity, without thee shedding tears? . . . I am more a friend to thee than such and such a one, for I have done for thee more than they; they would not have suffered what I have suffered for thee, and they would not have died for thee as I have done in the time of thy infidelity and cruelties" (B. Pascal, *Pensées* n. 552).

In repentance the Holy Spirit is already at work even if he works with our freedom and on our freedom. Jesus says: "He convinces the world of sin" (Jn 16:7). The Holy Spirit, God's finger of fire, touches the heart, that is the conscience, at a point that he alone knows and opens it to the light of truth. Then the sinner bursts into exclamations that express this new conscience of himself: *For I know my transgressions . . . Against thee, thee only, have I sinned and done that which is evil in thy sight, so that thou art justified in thy sentence* (Ps 51:5 ff.). God is acknowledged as being "just"; man begins to see suffering in all its forms with different eyes, no longer as being caused by God but by his own sin. God is exonerated from evil and proclaimed innocent; his love and goodness are saved. Truth, which was "imprisoned by injustice" is freed. The marvel of repentance is that as soon as man sides against himself, God sides in his favour and immediately defends him from condemnation, even that of his own heart (cf. 1 Jn 3:20 f.). As soon as the prodigal son said: "Father, I have sinned!," the father said: "Bring quickly the best robe . . ." (cf. Lk 15:21 ff.).

Indeed, repentance has nothing to do with "feeling like a slave" as has been said (cf. F. Nietzsche, *The Gay Science*, n. 135). Modern psychology has sometimes given the impression of indiscriminately condemning every guilt feeling as if it were a question of neurosis. But it was only able to demonstrate that such a feeling can degenerate and become a guilt complex. But who wasn't aware of this? Although in such cases the guilt feeling is not the cause but the revealing factor of a morbid state when it is not just the result of a wrong religious education. In fact, it becomes more and more obvious even to some great scholars of psychoanalysis, that a genuine and free guilty conscience and repentance are exquisitely worthwhile human feelings. Far from causing a person to regress to the morbid state of passivity and the infliction of self-injury, repentance becomes a constant source of renewal of life. On certain occasions there is nothing that renews hope and trust so much as saying either in the sight of man or of God: "I've sinned, I've done wrong!" (cf. P. Ricoeur, *Finitude et culpabilité,* Paris 1960). If "it is human to err," it is even more human to acknowledge that one has erred, that is to repent. Repentance is not useful to God but to us. God does not exact repentance for the pleasure of triumphing over man or of humiliating him but because he knows that this is man's salvation and that it is the only way worthy of man for him to enter back into life and truth after sinning. A psalm describes the wonderful transformation that repentance works:

> Blessed is he whose transgression is forgiven,
> whose sin is covered.
> When I declared not my sin, my body wasted away . . .
> for day and night thy hand was heavy upon me . . .
> I acknowledged my sin to thee,
> and I did not hide my iniquity.
> I said, "I will confess my transgressions to the Lord";
> then thou didst forgive the guilt of my sin (Ps 32:1 ff.).

As long as man keeps his sin hidden and refuses to acknowledge it, it consumes and saddens him; but when he decides to confess it to God he again experiences peace and beatitude.

The second step is, therefore, repentance for sin. To take this step doesn't necessarily mean that we at once feel cut to the heart and burst into a deluge of tears. This depends on grace and it may happen at once or come about slowly in time without our even realizing it. What is required now is that we start straight away to wish to repent, saying to God: "Make me know true contrition; don't refuse me this grace before I die!" The wish to repent is already repentance.

3. "Cease from sin"

The third step in our exodus is to cease from sin. God's word is once again our guide in this. St. Paul says: *Consider yourselves dead to sin*, and: *Let sin no longer reign in your bodies!* What St. Peter says is an echo of this: *Whoever has suffered in the flesh has ceased from sin, so as to live for the rest of the time in the flesh no longer by human passions but by the will of God . . . Let the time that is past suffice for the passions!* (1 Pet 4:1-3).

This passage, therefore, consists in saying "Enough!" to sin or, as St. Paul says, in "considering ourselves dead to sin." This is the time for decisions or *resolutions*. The question is simple. It involves making the sincere and resolute decision, as far as we can, to sin no longer. Put like that it might sound too ambitious and unrealistic but it is not so. No one of us will become faultless from one day to the next but that's not what God wants from us. Each one of us, if we examine our conscience well, will realize that apart from all the sins we commit, there is one that is different because we are more ready to commit it. It is that sin to which we are secretly attached and which we confess but without the real will to give it up. It's that sin we think we *can* never free ourselves of because, in fact, we don't *want* to free ourselves of it or, at least, not *right now*. In his *Confessions*, St. Augustine describes his struggle to free himself from the sin of sensuality. There was a time when he prayed to God saying: "Grant me chastity and continence . . ." and a voice secretly added: "But not right now!" Until the time arrived when he cried out to himself: "How long shall I go on saying '*tomorrow, tomorrow*'? Why not *now*? Why not make an end of my ugly sins at this moment?" (*Conf.* VIII, 7.12). He only had to say "enough of that" to feel free. Sin enslaves us until we truly say "enough!" Then it loses almost all its power over us. Jesus asks us as he did the paralytic: *Do you want to be healed?* (Jn 5:6). Do you really want it? Because if you really want it, you will be healed.

What takes place in nature takes place in our lives. You can at times see some very old olive trees with chopped and withered trunks but which nevertheless still have a few green branches on their tops which, in the olive season, are full of lovely olives. If you look closely at them you will discover the reason for this. It's because somewhere there is still a "vein" of live wood rooted in the soil which gives life to the tree. That's what happens sometimes to the evil tree of sin in our lives. It should be completely dead and unproductive from the moment we no longer want sin which we have often confessed and rejected. Yet it continues to produce its fruits and the reason is that there are still some "green branches" rooted in the living soil of our freedom . . .

To discover our "green branch" we must look for the thing we fear will be taken from us and which, without admitting it, we defend and keep on an unconscious level. We keep it hidden for fear that our conscience will oblige us to renounce it. More often than a single sin, it's a question of a sinful habit or of an omission which must be overcome. A religious who had got into the habit of putting off confession for months, asked himself what the "green branch" to be snapped off in his life could be and there didn't seem to be one until the Lord made him understand that it was precisely his act of putting off confession. The Word of God is inviting us to single out the "thread" which still keeps us bound and resolutely break it. St. John of the Cross said that it's of no importance whether a bird is kept tied by a silk thread or a cord because, in a certain way, the result is the same: the bird cannot fly (cf. St. John of the Cross, *The Ascent of Mount Carmel*, I, 11,4).

But what must we do exactly? In a moment of recollection, during a retreat or, even this very day, let us kneel down in God's presence and say to him: "Lord, you know my weakness and I know it too. Trusting therefore only in your grace and faithfulness I declare that from now on I no longer want that particular satisfaction, that particular freedom, friendship, resentment, that particular sin . . .; I want to accept the idea of having to live without it from now on. I have finished with sin and with that particular sin. I repeat 'enough of that!' Help me with your Spirit. Renew in me a *firm* spirit, keep my heart *generous*. I consider myself dead to sin." After this, sin no longer "reigns" simply because you no longer *want* it to reign; it was, in fact, in your will that it reigned. If sin repeats itself in your life—and it will almost certainly do so—you will no longer be "conniving" with sin but simply "living" with it; that is you will have to live reluctantly with it accepting it as part of your purification and struggle against it. But this is very different to the previous state when you were conniving with it, when you were its accomplice. There may be no apparent change, those around us may still notice the same faults in us but where God is concerned something has changed because our freedom is now on God's side.

However, we must insist on a certain point: this decision must be put into practice straight away, otherwise it can easily get lost. An action contrary to the vice or sinful habit must be done immediately as the first "no" to it. Otherwise it will get back its full power again. A Christian writer made this shrewd observation. The Word of God revealed to a certain person that his sin was the love of gambling and it was this that God asked him to sacrifice to him. (We could be talking about any other sinful habit such as drugs, drink, a grudge, telling lies, hypocrisy, an impure habit). The man was convinced of his sin and decided to stop gambling and he said: "I make a solemn and sacred vow never to gamble again . . . It will be the last time tonight!." He didn't solve anything; he'll continue gambling as before. At the most he should have said to himself: "All right, you can gamble every day for the rest of your life but not tonight!" If he keeps his promise and doesn't gamble that night he is saved; he will probably never gamble again in his life. The first resolution is a nasty trick that vice plays on the sinner whereas the second, on the contrary, is a nasty trick that the sinner plays on the vice (cf. S. Kierkegaard, *For Selfexamination, On the Letter of St. James* 1,22).

If we are to be sincere, our "enough of that" must not only concern sin but the occasion for sin. As traditional moral doctrine teaches us, we must flee from the occasion of sin because to hold on to it would be to hold on to sin itself. The occasion is like certain wild beasts that enchant and hypnotize their prey so as to then devour it without its being able to move an inch. The occasion starts off strange psychological mechanisms in man and manages to enchant his will with this simple thought: "If you don't grasp this opportunity, you'll never have it again and it would be foolish not to take advantage of it . . . ." The occasion makes those who do not avoid it fall into sin just as dizziness make those on the brink of a precipice fall in.

4. "Destroy the sinful body"

In our text, St. Paul alludes to one final thing that must be done against sin and that is to "destroy the sinful body": *We know that our old self was crucified with him so that the sinful body might be destroyed* (Rom 6:6). He is saying that on the cross, Jesus virtually destroyed the entire body, that is the reality, of sin and now he is offering us the opportunity of actually destroying *our* sinful body through his own grace.

I should like to try to explain what this implies through an example, or better, by telling you how the Lord made me understand it. One day I was reciting the psalm which says: *O Lord, thou hast searched me and known me . . . thou discernest my thoughts from afar . . . Thou searchest out my path . . .* (Ps 139:1ff.). While reciting this psalm one feels as if he were being X-rayed by God's look as if his light were penetrating his whole body. At a certain point I found myself, in thought, on God's side, as if I too were looking into myself with his eyes. A clear image came to my mind; it was the image of a stalagmite, that is one of those limestone columns that form at the bottom of certain millenial grottoes caused by the drops of limestone water from the roofs of the grottoes. At once the meaning of the image was clear to me. Over the years my own particular sins had fallen to the bottom of my heart like numerous drops of limestone water. Each one had deposited a little limestone, that is a little opacity, a little hardness and resistance to God which then piled up with that left by a preceding sin. As happens in nature, the biggest part slides away like water, thanks to confession, the Eucharist and prayer . . . But each time a small part remained undissolved because the repentance and the resolution were not absolute. They weren't perfect. And thus my stalagmite had grown like a column or a large stone weighing me down. Suddenly I grasped the meaning of "the sinful body" St. Paul talks of and of the "heart of stone" God talks of in Ezekiel when he says: *I will take out of your flesh the heart of stone and give you a heart of flesh* (Ezek 36:26). It is the heart we have ourselves created through compromise and sin. It is something more than the pain that remains once sin has been forgiven; it is guilt and pain together. It is the old self.

What can be done about this? I can't remove that stone with my own will simply because it is within my will. This is where man's part ends (what is called the *opus operantis* in theology) and God's part begins (*the opus operatum*), even if God was certainly not absent previously. As far as the Bible is concerned, the greatest thing by far on the question of sin is not that we are sinners but that God forgives sin. Man can commit sin but he cannot remit it. "Only God alone can forgive sins" (cf. Mk 2:7). St. Peter, on the day he cried out "repent!," added: *Be baptized every one of you for the forgiveness of your sins* (Acts 2:38), thus indissolubly uniting repentance to the sacrament. As it was a question of a first conversion to the faith, the sacrament was, in that case, baptism whereas as we have sinned after baptism the sacrament is the sacrament of penance, that which the Fathers called "the second table of salvation offered to those who are shipwrecked after baptism" (cf. Tertullian, *De Paenit*. 4:2; 12:9; CCL 1, p. 326.340). And St. John says: *My little children, I am writing this to you so that you may not sin; but if any one does sin, we have an advocate with the Father, Jesus Christ the righteous; and he is the expiation for our sins* (1 Jn 2:1-2). And again he says: *The blood of Jesus cleanses us from all sins* (1 Jn 1:7). The blood of Christ is the great and powerful "solvent" which, in the sacrament of penance and thanks to the power of the Holy Spirit working in it, can dissolve the sinful body. The Church received the power to remit sins in the name of Jesus and by virtue of the Holy Spirit. Jesus said to the Apostles: *Receive the Holy Spirit. If you forgive the sins of any, they are forgiven* (Jn 20:22 ff.). Therefore, the Holy Spirit doesn't stop at "convincing us of sin"; he also frees us from sin. Rather, he himself is "the remission of sins."

God certainly has the right to establish how sins will be forgiven. It would be dangerous for us to arrogate to ourselves the right to change this by saying that there's no need to turn to the Church and that placing oneself before God would suffice. Jesus joined the Church, his spouse, to himself so that it would be one with him as he is with the Father. "Therefore the Church *cannot* remit anything without Christ and Christ doesn't *want* to remit without the Church. The Church can remit nothing if not to those who have repented and that is, to those who have received Christ's grace; Christ doesn't want to consider as forgiven those who disdain to turn to the Church" (Bl. Isaac of Stella, *Disc*. 11; PL 194, 1729). The way God chose to remit sins through confession fulfils, after all, the very natural and deep need of the human psyche to free itself from what is oppressing it just by giving expression to it. Psychoanalysis itself is based on this fact and involuntarily confirms it. Experience shows that the abandonment of confession always leads to a progressive loss of sensitivity towards sin and of spiritual fervour.

Nevertheless, our way of approaching the Sacrament of reconciliation must also be renewed in the Spirit if it is to become truly efficacious and decisive in our struggle against sin. A renewal of the sacrament in the Spirit signifies living it not as a rite, a habit or an obligation but as a need of the soul, as a personal meeting with the risen Christ who, through the Church, gives us the restoring strength of his blood and gives us "the joy of being saved" (Ps 51:12); it signifies rediscovering the mysterious "power" hidden in this gesture, thanks to the Holy Spirit working in it who renews and strengthens us.

A renewal of the sacrament in the Spirit also signifies a review of the object of our confessions. In confession we usually only worry about our habitual and present sins or habits; we worry about sins and not about sin. The Apostle tells us at the beginning of his Letter that there is something which comes before individual sins such as pride, anger, impurity . . . and of which all these are, in a certain way, the natural consequences and punishment. Before all of these there is impiety which is the lack of glorifying and thanking God; God is lacking in our lives, he has been emarginated from it. Sin multiplies from this as from a root and if this root is not eliminated we shall continue to gather in our confessions great "bunches" of sins and faults without getting anywhere and nothing will really change in our spiritual lives. We must get rid of what causes divine anger and then little by little its consequences will disappear. In the present chapter too, the Apostle always talks of sin in the singular as if it were a unitary force hidden in man and which commands the members like an invisible tyrant. We know that many trees have a tap root, that is the main root, which goes down vertically into the soil below the tree trunk. If a person who is not expert wants to remove a tree or the stump of a tree, he will start moving away the soil and cutting the lateral roots as they emerge. Then he will push the tree or stump expecting it to come out on its own whereas the tree has no intention of doing so. A person who is expert knows, however, that he must go on digging until he gets to the main root to cut it. That's how it is with the tree of our lives . . . Our main root is our old "self," or our will, "the will of the flesh" as Scripture calls it.

What a liberating discovery it would be and how much more efficacious our confessions would be if we had the courage for once and all to
get down to the root where a person makes his fundamental decisions
about life. Sometimes I surprise myself imagining a different type of
confession to the usual one. Someone comes into the confessional and
says as usual: "Bless me father, for I have sinned!," and I would say to
him: "What have you done, my brother, what are your sins?" And he
would answer as if he had finally discovered the truth: "I have been im-
pious. I have lived for myself up to now and not for God." Then I would
say: "You are blessed, brother, because this was not revealed to you by
flesh and blood but by the Spirit of the Father in heaven! You have discovered the hiding place of sin, its brooding place. Go in peace and pray
for me too!" And I would give him absolution. At times, when going to
confession, I myself have felt a great desire to change the traditional formula and present myself to the priest saying: "Bless me father, because I
am sin (not I *have* sinned)." This is really taking the sinful body, my old
self and throwing it into the arms of Jesus crucified as you would throw
a large stone into a live limestone furnace to smash and dissolve it.

Once you have confessed your sin, you must forget your part, your
preparation and even your contrition and think of nothing but God's
work being accomplished through absolution so as not to miss the sweetness and comfort that comes from it: "Withdraw your gaze from your
contrition and listen with all your heart to the voice of the brother ab-
solving you; don't doubt that the words you hear in the sacrament, are
words divinely uttered by the Father himself, the Son and Holy Spirit so
as to depend entirely on what you are listening to and not on what you
are thinking or doing" (Luther, *Comm. on the Ps. LI*, WA, 40, 2, p. 412).

The sacramental action on our sin is not limited to the sacrament of
penance only, even if, as we know, this is necessary for serious sins. The
Fathers of the Church and theologians have always recognized the
general efficacy of the Eucharist for the liberation of sin (cf. St. Thomas,
S.Th. III, q. LXXIX, aa.3-6). The blood of Christ that we receive in the
Eucharist "purifies our conscience from dead works" (cf. Heb 9:14). In
the Eucharist we draw near to the very source of the remission of sins;

each time sin becomes a little smaller, like a block of ice when it is placed near a fire. St. Ambrose wrote: "Each time you drink this blood, you receive the remission of sins and you are intoxicated with the Spirit" (*De Ben.Patr.* 9, 39; CSEL 32, 2, p. 147). Before distributing the body of Christ at communion, the celebrant says: "Behold the Lamb of God who takes away the sins of the world!"

5. "Whoever has suffered in the flesh . . ."

We can cooperate with the destruction of the sinful body by backing up the work of the sacrament in two ways especially: through suffering and praise. The Church calls all of this *satisfaction* or *expiation* and the penance given to the penitent is a symbol of this. The penance is a "sign" and indicates an act or an attitude which must continue well beyond the sacrament. St. Peter, in the text we are now familiar with, says: *Since therefore Christ suffered in the flesh, arm yourselves with the same thought, for whoever has suffered in the flesh has ceased from sin* (1 Pt 4:1). He thereby establishes a very important principle: whoever suffers ceases to sin. Suffering, since the Son of God underwent it and sanctified it, has the mysterious power to "undo" sin, to unravel the plot of our passions and drive out sin from our members. It's the sort of thing that happens when a tree is strongly shaken and all its bad fruit falls off. We don't know why this happens but we know that it does happen. We see it in ourselves and around us every day. "To suffer means to become particularly sensitive to the action of God's saving power given to humankind in Christ" (John Paul II, Ency. *Salvifici Doloris* n. 23). Suffering is a channel uniting us in a unique way to Christ's passion from which comes all remission of sin.

It's not a question, usually, of looking for suffering but of welcoming with a new spirit that which already exists in our lives. We should be particularly careful not to waste the little "unjust" suffering we experience because this unites us to Jesus in a particular way: humiliations, unjust criticisms, insults, hostilities which seem prejudices to us and cause us great suffering. This is the only way to reach a certain degree of intimacy with the Redeemer, through "sharing his sufferings" (Phil

3:10). This is how the basic sin of autoglorification is overcome. So as not to waste this suffering it is especially necessary not to talk of it except out of real necessity or utility; it should be jealously guarded as a secret between oneself and God if it is not to lose its perfume and expiation power. "No matter how great your sufferings are—a Father of the desert said—your silence is your victory over it" (*Apoph. Patrum, Poemen* 37; PG 65, 332).

Suffering remains a problem for man but it's a problem which after Christ came on earth finds its solution in itself. In fact, suffering with faith you learn, little by little, the reason for suffering and what it serves. We experience the fact that since sin entered the world, we are no longer able to walk with God and advance in holiness without suffering. A few days without any cross are sufficient to make us again full of superficiality and weakness of spirit. We can thus guess why suffering often ceases to be a problem for the saints and becomes, instead, a grace, as the Apostle stated in his letter to the Philippians: *For it has been granted to you that for the sake of Christ you should not only believe in him but also suffer for his sake* (Phil. 1:29). Suffering could then become the only worthwhile reason for living, even to the point of asking God, as St. Teresa of Avila did: "Let me die or else let me suffer!" (*Life,* 40,20). But let us not pretend that we too have reached this point and let us be happy, at least, to accept the sufferings that come our way and to practise a little renunciation. In fact, we must start with the sacrifice of pleasure so as one day to reach the pleasure of sacrifice. . .

It's wrong to think that all of this can be detrimental to hope in the cross of Christ and lead us again to boasting of our good actions. On the contrary, "when a person has fulfilled the work of the cross and practised penance, day and night, it's then that he truly realizes that he is a useless servant and if he asks something of God, he does so not in the name of his own suffering but in the name of the suffering that Christ himself bore within it and for it" (Bl. Angela of Foligno, *op.cit.,* p. 438).

Side by side with suffering, the other powerful means of destroying "the sinful body" is *praise*. Praise is, par excellence, anti-sin. If, as the Apostle explained at the beginning, the mother-sin is impiety, that is a refusal to glorify and thank God, then the exact opposite to sin is not virtue but *praise!* Yes, the opposite to sin is not virtue but *praise!* The opposite to impiety is piety. We must learn to overcome sin with big means and not small ones, with positive ones and not negative ones and the greatest and most positive of all means is God himself. We wouldn't have sin if we had God; where God enters sin goes out. The Bible often talks of a sacrifice of praise and thanksgiving: *Offer to God a sacrifice of thanksgiving . . . He who brings thanksgiving as his sacrifice honours me . . . I will offer thee the sacrifice of thanksgiving* (Ps 50:14-23, Ps 116:17). What relationship could possibly exist between praise and sacrifice? Sacrifice indicates the immolation and destruction of something but what does praise immolate and destroy? It immolates and destroys man's pride! Whoever offers praise sacrifices to God the most acceptable victim that could exist and that is, his own glory. This is what the extraordinary purifying power of praise consists of. Humility is concealed in praise. The most extraordinary thing of all is that nothing exists that cannot be transformed, if we want, into a reason for praising and giving thanks to God, not even sin. There is no state of conscience, however difficult, that cannot be reversed if a person tears himself away from all the contrary reasoning of the flesh and decides to glorify God. As I have just said, I can glorify God even for my sins; not because I have sinned (that would be mocking God) but because of how God behaved in front of my sin, because he kept me alive and did not withdraw his mercy. The Bible gives many reasons for praising God but none greater than the fact that he is God who forgives sin: *Who is a God like thee, pardoning iniquity and passing over transgression for the remnant of his inheritance? He does not retain his anger for ever because he delights in steadfast love* (Mic 7:18). We can praise God because he who transformed from evil into good the sin committed by Adam to the point of causing the liturgy to exclaim: "O happy sin!" ("O felix culpa!"), will mysteriously transform into good and for his own glory also the sins of those who welcome salvation and which are certainly smaller sins than Adam's was. God assured a well-known mystic that "sin was necessary, but it is all going to be all right; everything is going to be all right." (Julian of Norwich, *Revelations*, ch. 27).

Having seen our liberation from sin as a paschal exodus, now that we have reached the end, it must be transformed into a feast as happened in the first exodus. The Hebrews were reluctant to move out of Egypt and when they reached the Red Sea they were dismayed for a moment and they murmured; but as soon as they had crossed the sea, they were seized by irrepressible joy and following Moses and Maria, they started to sing this song:

> I will sing to the Lord,
> for he has triumphed gloriously;
> the horse and his rider he has thrown into the sea . . . (Ex 15:1).

That's what we want to do now. The Pharaoh that God has thrown into the sea is our "old self," the horses and riders are our sins. He "will cast all our sins into the depths of the sea" (Mic 7:19). Having crossed the Red Sea we shall start our journey towards Sinai. Easter has been celebrated, let us prepare to celebrate Pentecost. Our hearts are now new wineskins, ready to receive the new wine which is the Holy Spirit.

VIII. The Law of the Spirit Which Gives Life

The Holy Spirit, the principle of the New Covenant

In the Acts of the Apostles, the account of the coming of the Holy Spirit begins with these words: *When the day of Pentecost had come, they were all together in one place* (Acts 2:1). It may be inferred from these words that Pentecost existed before Pentecost. In other words there was already a Pentecost feast in Judaism and it was during this feast that the Holy Spirit, descended. Actually, even for some years after the coming of the Spirit the Apostles continued to celebrate the Jewish Pentecost (cf. Acts 20:16). We know that Easter also already existed and the fact that Jesus died precisely on the occasion of a paschal feast didn't just take place by chance but to make it clear that he was the true paschal Lamb and the final fulfilment of all that had previously occurred in the Old Testament in prefiguration. We cannot comprehend the significance of the new Passover if not as a continuation of the old one of the exodus and Hebrew liturgy. But whereas everyone knows that a Hebrew paschal feast existed and what it commemorated, very few, on the other hand, know that a Pentecost feast existed and what it commemorated. Yet, just as we cannot comprehend Easter without considering the Hebrew paschal feast, so we cannot comprehend the christian Pentecost without considering the Hebrew Pentecost. The coming of the Holy Spirit also fulfils a prefiguration and we must now try to understand which prefiguration this was.

1. Pentecost and the Law

In the Old Testament there existed two fundamental interpretations of the feast of Pentecost. At the beginning Pentecost was the festival of the seven weeks (cf. Tob 2:1), the day of the first fruits (cf. Num 28:26 ff.) when a sheaf of the new crop was offered to the Lord (cf. Ex 23:16; Dt 16:9). Later on in the time of Jesus, the festivity was given a new meaning; it was the feast celebrating the giving of the law on Mount Sinai and of the covenant, the feast, that is, that commemorated the events described in Exodus 19-20. According to Biblical reckoning the law was, in fact, given on Sinai fifty days after the Passover. From being a feast associated with the cycle of *nature* (the harvest), Pentecost had become a feast associated with the *history* of salvation. A text from the present Hebrew Liturgy of Shavuoth says: "This day of the Feast of Weeks is the time of the gift of our Torah." When the people left Egypt, they walked for fifty days in the desert and at the end God gave Moses the law and he made a covenant with the people making them "a kingdom of priests and a holy nation" (cf. Ex 19:4-6). It would seem that in Acts, St. Luke deliberately describes the descent of the Holy Spirit so as to evoke the theophany of Sinai. Church Liturgy confirms this interpretation as it has inserted Exodus 19 among the readings for the Pentecost vigil.

What does the comparison tell us of our Pentecost? What, in other words, is the significance of the fact that the Holy Spirit descends on the Church precisely on the day Israel recalls the gift of the law and the covenant? Even St. Augustine wondered about this: "Why—he asked himself—do the Jews too celebrate Pentecost? It's a big and wonderful mystery; if you think about it, they received the law written by God's finger on the day of Pentecost and the Holy Spirit also came on the day of Pentecost" (St. Augustine, *Ser. Mai* 158,4; PLS 2, 525). Another Father, this time from the East, tells us how this interpretation of Pentecost was the common patrimony of the whole Church in the first centuries. He writes that "On the day of Pentecost the law was given; it was convenient therefore that on the same day the old law was given the grace of the Holy Spirit should also be given" (Severian of Gabala, in *Cat. in Act. Apost.* 2, 1; J.A. Cramer 3, Oxford 1838, p. 16). At this point, the answer to why the Holy Spirit descended on the Apostles precisely on Pentecost day is clear. It was to show that he is the new law, the spiritual law, which seals the new and eternal covenant and who consecrates the royal and priestly people that form the Church. What a wonderful revelation on the meaning of Pentecost and on the Holy Spirit himself! St. Augustine exclaimed: "Who wouldn't be struck by this coincidence and at the same time by this difference? Fifty days pass between the celebration of the Passover and the day on which Moses received the law written by God's finger on tablets of stone; similarly, fifty days after the death and resurrection of the one who like a lamb was slaughtered, the finger of God, that is the Holy Spirit, filled the faithful who were gathered together" (St. Augustine, *De Spir. Litt.* 16, 28; CSEL 60, 182). Suddenly the prophecies of Jeremiah and Ezekiel on the new covenant become clear: *This is the covenant which I will make with the house of Israel after those days, says the Lord: I will put my law within them and I will write it upon their hearts* (Jer 31:33). He will no longer write it on tablets of stone but upon their hearts; it will no longer be an exterior law but an interior one. Ezekiel explains what this interior law consists of when he takes up again Jeremiah's prophecy and completes it: *A new heart I will give you, and a new spirit I will put within you; and I will take out of your flesh the heart of stone and give you a heart of flesh. And I will put my Spirit within you, and cause you to walk in my statutes and be careful to observe my ordinances* (Ezek 36:26-27).

What St. Paul says about the gift of the Spirit in chapter eight of his Letter to the Romans can only be understood in the light of these premises on the meaning of Pentecost and the new covenant. In fact he begins by saying: *The law of the Spirit of life in Jesus Christ has set me free from the law of sin and death* (Rom 8:2). The whole discourse on the Spirit in the Letter to the Romans is a counterpoint to the discourse on the law. The Spirit himself is defined as being the law: the "law of the Spirit" means, in fact, "the law which is the Spirit." On the other hand, the fact that the Apostle has in mind all the prophecies linked to the theme of the new covenant is clear from the passage where he calls the community of the new covenant a "letter from Christ, written not with ink but with the Spirit of the living God, not on tablets of stone but on tablets of human hearts" and where he calls the apostles "ministers of a *new covenant* not in a written code but *in the Spirit*; for the written code kills, but the Spirit *gives life*" (cf. 2 Cor 3:3-6).

We have thus discovered the key to understand Paul's illuminating discourse on the Spirit. Once again the key is a "spiritual reading" of Scripture. Chapter eight of the Letter to the Romans is a kind of typological catechesis on the Holy Spirit. The Apostle has the prophecies of the Old Testament in mind which foretold the great outpouring of the Spirit in the time of the new covenant and he wants to demonstrate that all of these were fulfilled in Christ and in the Church and that they were fulfilled even beyond all expectation. In our spiritual journey this is an "illuminative" catechesis; it must serve to illuminate our minds rather than encourage practical proposals; its purpose is to widen the horizon of our faith allowing, so to say, our spirit to breathe deeply and fully so that we shall not be happy with meaningless exterior practices of devotion but we will aim at being aware of the fullness of the christian mystery.

2. The "Spirit of Christ"

The Old Testament talks of the Holy Spirit as the breath of God that creates and gives life, which pours its strength into certain men bestowing on them extraordinary powers to fight, govern and prophesy. But it is only in the prophets, in Jeremiah and Ezekiel in particular, that we pass from the outward and public view of the action of the Spirit to an interior and personal view in which the Holy Spirit is seen to be at work in the hearts of all as the principle of interior renewal which will enable each one to observe God's law thus becoming the principle of the new covenant and a new life. The most explicit text on this new point of view is that already mentioned in Ezekiel. Paul's discourse on a new life in the Spirit belongs to this "interior" view. What he is really saying is that God has written his law in our hearts with the Holy Spirit. This new law is the love he has poured into our hearts, in Baptism, through the Holy Spirit (cf. Rom 5:5). This also enables us to put the other laws into practice, which can be either written or stated; in short, it allows us to walk according to the Spirit in obedience to the Gospel.

Let us now see where the newness brought by Christ and the coming of the new covenant is in all this. St. Paul affirms that the ancient law, that is every written and external law, gives only "knowledge of sin" (Rom 3:20), but it does not take sin away; it does not grant life but only brings to light the state of death and enmity with God: *For if a law had been given which could make alive, then righteousness would indeed be by the law* (Gal 3:21). The mosaic law, being external to man, and in general every positive law, does not modify an interior state and does not influence the heart. Life and death come before the law; they depend on whether one turns one's heart towards God or towards oneself. In both cases, whether in observance as in transgression, the law is the external manifestation of what has first been decided in the heart. That is why the basic sin of egoism, "love of oneself to the point of hating God," as St. Augustine says (*De Civ. Dei*, XIV, 28; CCL 47, 360) cannot be removed through observance of the law but only through re-establishing the state of friendship that existed at the beginning between God and man and which the serpent, out of envy, persuaded man to destroy. And this is precisely what happened when Christ redeemed us: *God has done what the law, weakened by the flesh, could not do: sending his own Son in the likeness of sinful flesh and for sin, he condemned sin in the flesh* (Rom 8:3). On the cross Jesus took the heart of stone from the whole of mankind; he took away all the ill feeling, enmity and resentment against God that mankind had accumulated under the law. Jesus "crucified the old self" and "destroyed the sinful body" (Rom 6:6). He took on our death and gave us his life in exchange, that is his love for the Father, his obedience, his new relationship with God, his "spirit of son." St. Paul expressed all of this by calling the Holy Spirit the "Spirit of Christ" and by saying that the Spirit gives life in "Christ Jesus" (Rom 8:2).

The Holy Spirit which at Pentecost is poured into the Church comes therefore from Christ's death and resurrection; it is a paschal Spirit. It is the breath of the risen Christ. With the resurrection the new Adam became "a life-giving Spirit" (1 Cor 15:45). The fourth Gospel expresses the same certainty of the nascent Church. On the cross Jesus "gave up his spirit" (cf. Jn 19:30) and in John's language this has a twofold meaning: a natural meaning, "he drew his last breath," that is, he died and a mystical meaning, "he emitted his Spirit." To John the Evangelist, the last breath of Jesus was the first breath of the Church. The Church, symbolized by the Sacraments of Baptism and the Eucharist (water and blood) was *born* of Christ's *death*. This mystical significance is confirmed shortly after when on the evening of Easter day in the Cenacle,

Jesus breathed on the disciples and said: *Receive the Holy Spirit* (Jn 20:22).

The Holy Spirit we have received is certainly more than just a thing, it is a "person"; it is the third person of the Trinity and as such comes primarily from the Father. Nevertheless, in redemption, it comes to us from Christ; it is the Holy Spirit who in Christ "became accustomed to living with man" (St. Ireneus, *Adv.Haer.* III, 17, 1), which filled and sanctified the Head and from him is poured into all the members to form with them "one body and one Spirit." We can now see how absurd it is to think that Pentecost could overshadow the role of Easter and that insisting on the Holy Spirit could overshadow Jesus almost as if the Holy Spirit were representing a third form of economy or a "third era" superior to Christ's. On the contrary, the Holy Spirit keeps the memory of Jesus "alive," he who "bears him witness," who "takes what is his" and declares it to us (cf. Jn 16:4). The Holy Spirit does not make new things but makes things new!

3. A "new heart"

Christ's Spirit, when it is poured into a believer through the sacraments, the Word and all the other means at our disposal, in the measure in which it is welcomed and listened to, is finally able to change the interior state that the law was unable to change. This is how it comes about. So long as man lives "for himself," that is in sin, he inevitably sees God as an antagonist and an obstacle. Between him and God there is a silent hostility which the law does nothing but emphasize. Man "lusts" after certain things and it is God who, through his commandments, blocks his way and opposes man's desires with his own "you must" and "you mustn't." St. Paul says: *The mind that is set on the flesh is hostile to God; it does not submit to God's law* (Rom 8:7). The old self is in revolt against its Creator and, if it were possible, would even want him not to exist. It is sufficient that, either through our own fault, or because of a contradiction or simply by God's permission, we lose the sense of God's presence and we can immediately discover that we feel only anger and rebellion and a whole front of hostility before God and our brethren which comes from the old root of our sin, to the point of overshadowing our spirit and making us dread ourselves. This is our state until we reach the constant state of complete peace in which, as Julian of Norwich says, we are "wholly content with God, his actions and decisions; until we are in love and at peace with ourselves, our fellow Christians and with all that God loves" (*Revelations,* ch. 49). When in the present state, at times characterized by peace and at other times by struggle, the Holy Spirit takes possession of a heart a change comes about. If before, there was a "secret rancour against God" in the depths of a man's heart, now the Spirit comes to him from God and attests that God is truly favourable and benign, that he is his ally and not his enemy; he opens his eyes to all that God has been capable of doing for him and to the fact that he did not spare his only Son for him. The Spirit puts "God's love" into man's heart (cf. Rom 5:5). In this way he makes him a new man who loves God and who willingly does what God asks of him (cf. Luther, *The Whitsuntide Sermon,* Weimar edit. 12, p. 568 ff.). God, in fact, no longer limits himself to telling man what he should do or not do but he himself does it with him and in him. The new law, the Spirit, is much more than an "indication" of a will; it is an "action," a living and active principle. The new law is new life. That's why it is more often called grace than law: *You are not under law but under grace* (Rom 6:14).

In a strict sense, therefore, the new law or the law of the Spirit is not that which Jesus proclaimed on the mount of the Beatitudes but that which he engraved in man's heart at Pentecost. The evangelical precepts are certainly higher and more perfect than the mosaic ones were; yet, on their own, they too would have been inefficacious. If it had sufficed to proclaim the new will of God through the Gospel, we wouldn't be able to explain why Jesus died and why the Holy Spirit came. The Apostles themselves show that it wasn't enough; they had heard everything, for example that we should turn the other cheek to those that strike us, and yet at the moment of the passion they were not strong enough to carry out anything of what Jesus had commanded. If Jesus had limited himself to proclaiming the new commandment saying: *A new commandment I give to you, that you love one another* (Jn 13:34), it would have remained what it was before, just an old written law. It was at Pentecost when he poured his love into the hearts of his disciples by means of the Spirit that it became, by right, a new law, the law of the Spirit that gives life. It is by the Spirit that this commandment is "new" and not by the letter; it was "old" by the written word and John the Evangelist seems to be aware of this fact because he tells us: *I am writing you no new commandment but an old commandment.* Then he immediately and forcefully adds: *Yet I am writing you a new commandment* (1 Jn 2:7-8).

Therefore, without the inner grace of the Spirit, the Gospel and the new commandment too would have remained an old law, a written word. St. Thomas Aquinas, commenting on a daring thought of St. Augustine's wrote: "By the 'letter' is meant every written law that remains external to man, even the moral precepts contained in the Gospel. So the letter of the Gospel would also kill if the grace of healing faith were not added interiorly" (St. Thomas, *S.Th.* I-IIae, q. 106, a.2). Even more explicit is what he stated a little earlier on: "Primarily the new law is the grace itself of the Holy Spirit given to believers in Christ" (*Ib.*, q. 106, a.1). We are dealing with a certainty of faith that is truly ecumenical, that is with something that is common inheritance in all the great Christian traditions. In fact not only does catholic and protestant theology, heirs to Augustinian theology, share this view but so does orthodox theology as well. A great upholder of this tradition wrote: "The Apostles and fathers of our faith had the advantage of being instructed in every doctrine and furthermore they were instructed by the Saviour himself; . . . yet, having seen all this, they showed nothing new or noble or spiritual that was better than the old state until they were baptized with the Spirit at Pentecost. But when they were baptized and the Paraclete had been poured into their souls they were renewed and embraced a new life. They became guides for others and made the flame of love for Christ burn within themselves and in others . . . In the same way God leads all the saints that came after them to perfection. They know him and love him not because they are attracted by mere words but because they are transformed by the power of baptism while the Beloved one moulds and transforms them creating in them a heart of flesh and removing all insensitivity. He writes but as Paul says, not on tablets of stone but on tablets of human hearts (2 Cor 3:3), and he does not simply engrave the law but he engraves "the lawgiver himself." (N. Cabasilas, *Life in Christ*, II, 8; PG 150, 553).

But how does this new law of the Spirit work in practice and in what way can it be called a "law"? It works through love! The new law is nothing other than what Jesus called the "new commandment." The Holy Spirit has written the new law on our hearts by pouring his love into them: *God's love has been poured into our hearts through the Holy Spirit who has been given to us* (Rom 5:5). This love is the love God loves us with and through which, at the same time, he makes us love him and our neighbour. It is a new capacity to love. Love is the sign that reveals the new life given by the Spirit. St. John writes: *We know that we have passed out of death into life because we love the brethren* (1 Jn 3:14).

Those who approach the Gospel in a human way find it absurd that love should be a "commandment"; they question what kind of love it could be if it is not freely given but commanded. The answer is that there are two ways in which man can be driven to do or not do something: either by *force* or by *attraction*—either by pushing or by pulling. In the first case the law forces him under the threat of punishment; in the second case love makes him act because he is attracted to something. In fact, each one of us is drawn to what we love without feeling obliged by external factors. Show a child some nuts and he'll stretch out his hand to seize them. He doesn't need to be pushed; he is attracted by the object he desires. Show the Supreme Good to a soul thirsting for truth and it will reach out for it. Nobody pushes the soul, it is attracted by what it desires. Love is the "weight" of a soul which draws it as if by a law of gravity to what it loves and where it finds its rightful rest (cf. St. Augustine, *In Ioh.* 26, 4-5; CCL 36, 261 f.; *Confess.* XIII, 9). It is in this sense that the Holy Spirit or love, is a "law," a "commandment"; it gives the Christian an energy which makes him do all that God wants, spontaneously and without even thinking about it, because he has made God's will his and he loves all that God loves. Love draws God's will from its very source. Through the Spirit it reaches the living will of God. It's like "being in love" when, full of love, everything is done joyfully and spontaneously and not out of habit or self-interest. "He who loves flies, runs, rejoices, is free and cannot be held back . . . Often love has no limits. Love knows no burden and pays no heed to weariness, it wants to do more than it can; it doesn't admit that anything is impossible because it believes that everything is right and possible. Love is capable of all things and, in fact, it manages to do most of them whereas he who does not love fails to do what he wishes and gives in" (*Imitation of Christ*, III, 5). We could say that to live in grace, governed by the new law of the Spirit, is to live "in love," that is, transported by love. The same change that falling in love creates in human life and in the relationship between two people is created by the coming of the Holy Spirit in the relationship between God and man.

4. Love Protects the Law and the Law Protects Love

In this new economy of the Spirit what is the place of the observance of the commandments? This is a crucial point that must be cleared up, also because it could help us to overcome one of the greatest obstacles met with in the dialogue with Jews who rightly do not intend to give up what "the Law" means to them. The written law still exists after Pentecost: there are God's commandments—the decalogue, and the evangelical precepts; later on Canon law was added to these. What is the significance of the Code of Canon law, monastic rules, religious vows, everything, in fact, that indicates an objective will which is imposed on us from outside? Are these things foreign bodies in the Christian organism? We know that in the course of the history of the Church there have been movements that shared this idea and in the name of freedom of the Spirit rejected all laws so much so as to call themselves "anomists," that is without law, but these have always been repudiated by the Church authorities and by the christian conscience. Nowadays, in a cultural context of atheistic existentialism, the law is no longer rejected in the name of freedom of the Spirit but purely and simply in the name of human freedom. J.P. Sartre makes one of his characters say: "There is nothing left in heaven, neither Good nor Evil, nor anyone who can give me orders . . . I am a man and every man must invent his own way" (*Les Mouches*, Paris 1943, p. 134 ff.).

The christian answer to this problem is to be found in the Gospel. Jesus says he didn't come to "abolish the law" but to "fulfill it (Mt 5:17)." What is the "fulfillment" of the law? *Love is the fulfilling of the law*, St. Paul answers (Rom 13:10). Jesus says that on the commandment of love depend all the law and the prophets (cf. Mt 22:40). Therefore love does not substitute the law but fulfills it. Actually, it is the only force that can make it observed! In the prophecy of Ezekiel the possibility to observe God's law is attributed to the future gift of the Spirit and a new heart: *And I will put my Spirit within you and cause you to walk in my statutes and be careful to observe my ordinances* (Ezek 36:27). In the same sense Jesus says: *If a man loves me, he will keep my word* (Jn 14:23), that is he will be able to observe it. In the new economy there is no contrast or incompatibility between the interior law of the Spirit and the written external law; on the contrary there is full collaboration; the one is given to guard the other: "Law was given so that we might seek grace and grace was given so that we might observe the law" (St. Augustine, *De Spir. Litt.* 19, 34). The observance of the commandments and, in fact, obedience, is the proof of love; it is the sign that shows whether we are living "according to the Spirit" or "according to the flesh." *This is the love of God, that we keep his commandments* (1 Jn 5:3). That's what Jesus himself did; he made of himself the sublime model of a love which is expressed in the observance of his commandments, that is, in obedience. He says: *I have kept my Father's commandments and abide in his love* (Jn 15:10).

The commandment doesn't therefore cancel out the commandments but it guards them and fulfils them. And not only in the sense that whoever loves has the strength to observe what is commanded but also in the deeper sense that whoever loves realizes in himself the ultimate end of every law which is to be in harmony with God's will. Let us suppose one were to observe every law to perfection but didn't have the interior disposition of the heart that comes from love, he wouldn't in fact be observing the law but pretending to observe it. St. Paul is right then when he says that all his discourse doesn't tend to "overthrow the law" but, on the contrary, it "upholds the law" (cf. Rom 3:31). He says that "the just requirement of the law" and that is all that in the law is eternally valid and holy, is fulfilled in us when we walk according to the Spirit (cf. Rom 8:4). The law doesn't therefore suddenly become a giver of life; it remains exactly what it was, that through which the will of God is shown and nothing more. The difference is, though, that now, after the coming of the Spirit, its limited function is openly recognized and therefore it is positive whereas before, when it was expected to give life, it was misleading and only encouraged the pride of man and sin. The very "letter" is, in other words, only safe in the "Spirit."

To understand the positive relation that is established in the regime of grace and love let us take the example of an expectant mother. The doctor or the midwife or relatives, depending on the place and the customs, tell the young woman what rules to observe during her pregnancy; they tell her what she should do and what she shouldn't do in her condition, what she should and shouldn't eat, what she should and shouldn't wear . . . Especially if it is her first baby the woman will be so completely caught up in the miracle of the new life growing in her that she will certainly observe all the "rules" imposed on her and will be grateful from the bottom of her heart to those transmitting them to her; but she will not observe them because "it is written" somewhere or for a question of honour or to avoid criticism but simply because she loves her child. Her law is love. She doesn't act because she is obliged to do so but because she is drawn to do so and yet no one could be more zealous or diligent in doing what she has to do. She loves her child and wants only his good but she is young and inexpert and doesn't know exactly what is good or bad for her and so she is happy to do what is indicated by experience and authority. This is precisely the position and meaning of the law under grace! It's understandable why the Apostle himself, after dedicating whole chapters of his Letter to show us the end of the law, gives numerous laws to Christians in the second part: "Charity has no pretence," "let each one be subject to governing law". . . A certain way of seeing the law has been surpassed but a new way has been opened.

These laws are now at the service of the new life enkindled in us at Baptism, they are like the rules given to the woman carrying a new life in her womb.

As we can see, a wonderful exchange, a sort of reciprocity, exists between law and love. If it's true, as we have just seen, that love protects the law, it's also true that *the law protects love*. Love is the strength of the law and the law is the defence of love. In different ways the law is at the service of love and defends it. First of all, we know that "the law is laid down for sinners" (cf. 1 Tim 1:9) and we are still sinners. It's true that we have received the Spirit but only as first fruits; the old self lives on in us together with the new self and as long as there is concupiscence in us, it is providential that the commandments should exist to help us recognize it and struggle against it even if under the threat of punishment. The law is a support given to our freedom which is still uncertain and wavering in doing good. It is *for* and not *against* freedom and it must be said that those who thought they should reject every law in the name of human freedom, were mistaken and disregarded the concrete and historical situation in which this freedom works.

Together with this so called negative function, the law also has the positive function of discernment. Through the grace of the Holy Spirit we globally adhere to God's will, we make it ours and desire to fulfil it but we still don't know it in all its implications. These are revealed to us by the law other than by the events of life. In this sense St. Thomas Aquinas says that also the moral precepts of the Gospel are a "new law," although in a secondary sense. They concretely express in fact the demands of God's will and the direction in which the interior law is pushing us which is not always recognizable in us due to our passions (cf. St. Thomas, *St. Th.* I-IIae, q. 106, a. 1-2).

But there is yet a deeper sense in which we could say the law protects love. Kierkegaard wrote that "only when the *duty* to love exists is love guaranteed for ever against every change; it is eternally liberated in blessed independence, assured in eternal beatitude against all despair" (S. Kierkegaard, *Works of Love,* I, 2, 40). These words mean that the more a lover loves, the stronger is his anguished perception of the risk his love runs. This risk doesn't come from others but from himself as, in fact, he is well aware of his volubility and knows that tomorrow, alas, he could become weary and no longer love. And as now, loving, he clearly sees the irreparable loss this would be, he protects himself by "binding" himself to love through the law and thereby anchoring his act of temporal love to eternity. Today, man wonders more and more what relationship can possibly exist between the love of a young couple and the law of matrimony and what need love has to "bind" itself. Consequently more and more couples reject in theory and in practice the institution of matrimony and opt for so-called free love or simply live together. Only by discovering, through God's Word, the deep and important relation that exists between law and love, between decision and institution, can we rightly answer these questions and give young people a convincing reason for "binding" themselves to love for life and for not fearing to make love a "duty." The duty to love protects love from "despair" and makes it "free and independent" in the sense that it protects from the despair of not being able to love for ever. It has been rightly said that "to be truly free, man must begin by binding himself" (Silvanus of Mount Athos).

This consideration is not true of human love only but also, and more rightly so, of divine love. We could ask ourselves: Why should we bind ourselves to loving God, submitting to a religious rule; why take the vows that "oblige" us to be poor, chaste and obedient when we have an interior and spiritual law which can obtain all of this by "attraction"? It's because in a moment of grace you were drawn to God, you loved him and desired to possess him for ever, completely, and dreading the thought of losing him because of your instability, you "bound" yourself to guarantee your love from every possible change. In a different way the same thing happens to whoever converts himself and decides to give himself truly to God . . . even on this journey of ours. In a flash he discovers who God is and what irreparable damage it would be to lose him; so while he is still in the lucky state of love, he binds himself with a decision, a promise, a personal vow or any other way the Spirit might suggest to him. He binds himself for the same reason that the ancient navigator bound himself to the ship's mast because he wanted at all costs to see his native land and his wife again, but he knew he had to pass through the place of the mermaids and feared he would be shipwrecked like many before him . . . One of the most necessary and efficacious ways of safeguarding this "bond" of love is to choose a spiritual director or a confessor, committing oneself to submit regularly to him any important decision in one's life and to obey him.

In a certain sense, man is called to reproduce in himself by his will what comes about in God by nature. Love is a duty in God; God "must" love by necessity of his nature because he "is love." He is bound to love and cannot do anything else. And yet nothing is freer and more gratuitous than God's love. In him the duty to love is not opposed to the freedom to love; the two things coincide perfectly. Man draws close to God and imitates God when he freely binds himself to love for ever. He makes love a duty and a law or better still, he accepts the law God's love gives him: *You shall love the Lord your God with all your heart and with all your soul, and with all your mind and your neighbour as yourself* (Mt 22:37 ff.).

5. A New Pentecost for the Church

To know the difference between the old law and grace is not only a theoretical question or a question of greater or less understanding of the faith. It is also a practical question from which immediate consequences for our way of life spring. In fact we mustn't only "understand" what the passage from law to grace consists in but we must put it into practice too. *Historically* speaking, the passage from the Old to the New Testament came about once and for all two thousand years ago, with Jesus Christ who established the new covenant in his blood but, *existentially* and spiritually speaking, it must happen anew all the time, in every epoch and in every believer. We are born with the desires of the flesh in revolt against God; we are born with the dread, the boast and confidence in works. It is true to say that we are born "under the law." At birth we are already old people! The right of passing to the new covenant comes about at the moment of Baptism but the moral, psychological or actual passing takes up a whole life. It's possible to live objectively and historically under grace while being subjectively under the law at heart.

It is also possible to imperceptibly fall back under the law even after experiencing freedom of the Spirit and grace. St. Paul had to fight two big battles in his apostolic life, that of urging Judaism to pass from the law to grace, from the old to the new covenant and that of preventing entire communities who had made the passage to turn back and allow themselves to be swallowed up again by the law and by works. This was the battle he fought against the Galatians. He rebukes them for ending with the flesh, having begun with the Spirit (cf. Gal 3:3). He says to them: *The freedom of Christ has set us free; stand fast therefore, and do not submit again to a yoke of slavery* (Gal 5:1). He shows us that we can fall away from grace in other ways as well as by sinning. *You have fallen away from grace!*, he cries at a certain point (Gal 5:4). We know of only one way to fall away from grace and that is precisely by mortal sin because we have impoverished the meaning of the word "grace" and made it just a "thing." We can fall away from grace by legalism, by seeking our own justice and by fear. That's why St. Paul warns the Romans by saying to them: *You did not receive the spirit of slavery to fall back into fear* (Rom 8:15).

The danger of "ending with the flesh" and of falling back to the Old Testament with the mind and heart didn't end with Paul's death; it has always existed and will always exist and we must fight against it and avoid it just as Paul did in his time. To live in the new covenant is like swimming against the current. Origen wrote: "Don't think that the renewal of life that came about once and for all at the beginning is enough; it is necessary to continually renew the newness every day" ("ipsa novitas innovanda est") (Origen, *Comm.in Rom:* 5,8; PG 14, 1042 A). The revealing factor is to see what idea Christians have of God in their lives and how they see him, whether it's with the fearful and interested eye of a slave or the trusting eye of a son. Today there is a new way of making Church history, which consists in not dwelling only on exterior things, on institutions or on famous people but in getting down to the "real life" of the Christian people and trying to discover the quality of the religious life of a part of the Church in a given historical moment. If, for example, through the archives we were to examine the preaching of a certain priest during the whole time he spent in a particular parish, we could clearly see what kind of religion and idea of God was inculcated into the people of that parish. Very often the conclusion is that the sense of religion given was basically that which was predominant in the Old Testament, that is "a religion of fear" (cf. J. Delumeau, *Histoire vécue du peuple chrétien*, Ed. Privat 1979). It was not even therefore a religion based on what was most alive and lasting in the Old Testament but a religion based on what was most contingent and destined to be perfected by Christ. This shows us how misleading it is to underline the rigid opposition between *Law-Gospel* to the point of making it mechanically coincide with the opposition *Synagogue-Church* or *Jews-Christians*. Actually in this particular case we could apply what St. Augustine said in general about belonging to the Church: "How many wolves there are inside the fold and how many sheep outside it!" (*In Ioh.* 45, 12; CCL 36, 395). How many live in the spirit of the new covenant outside the Church amidst the people of the old covenant and how many live in the spirit of the old covenant inside the Church amidst the people of the new covenant!

The newness of the Christian message becomes clouded when preaching, catechesis, spiritual guidance and all other formative activities of faith unilaterally insist on duties, virtues, vices, punishment and, in general, on what man "should do," presenting grace as an aid that comes to man in the course of his commitment to make up for what he is not able to do alone and not, on the contrary, as something that comes before these efforts and which makes them possible; when "duty" is created by the law and not by grace and when duty is consequently not conceived as our debt of gratitude to God but rather as something that creates, if we accomplish it, a debt of gratitude on God's part towards us; when, in other words, morals become separated from the *kerygma*. In a stricter sphere, the religious life is similarly clouded when in the formation given to young people and novices, in retreats and in other occasions, more time is spent on talking about the charism, traditions, rules and constitutions and the particular spirituality of the order (often very poor and inconsistent) than talking of Christ the Lord and his Holy Spirit. The barycentre of attention imperceptibly moves from God to man and from grace to the law. St. John says that "the law was given through Moses but grace and truth came through Jesus Christ" (cf. Jn 1:17) and if we apply this today to us in the Church, it means that man can make the law and founders can make rules of life but that only Jesus Christ, with his Spirit, can give the strength to live them.

From our meditation therefore comes the appeal and impulse for a deep renewal in the Spirit and a "conversion to the Lord." St. Paul talks of "a veil put over the heart" which prevents us from seeing the surpassing splendour of the new covenant and which is removed "when a man turns to the Lord" (cf. 2 Cor 3:14 ff.). Such conversion must start with the spiritual leaders of the people. At the beginning of the 5th century, the people of Hippo were a simple and illiterate people but they were perfectly aware of the difference between law and grace, fear and love. They were really a people of the new covenant simply because their bishop, Augustine, explained the Scriptures to them and spoke to them of these things day after day. He didn't fear addressing them with these words: "Remove what is old in you, you have known a new canticle. A new man, a New Testament, a new canticle. The new canticle doesn't belong to the old man; it can only be apprehended by the new man, renewed by means of grace, and already belonging to the New Testament which is the kingdom of heaven" (*Enarr.Ps.* 32:8; CCL 38, p. 253). Another time when preaching to the people, he said: "Christ has given us a new commandment, to love one another as he loved us. It is this love that renews us and makes us new men, heirs to the New Testament, cantors of the new canticle" (*In Ioh.* 65:1; CCL 36, p. 491).

In our century the risen Lord has diffused here and there in various parts of his mystical body, the yearning for and the experience of a "new Pentecost." With the ecumenical council, Vatican II, this yearning took strong shape also within the Catholic Church. It didn't just remain a prayer on the lips of a Pope but started to become a fact through many signs. But what is a "New Pentecost" for the Church? It can't consist only in a new blossoming of charisms, of ministries, of power or in a breath of fresh air in the Church. These things are just a reflection and a sign of something deeper. We've seen what the first Pentecost consisted in and that is in the gift of a new law which creates a new heart and a new covenant and makes it possible again to love and serve God in Christ. Pentecost wasn't just the fulfilment of the prophecies of Joel who spoke of all sorts of charisms: dreams, visions and wonders (cf. Acts 2:17 ff.), but also and first of all of the prophecies of Jeremiah and Ezekiel of a new heart and a new spirit. The Spirit of Christ which characterizes the new covenant is not primarily an exterior manifestation of thaumaturgical and charismatic power but it is the principle of a new life. To be really so, a new Pentecost must take place at this depth; it must renew the heart of the Spouse and not only her garments. In other words, it must be "a renewal of the covenant."

For each one of us, the entrance to this new Pentecost taking place in the Church is a renewal of our Baptism. The fire of the Spirit was given to us at Baptism. We must remove the ashes suffocating it so that it can flame again and make us capable of loving. If this meditation has made us yearn for the newness of the Spirit and if we desire it and invoke it, God will not delay in offering us too the occasion of this experience so that we too can knowingly and really become "new men, heirs of the New Testament and cantors of the new canticle."

IX. The Spirit Intercedes for Us
Prayer "in the Spirit"

Chapter eight of the Letter to the Romans is the chapter on the Holy Spirit. The word "Spirit" is repeated thirty times in the letter and nineteen of these occur in this chapter. The Apostle now talks about some of the most important works of the Spirit and he places prayer in the foreground. The Holy Spirit, the principle of a new *life* is consequently the principle of a new *prayer*. Among the good works that redeemed man can do so as to grow in grace, prayer is unique in that it is "good for everything" (cf. 1 Tm 4:8). It is the indispensable tool for advancement in all the virtues. If you wish to begin to possess God's light, prayer; if you have already undertaken the climb towards perfection and you wish this light to increase in you, pray; if you wish to possess hope, pray; if you wish to possess obedience, chastity, humility, meekness, strength, pray. For whichever virtue you desire, pray. . . . The more you are tempted the more you should persevere in prayer. It is by virtue of your constant prayer that you deserve to be tempted and it is by virtue of your constant prayer that you merit to be freed from temptation; prayer, in fact, gives you light, frees you from temptation, purifies you and brings you closer to God" (*The Book of Bl. Angela of Foligno*, cit. p. 454 f.). If, with Augustine, it is right to say—as Western Christians do: "*Love* and then do what you will!" it is equally as right to say—as Orthodox Christians do—"*Pray*, and then do what you will!" (Anonymous, *Tales of a Russian Pilgrim*, VI). To pray is to recollect oneself and lose oneself in that infinite abyss that God is. Prayer is the breath of the soul. Just as a good breathing capacity is essential for all the organs of the body to function healthily, especially if they are to be called upon for arduous athletic performances, so a strong will for prayer is essential for the soul, especially when one wants to set out on a spiritual "ascent." This meditation dedicated to prayer "in the Spirit" is, therefore, the hinge between the first or kerygmatic part of our journey, in which, through faith, we have appropriated to ourselves the actions of Christ and the second or parenetic part, in which we are exhorted to imitate the actions of Christ in our lives.

1. The "weakness" of our Prayer

The whole of the second half of chapter eight of the Letter to the Romans speaks of the Holy Spirit as the inspirator of prayer in the heart of creation and in the heart of man. We shall start with the two verses of closest interest to us: *Likewise, the Spirit helps us in our weakness; for we do not know how to pray as we ought, but the Spirit himself intercedes for us with sighs too deep for words. And he who searches the hearts of men knows what is the mind of the Spirit because the Spirit intercedes for the saints according to the will of God* (Rom 8:26-27). These two verses tell us a lot about prayer. First of all they explain the "why" and the "wherefore" of prayer; they help us, that is, to discover its theological basis. In fact, if we think carefully about it, the constant need to pray after Christ came on earth constitutes a problem; it is not self-evident. If, now, thanks to redemption, we lack nothing and "no grace is missing to us" (1 Cor 1:7), if there is "no further condemnation for those who are in Christ Jesus" (Rom 8:1), if we have been freed from the law of sin and death, how is it that this "sigh" exists and this need to pray which rises from creation itself, other than from the Church and the heart of man? And what is this "weakness" to which, it is said, the Spirit comes in our help? Have we or have we not been redeemed? Have we or have we not received the Spirit? Our context gives us a clear answer: it is true that we have the Spirit, but in the "first fruits"; we have redemption but not yet *full* redemption, for *in hope we were saved* (Rom 8:23 f.). The state of believers in the world becomes clear at this point, a state taut between the "already" and the "not yet." The reason for prayer lies exactly in this; it is precisely prayer that shows up this state: we wouldn't be able to pray if we didn't have the first fruits of the Spirit and we wouldn't have to pray, if we already possessed the fullness of the Spirit. The prayer of redeemed man springs exactly from the tension between faith and hope, between what we already possess and what we still hope for. Fundamentally, it is an agonizing yearning for the full freedom of the children of God and for glory, and it is similar—the Apostle says—to the groaning of travail (Rom 8:22). Here we are dealing, above all, with prayer in the stricter and more common sense of the word, that is, of the prayer of petition and intercession (*proseuche*) which is the right and most apt prayer in time of "need," just what our present state as pilgrims is.

The present state of "weakness" in which we live, is reflected, first of all, in our prayer. Our prayer is weak; in fact, we don't know "what" to ask for and we don't know "how" to ask it: both aspects are dealt with in the pauline text, even if this is not always clear in modern translations. It was well translated in the Latin Vulgate: "*Quid* oremus, *sicut* oportet nescimus": we don't know *what* we should ask for and we don't know *how* to ask it. St. Augustine also distinguished between the two things: "*what* you pray for and *how* you pray for it," "quid ores" and "qualis ores" (cf. *Ep* 130, 4, 9; CSEL 44, p. 50).

The imperfection is not, therefore, only in what we pray for but also, and more deeply, in the attitude and spirit with which we pray. The inefficacy of our prayer comes—according to a latin maxim—from the fact that we "mali, mala, male petimus," that is, we being evil (*mali*) ask for evil things (*mala*), in an evil way (*male*). The Spirit comes to our help rectifying all the evil or imperfection that is in us because of our lasting egoism.

First of all, let us take the imperfection that lies in what we ask. St. Paul affirms that we don't know "what" to ask, but, in fact, this would not seem to be true. We seem to know all too well what to ask of God; as soon as we start praying we always have an infinite number of things to ask him; they tumble from our lips. This is true. But we are often like the peasant mentioned by an old spiritual master, who was granted an audience with the king. At last he can talk to the king in person and place his petition directly before him; it is the chance of his life! But when the moment comes and he finds himself in the presence of the king, what does he ask for? He asks the king to grant him . . . a hundred kilos of manure for his fields! (cf. Isaac of Nineveh, *Mystic Treatises,* III, Amsterdam 1923). More often than not we ask God for small things; things that concern our material welfare and are useful only for this life.

They are "manure" with respect to what God is willing to grant us; they are what he gives "over and above" to his friends who seek his kingdom. The Holy Spirit assists us in our uncertainty about what to ask for by the fact that he intercedes for us "according to the will of God." He asks, that is, for precisely those things he knows the Father wants to grant us through prayer and so prayer actually becomes infallible. He who scrutinizes the "depths of God" knows what designs God has for us.

2. At the School of Prayer in the Bible

The biggest imperfection in our prayer lies not so much in the *object* of the prayer as in the *subject*; it's not so much that enclosed in the noun "mala" as that enclosed in the adjective "mali." The Holy Spirit comes to help us in our weakness rectifying above all the heart which is the very source of our prayer. He teaches us to pray no longer with the attitude of slaves but of sons. It is on this point that we want to let him teach us from now on.

St. Paul affirms that the Spirit prays in us "with sighs too deep for words" and in telling us that the Spirit "prays" it's as if he were telling us "he makes us pray." If we could decipher the meaning of these "sighs too deep for words," if we could discover for what and how the Spirit prays in the heart of the believer, we would have discovered the very secret of prayer. Now, it seems to me that this is possible. In fact, the Spirit that prays secretly and silently within us is the same identical Spirit that prayed in the Scriptures. He who "inspired" the pages of Scripture also inspired the prayers in Scripture. In a certain sense we could say that there is nothing more surely and clearly "expressed" than those "unexpressed" sighs of the Spirit. If it is dogmatically true that the Holy Spirit continues to speak today in the Church and in souls, repeating in a new way, what he said to the prophets in Sacred Scripture, it is also true that he prays today in the Church and in souls, in the same way he taught us to pray in Scripture. The Holy Spirit doesn't utter two different prayers.

We must, therefore, learn how to pray from the Bible, so as to learn to be in harmony with the Spirit and pray as he prays. Let us discover the sentiments of the biblical man of prayer through the prayer of some of God's great friends such as Abraham, Moses, Jeremiah, whom the Bible itself presents as the greatest of intercessors (cf. Jr. 15:1; 2 M 15:14). The first thing that strikes us in these "inspired" men of prayer is the great trust and incredible boldness with which they address God. There is none of the servilism that men usually associate with the word prayer itself. Abraham's prayer in favour of Sodom and Gomorrah is well known to us (cf. Gn 18:22 f.). Abraham started by saying: *Will you really destroy the upright with the guilty?*, as if to say: I can't believe you want to do a thing like that! To every request for pardon that follows, Abraham repeats: *It is presumption of me to speak to the Lord!* His prayer is presumptuous and he knows it. But Abraham is "God's friend" (Is 41:8) and friends know how far they can go with one another.

Moses goes even further in this presumption. We have an extraordinary example in chapter 29 of Exodus and chapter 9 of Deuteronomy. After the people had built the golden calf, God says to Moses: *Arise, go down quickly from here; for your people whom you have brought from Egypt have acted corruptly.* Moses answers saying: *They are thy people and thy heritage, whom thou didst bring out by thy great power* (Dt 9:12-29; cf. Ex 32:7-11). Rabbinic tradition well understood the meaning underlying Moses' words: "When this people is faithful to you, then it is your people which you brought out of Egypt but when it is unfaithful, then it is my people which I brought out of Egypt!" God uses the weapon of seduction. He flashes before his servant the idea that, once the rebellious people has been destroyed, he will make "a great nation" of him (Ex 32:10). Moses falls back on a little blackmail and says to God: Be careful, if you destroy this people, it might be said you did so because you were not able to bring them to the country you had promised them! (cf. Ex 32:12; Dt 9:28). The Bible comments saying that the Lord spoke to Moses "as a man speaks to his friend" (Ex 33:11), almost as man to man. And it was the Holy Spirit who inspired this audacious prayer!

Jeremiah reaches and explicit protest and cries to God: *Thou hast deceived me!* and: *I will not mention him or speak any more in his name* (Jer 20:7-9).

Looking at the psalms it would seem that God puts the most efficacious words of lament against himself into man's mouth. One of the
greatest scholars of the psalms called his book "Praise and Lament," because the Psalter is, in fact, a unique intertwining of the most sublime
praise and the most mournful lament. God is often openly called into
cause: "Wake, Lord! Why are you asleep?", "Has your word come to an
end for all time?" "How much longer, Lord, will you look on in the time
of onslaught?," "For your sake we are being treated as sheep to be
slaughtered!," "Give ear to my words, Lord!," "How much longer, Lord,
will you look on?"

How can all this be explained? Is God pushing man towards ir-
reverence to himself, as, in ultimate analysis, he is the one who inspires
and approves this type of prayer? The answer is that it is all possible because biblical man is well aware of his state of creature in relation to
God and he accepts it. The biblical man of prayer is so intimately filled
with a sense of the majesty and holiness of God, so totally submitted to
him, God is so much "God" to him, that on the basis of this given fact,
everything else is safe. The answer lies, all told, in the heart with which
these men pray. They do not pray as "evil beings" (*mali*) and do not,
therefore, pray in an "evil way" (*male*). In the midst of his tempestuous
prayer, Jeremiah reveals the secret that explains all this and puts things
in their proper place: *But thou, O Lord, knowest me, thou seest me and
triest my mind toward thee* (Jer 12:3). The psalmists also insert similar
expressions of absolute faithfulness into their laments: *God is the
strength of my heart and my portion forever* (Ps 73:26). Moses reminds
the people: "Know that the Lord your God is God" (cf. Dt. 7:9). It's as if
the hearts of these men and the heart of God have been welded together
and nothing and no one can separate them. The contrast, the anguished
"why?," the bewilderment are in their minds (because the mystery of
God's ways continues), but not in their hearts. This is so true that
whatever God does, this worshipper is always ready to admit that God is
right even when he is angry with him (cf. Is 12:1) or when man is strick-
en by his anger (Ps 76:11). Man knows who he is dealing with and accepts this entirely. He also knows that he has sinned and that herein lies
the explanation of all that he doesn't understand of God. His favorite

prayer in time of trial is always the same: *For you are upright in all that you have done for us, all your deeds are true, all your ways right, all your judgements true . . . Yes, we have sinned* (Dn 3:28 f.; Dt 32:4 f.). "You are upright, Lord!": after these few words—God says—man can say what he wants to me: I am disarmed!

3. The Prayer of Hypocrites

Biblical prayer starts, therefore, with the serene and joyful acceptance of God as God and of ourselves as creatures of God. A comparison between this "good" prayer and the "evil" prayer, also mentioned in the Bible, will help us towards a better appraisal of what "good" prayer means. We have so far seen how biblical man prays, that is, the man approved of by the Word of God; let us now look at the prayer of the man of whom the Bible disapproves, that is "human" or carnal man.

In the prophet Isaias we find this lament by God (this time it is God who laments about man): *This people draw near me with their mouth and honor me with their lips while their hearts are far from me* (Is 29:13). Jesus, one day quoting these words to the pharisees, said: *Hypocrites, how rightly Isaias prophesized about you when he said . . .* and he quotes the text of Isaias just mentioned (Mt 15:7-8). The biblical man of prayer is he who can say with the words of Jeremiah: "My heart is with you and you know it!"; the hypocritical worshipper is he of whom God says: "His heart is far from me!" The heart of the biblical man of prayer is with God while his words are often against God, in the sense that, as we have seen, he uses harsh words of lament and even accusation against God, whereas the hypocritical worshipper's words are with God (he would never use disrespectful words against God) but his heart is against him. In fact, a psalm says of such worshippers: *But they flattered him with their mouths and lied to him with their tongues. Their hearts were not steadfast toward him* (Ps 78:36 f.) and Jeremiah addressing God, says of them: *Thou art near in their mouth and far from their heart* (Jer 12:2). When God laments saying: "This people honors me only with lip-service while their hearts are far from me," we are dealing with something much worse than just simple distraction in prayer when the mind is not on what is being said. It is the heart that is deceiving and contradicting the words. This is what happens when man wants the things of God more than he wants God himself! God is no longer God, that is, above all other things. He is exploited and placed at man's disposal. It is not the prayer of a friend but of a cunning and opportunistic slave who admits his own smallness and the greatness of his lord only to exploit him. Such prayer is mercenary and no longer heartfelt.

Such a state of mind gives rise to an odd and contorted type of prayer which I would call diplomatic prayer. In human experience it is easy to distinguish between a friendly and cordial conversation and a diplomatic one. In the first you feel an inner sense of freedom, you look the person in the eye and you don't measure your words at the back of your mind. It is not necessary to say much as just a simple glance suffices. In the second case it is difficult to hide a sense of awkwardness: people avoid looking at one another, the words used are studied, they *talk* a lot being careful not to *say* anything and they can't wait for the conversation to end. The difference, where prayer is concerned, is that man "sees the face" while God "scrutinizes the heart" and therefore, man can be deceived whereas God cannot be deceived. The hypocrite doesn't deceive God, but himself. God's scrutiny goes straight to the heart. Above all, he looks for sincerity of heart in the person praying to him: *You delight in sincerity of heart . . .* (Ps 51:8). If this is present all the rest is acceptable but without it nothing is acceptable.

It must be said that the veil of diffidence and hypocrisy impeding genuine prayer has greatly increased in modern man. The various humanistic trends have—even unintentionally—created a sort of unspoken rivalry between man and God. The idea is that God is acceptable so long as man's freedom and autonomy are in no way interfered with. Man, foolish as he is, is completely taken with defending his freedom not from Satan and sin but from God, as if he who created it were the threat! In the minds of certain thinkers God would appear to be man's rival so that the more space is given to God, the more is taken from man. That's why modern man's prayer is often so contorted. It has become very difficult for us to pray with the simplicity and presumption of

Abraham, Moses and the psalmists. A bad conscience rightly brings with it a sense of guilt because the interior conditions essential to such prayer are missing, at least until we restore a biblical heart in ourselves.

4. The Prayer of Job and that of His Friends

The Bible presents us with an exemplary case of prayer in that of Job and his friends, in which we can distinguish and assess—as in a diptych—the two types of prayer outlined so far. God puts his friend Job through a terrible trial. As soon as the trial overtakes him, the first thing Job does is to place himself on the safe side with God. Just as when a hurricane is approaching an island, a man rushes into this house and hastens to put his dearest and most precious belongings in a safe place, so Job withdraws into himself and hastens to make his submission to God safe. *Then Job stood up, tore his robe and shaved his head. Then falling to the ground he prostrated himself and said: Naked I came from my mother's womb, naked shall I return again. The Lord gave, the Lord has taken back. Blessed be the name of the Lord* (Job 1:20-21) (Job acts and speaks rapidly, almost breathlessly, as if he were afraid of not getting to the end).

Let us now follow the development of the events. Job's friends arrive and observe silence for seven days. Then the dialogue starts which takes a strange and unexpected turn. Job curses the day he was born and his friends make their long and passionate defense of God (4:1 f.). *Can a mortal seem upright to God?* they ask. Job cries out: "Man of grief that I am," and they answer: "Blessed are those whom God corrects!" Thus the scene of how the rest of the drama developed is outlined. On the one hand we have poor Job talking nonsense and imploring, defying God and accusing him. He passes from cries to invocations and uses heart-rending words with God: "Do not condemn me! Soon you will look for me and I shall be no more; why do you look on me as your enemy? What have I done to you?" On the other hand we have the three friends who take turns in upholding God's side against Job and say wonderful things in favor of the divinity and against man. Job is bewildered by God's actions and confesses that he can't understand them. God's defenders, instead, know everything. It's all clear to them: where there is suffering, there has been sin. They don't even suspect a different judgement on God's part, which is still to be revealed. Revelation could have ended here for them. Seen thus, nothing else was necessary, not even the coming of Jesus Christ. Job accuses his friends of "partiality" towards God and of hypocrisy. He says that if God were to scrutinize the bottom of their hearts, he would find deceit in their words (13:7 f.). But then, in his anguish he implores them too and says: "Pity me, pity me, my friends, since I have been struck by the hand of God!" (19:21).

How does God respond to all those contradictions? God enters the scene in chapter 38. He first speaks directly to Job about his greatness and incomprehensibility and Job immediately repents laying his hand over his mouth (40:4; 42:2). But the most disconcerting thing is what comes immediately after. When this tête-à-tête with Job ends, God addresses Eliphaz of Teman, saying: *I burn with anger against you and your two friends, for not having spoken correctly about me as my servant Job has done* (42:7). This is strange! Why does God give such a disconcerting verdict in favour of his accuser and against those who defended him? It's because God looks at the sincerity of the heart. Job was sincere with God; in the vice of suffering he cried to God: "Why, why?," but his spirit held fast under the terrible strain even if at times he wavered. He did not break with God, nor did he withdraw his initial submission to God; his deep relationship with God was "safe." "My footsteps have followed close in his," he can say of God (23:11). God knew that he could go a long way in testing his Job and Job knew that he could go a long way in complaining to his God. On the contrary, the defense of God made by Job's friends is basically hypocritical and false as it has not been put to the test. It is the presumptuous defense of he who is convinced that in the same circumstances, he would do better; of the one who thinks he knows everything about God and thus offends him deeply because he ignores who God really is and lacks respect towards suffering which is sacred to God. God knows well how to distinguish between admirers and adulators. Job's friends were more adulators than sincere admirers of God and Job had realized this. God doesn't want adulators, he doesn't need them. There is always a little self-interest hidden in adulators and maybe Job's friends thought they would thus avoid falling into the same situation as their friend.

This condemnation of Job's friends makes me reflect a lot because I think I can see in us "ministers of God," theologians and preachers, the danger of appertaining to the same category. It is easy to fall under the presumption of being counsel for God's defense and his justice. This happens whenever we give people the impression that neither God's ways nor human existence hold any mystery for us, that everything is clear and has been established for all time and whenever, faced with great suffering, we don't know how to keep silent and cry—as Jesus did before the suffering of the widow of Naim and before the tomb of Lazarus—but we lose ourselves in vain talk and explanations.

5. The Prayer of Jesus and of the Spirit

The Book of Job is not just a "wisdom book," it is also a "prophetic book," that is, it does not contain just a moral teaching but it also contains a prophecy. In fact, in Jesus, the case of the suffering righteous man will be repeated on an infinitely higher level and without the uncertainties we notice in Job. Jesus, too, in his hour of trial offered up to God "prayer and entreaty with loud cries and with tears" (cf. Heb 5:7). The counsel for God's defense—the pharisees and the doctors of the law—said of him (as Job's friends said of Job): "He has spoken blasphemy!" (Mt 26:65) and they constantly sought to find him in contrast with God. But he answered them: *Can any of you convict me of sin?* (Jn 8:46). In Job innocence was only relative, in Jesus it is absolute. Even Jesus addresses his deeply distressed "why" to the Father: *Why have you abandoned me?* (Mt 27:46). But God's sentence is once again in favor of the one he has stricken. In Job's case—in accordance with the still imperfect state of the Old Testament faith—restoration came about on the earthly level of children and flocks ("God gave Job double what he had before!"). In the case of Jesus it came about on a spiritual and eternal level, in the resurrection. Job is restored to his previous life; Jesus enters into another life.

If it is important to know how the Spirit prayed in Moses, in the psalms, in Jeremiah and in Job, it is even more important to know how he prayed in Jesus, because it is the Spirit of Jesus who now prays in us with groans that cannot be put into words. In Jesus is perfected that interior adhesion of the heart and of the whole being to God which forms, as we have seen, the biblical secret of prayer. The Father always heard him because he always did what pleased the Father (cf. Jn 4:34; 11:42); He heard him "for his piety," that is, for his filial submission (Heb 5:7). At such a level as that reached in the prayer of the Son of God, as man only asks what God wants, it happens that God wants all that man asks.

The Word of God, culminating in the life of Jesus, teaches us, therefore, that the most important thing in prayer is not so much what we *say* as what we *are*. It's not so much in the object of prayer as in the subject. Praying, like acting, "follows being." The change brought about by the Holy Spirit in prayer consists in the fact that he reforms precisely the "being" of the one who prays and—as we have seen in the previous chapter—creates a new man, a man who is God's friend and ally, changing the heart that is slave-like, hypocritical and hostile to God. The Spirit doesn't stop at teaching us how to pray, but prays in us, just as—where the law is concerned—he doesn't stop at telling us what we must do but does it with us. The Spirit doesn't give a *law* of prayer but a *grace* of prayer. Biblical prayer doesn't come to us, therefore, through exterior and progressive learning, that is in so far as we try to imitate the prayer we have so far come across in Abraham, Moses, Job and Jesus himself (even if all this will be necessary and required of us later on), but it comes to us by infusion, as a gift. This is the "good news" concerning Christian prayer! The very principle itself of such new prayer comes to us and this principle consists in the fact that God *has sent into our hearts the Spirit of his Son crying, Abba, Father* (Gal 4:6). This means praying "in the Holy Spirit" or "through the Spirit" (cf. Eph 6:18; Jude 20).

In prayer, as in everything else, the Spirit doesn't talk on his own authority, he doesn't say anything new or different. He simply revives the prayer of Jesus and makes it live in the hearts of believers: *All he reveals to you will be taken from mine*, Jesus says of the Paraclete (Jn 16:14). He will take my prayer and give it to you.

On the strength of this we can exclaim in all truth: "It is not I that pray, but Christ prays in me!" The cry *Abba* itself denotes that it is Jesus, the only Son of God, who prays in us through the Spirit. In fact, the Holy Spirit could not address God for himself, calling him "Father," as he was not generated by the Father but only proceeds from him and is not therefore his "son." When the Holy Spirit teaches us to cry "Abba!"—an ancient writer said—"it's like a mother teaching her child to say 'daddy' and she repeats this name with him until he becomes so familiar with it that he even says it in his sleep." (Diadochus of Photike, *Chapters on perfection* 61, SCh 5 *bis*, p. 121).

It is the Holy Spirit, therefore, who instills the sentiment of divine sonship into the heart, who makes us *feel* (not just know!) that we are children of God. *The Spirit himself joins with our spirit to bear witness that we are children of God* (Rm 8:16). This fundamental work of the Holy Spirit sometimes takes place in an sudden and intense way in the life of a person and the whole splendor can then be contemplated, like the blossoming of a flower in a color film where the whole process is accelerated. On the occasion of a retreat, of receiving a sacrament when one is particularly disposed, or on the occasion of prayer for a new releasing of the Spirit (the so-called "Baptism in the Spirit") the soul is filled with a new light in which God reveals himself in a new way as Father. One experiences what the paternity of God really means, the heart is touched and the person feels born again. A feeling of great trust and confidence and a completely new sense of the condescension of God are experienced. At other times, instead, this revelation of the Father is accompanied by such a strong feeling of God's majesty and transcendence that the soul is overwhelmed and can no longer, for a certain time, even say the word "Father," because on pronouncing it, the person is filled with a sense of awe and wonder and cannot go on praying. To say then "Our Father!" is no longer just a simple and harmless thing. It would seem to be such an undertaking and risk, such a beatitude, such a concession and condescension that the soul is afraid of spoiling everything and withdraws into silence. We can understand how some saints used to start reciting the "Our Father" and were still at the first two words after hours. Blessed Raymond of Capua, St. Catherine of Siena's confessor and biographer, said that she "seldom reached the end of an 'Our Father' without already being in ecstasy" (*Legenda Maior,* 113). When St. Paul speaks of the moment when the Spirit bursts into the heart of the believer and makes him cry "Abba, Father!", he is referring to this way of crying, to this repercussion on the whole being at its deepest level. "Blessed are those who know the Father!" ("Felices qui Patrem agnoscunt") Tertullian used to exclaim at the beginning of Christianity (*De Orat.* 2,3; CCL 1, 258); and we repeat the same thing: blessed are those who know the Father in this way.

But here on earth this strong way of knowing the Father doesn't usually last all that long. The time soon comes when the believer says "Abba!" without feeling anything and continues saying it only on the word of Jesus. This is the time to remember that the more unhappy the soul saying it, the happier the Father listening, because it is a cry of pure faith and abandonment. We are, then, like the well-known musician who, after he had become deaf, continued to compose and perform wonderful symphonies to the joy of his audiences, without being able to enjoy a single note himself, to the point that, when after listening to his masterpiece (the *Ninth Symphony*) the audience burst into a storm of applause, they had to pull the hem of his coat to get him to turn round. Instead of putting a stop to his music, his deafness made it purer and that's what aridity does to our prayer. In fact, when we talk of the exclamation "*Abba*, Father!", we usually only have what the word means to the person saying it in mind, what concerns us. We never think of what the word means to God who is listening to it and what it brings about in him. We never think, that is, of God's joy in being called Father. But anyone who is a father knows what it means to hear himself being called such by the unmistakable timbre of his child's voice. It's as if he were becoming a father again each time because each time that cry makes him again realize that he is a father. It touches the most intimate part of man's heart. Jesus was aware of this so he often called God *Abba*! and he taught us to do the same. The joy we give God in calling him Father is simple and unique, it is the joy of paternity. His heart "is overwhelmed" within him and "fever grips" his inmost being when he is thus called (cf. Hos 11:8). And—as I have said—we can do this even when we "feel" nothing.

It is exactly during this time of God's "absence" and our aridity that we discover the importance of the Holy Spirit in our prayer life. Although not seen or felt by us, the Holy Spirit fills our words and sighs with the longing for God, with humility and love, "and he who scrutinizes the heart knows the desires of the Spirit." We don't know but he does! The Spirit then becomes the strength of our "feeble" prayer, the light of our blind prayer, in a word, the soul of our prayer. Indeed he "irrigates what is arid" as we say in the sequence in his honor. All of this comes about through faith. All I have to say or think is: "Father, you gave me the Spirit of Jesus. Therefore, forming one only Spirit with Jesus, I'm saying this psalm, celebrating this Mass, or just simply being silent, here in your presence. I want to give you the same glory and joy that Jesus would give you if he were praying again on this earth." A fragrance rises to God from such prayer and I like to see the biblical figure of Isaac come to fulfillment here when he smelt his son's clothes and exclaimed *Ah, the smell of my son is like the smell of a fertile field which the Lord has blessed* (Gn 27:27). We are, in fact, "the fragrance of Christ" and we are so, above all, to the Father, "in God's presence," as the Apostle says (cf. 2 Cor 2:15).

When I want to be certain of really praying with the Spirit of Jesus, I've discovered that the simplest way is to pray with the words of Jesus, saying the "Our Father." I've discovered the continuous "Our Father" which consists in repeating over and over again, even for hours, the words of the "Our Father," not as if it were a repetition of many "Our Father"s one after the other, but as if it were one uninterrupted "Our Father." The "Our Father" thus becomes a particularly biblical way of developing that prayer of heart which has been cultivated by many through invoking the name of Jesus. Instead of praying to Jesus, we thus pray with Jesus. It is certainly not possible (at least for me it isn't) to pay attention all the time to all the words, especially if one has other things to do in the meanwhile; but just the same a mental rhythm of prayer is formed. Every now and then the attention is caught and one can in all simplicity concentrate on the word the mind has paused on even while continuing to pray: "Thy Kingdom come," or "Thy will be done," or "Forgive us our trespasses," or "Deliver us from evil." There is not a spiritual or temporal need and there is no state of soul which can't be expressed in prayer in the "Our Father." Yet it would seem that the most important thing of all, the Holy Spirit, is not prayed for in the "Our Father." In ancient times somebody tried to fill in the gap because in some manuscripts, after the invocation for our daily bread, we find the words: "May the Holy Spirit descend upon us and purify us." But it is simpler to think that the Holy Spirit is not among the things asked for, precisely because it is he who is asking. "*God*—it is written—*has sent into our hearts the Spirit of his Son crying, Abba, Father!*" (Gal 4:1). It is the Holy Spirit, therefore, who starts to pray the "Our Father" in us; without him, whoever cries "Abba!" does so in vain.

As I have said, there isn't a state of soul that is not reflected in the "Our Father," and that cannot be expressed in prayer: joy, praise, adoration, thanksgiving, repentance. But the "Our Father" is, above all, the prayer of the hour of trial. There is a certain similarity between the prayer Jesus left to his disciples and the prayer he himself offered up to the Father in Gethsemane. He left us, in fact, *his* own prayer: In Gethsemane he addresses God as "*Abba*, Father" (Mk 14:36), or "My Father" (Mt 26:39); he says "your will be done"; he asks that the "cup may pass him by," just as we ask to be "delivered from evil" and "led not into temptation." What a comfort it is in the hour of trial and darkness to know that the Holy Spirit continues in us the prayer of Jesus in Gethsemane, that the "groans that cannot be put into words" with which the Spirit intercedes for us at such moments, reach the Father mixed with "prayer and entreaty, with loud cries and with tears," which the Son offered up to him "during his life on earth" (cf. Heb 5:7)!

"Our Lord Jesus Christ, Son of God—says St. Augustine—is he who prays for us, who prays in us and who is prayed to by us. He prays for us as our Priest; he prays in us as our Head, and is prayed to by us as our

God. Let us, therefore, recognize in him our voice, and his voice in us (*Enarr. Ps.* 85, 1).

6. "Give me the grace to do what you command!"

There's a sort of hidden vein of prayer in us due to all of this. There's "a hidden treasure" in our hearts! Speaking of this interior voice of the Spirit, St. Ignatius of Antioch wrote: "I feel a spring of living water within me murmuring: come to the Father" (*Ad Rom.* 7, 2). What is left unattempted in countries afflicted by drought when a water vein is detected in the earth? They go on digging until the vein is reached and brought to the surface. We too should not spare ourselves in the effort to bring ever anew into the light of our spirit that "spring of water, welling up for eternal life" (Jn 4:14) which is in us through Baptism. I say bring "ever anew" into the light because we throw rubble and soil over that spring and cover it each time we fill our souls with noise, dissipation and vain activity, each time we give free reign to the thoughts and desires of self-indulgence which are "in opposition to the Spirit" (Gal 5:17).

I should like to ask those Christians who are today rediscovering the need and zest for prayer and who are, at times, tempted to go far away, or restlessly search outside themselves for places of prayer or someone to guide them: Where are you going? Where are you searching? "Look within yourselves: the truth dwells within man" (St. Augustine, *De vera rel.* 39, 72; CCL 32, 234). Prayer is within you, so why seek it outside?

This interior vein of prayer due to the presence of the Spirit of Christ in us, doesn't just give life to the prayer of petition but makes every other form of prayer alive and real: the prayer of praise, spontaneous prayer and liturgical prayer. In fact, when we pray spontaneously in our own words, it's the Spirit who makes our prayer his but when we pray with the words of the Bible or the liturgy, it is we who make the prayer of the Spirit ours and this is a safer type of prayer.

Also the silent prayer of contemplation and adoration benefits immensely if it is done "in the Spirit." According to St. Basil, the Holy Spirit is the "place" into which one must enter to contemplate God and adore him. In a spiritual sense, he applies to the worshipper what is read of Moses who went into "the cleft of the rock" so as to comtemplate God who was going past: "Scripture says of the Spirit: *Here is a place near me. You will stand on the rock* (Ex 33:21). What is this place—continues St. Basil—if not contemplation in the Spirit? It was thus that Moses was able to see God openly revealing himself to him. This is the suitable place for true adoration: *Take care*—Scripture again says—*you do not offer your burnt offerings in all the sacred places you see; only in the place that God chooses* (Dt 12:13-14). The spiritual burnt offering is the sacrifice of praise and the place in which we offer it is 'in the Spirit.' From whom did we learn this? From the Lord in person who said: *True worshippers will worship the Father in Spirit and Truth* (Jn 4:23)" (St. Basil, *De Spir.S.* XXVI; PG 32, 181 f.). It is not, therefore, only the soul that is the temple of the Holy Spirit but the Holy Spirit is the temple of the soul too. In this temple, "not man-made" but real, it is possible to contemplate God "close up"; in fact, the Holy Spirit belongs to God's world, he himself is God; through him we reach God himself and not some intermediary. He is in us and in God. To adore "in the Spirit" means to adore in the divine uncreated light of the Holy Spirit who reveals, from within, the mystery of Christ and through him leads us back to the Father. This is his secret, his prerogative.

The ability to pray is our great resource. Many Christians, even those really committed, experience their impotence when faced with temptation and the impossibility of conforming to the exacting requirements of evangelical morality. They sometimes end up thinking that it is all beyond them, that is impossible to live an integral christian life. In a certain sense, they are right. In fact, it's impossible to avoid sin on our own; we need grace; but even grace—we have been taught—is a free gift and cannot be merited. What should we do then: fall into despair and give up? The Council of Trent tells us: "God, in giving you grace, commands you to do what you can and ask for what you can't do" (DS, 1536). When a person has done his utmost and hasn't succeeded, there is always another possibility: prayer, and if he has already prayed, pray again! The difference between the new and the old covenant lies in this: in the Old Testament God *commands* saying to man: "Do what I ask you to do!"; in the New Testament man *demands* saying to God: "Grant me what you ask from me!" Once he discovered this secret, St. Augustine, who up to then had struggled in vain to be chaste, changed his tactics and instead of struggling against his body, began struggling with God; "O God—he said—you command me to be continent; well then, give me the grace to do what you command and then command me to do what you will!" (*Conf.* X, 29) and he obtained chastity! Prayer—as I said at the beginning—is the breath of the soul. Just as a person who is about to faint or make some strenuous physical effort, is told to breathe deeply, so a person about to give in to temptation or to difficulties or weariness should be told to pray, to take very deep breaths of prayer. Lots of people could bear witness to the change that took place in their lives the moment they decided to insert an hour's personal prayer in their daily timetable, defending it at length against all and everything.

7. The Prayer of Intercession

The strength of prayer is especially expressed in the prayer of intercession. The Holy Spirit—it is written—intercedes for us. The safest way for us to be in accord with the prayer of the Spirit is, therefore, to intercede in our turn for our brethren, for the people. The prayer of intercession means uniting ourselves, through faith, with Christ who was raised from the dead and who lives forever to intercede for the world (cf. Rom 8:34; Heb 7:25; 1 Jn 2:1). Jesus, in the great prayer with which he concluded his life on earth, gave us the most sublime example of intercession. "It is for them that I pray—he says—for those you have given me . . . keep them true to your name. I am not asking you to remove them from the world but to protect them from the evil one. Consecrate them in truth . . . I pray not only for these but also for those who through their teaching will come to believe in me . . ." (cf. Jn 17:9 f.). Jesus dedicates relatively little space to praying for himself ("Father glorify your son!") and much more to praying for others, that is to intercession. Through the Holy Spirit who intercedes for us, it is Jesus himself who is still interceding for us.

The efficacy of the prayer of intercession doesn't depend on "using many words" (cf. Mt 6:7), but on the level of union one manages to reach with the filial disposition of Christ. Rather than multiplying the words of intercession, it would probably be more useful to multiply the number of intercessors, that is to invoke the help of Mary and the Saints, as the Church does on the feast of all Saints when it asks God to grant what is being asked "through the many intercessors." The intercessors are also multiplied in number when we pray for one another. "If you pray for yourself—says St. Ambrose—you are the only one praying for yourself and if each one prays only for himself, the grace the person praying receives will be smaller with respect to that obtained by him who intercedes for others. Now, as the individual prays for all, it comes about that all pray for the individual. Therefore, if you pray only for yourself, you will be the only one praying for yourself. If, on the other hand, you pray for all, all will be praying for you, as you are included in that all" (St. Ambrose, *De Cain et Ab.* I,39; CSEL 32, I, p. 372).

Not only, therefore, does the Holy Spirit intercede for us but he teaches us to intercede, in our turn, for others. The Holy Spirit has revealed to us in the Bible that the true man of prayer is "daring" in prayer especially when interceding for others. The prayer of intercession is very acceptable to God because it is the most free from egoism, it closer reflects divine gratuitousness and is in agreement with the will of God, who wants "everyone to be saved" (cf. 1 Tm 2:4). At the end of the Book of Job, we read that God pardons the three friends because "Job interceded for them" and that he restored Job's condition to former times because he had prayed for his three friends (cf. Job 42:8-10). It would seem, therefore, that the decisive factor in all of this was the prayer of intercession. Of the servant of God—that is, in fact, of Jesus—it is written that God "gave him a portion with the great, because he was interceding for the rebellious" (cf. Is 53:12). God is like a compassionate father whose duty is to punish, but who makes all the allowances possible so as not to have to do so, and who is deeply happy when the brothers of the sinner hold him back from doing so. When these outstretched fraternal arms are missing, God laments about it in Scripture: *He saw there was no one and wondered there was no one to intervene* (Is

59:16). Ezekiel transmits the following lament of God to us: *I have been looking for someone among them to build a barricade and oppose me in the breach, to defend the country and prevent me from destroying it; but I have found no one* (Ezek 22:30).

The word of God emphasizes the extraordinary power the prayer of those placed in charge of his people has with God by his very own wish. Once, it says, God had decided to put an end to his people because of the golden calf if "Moses hadn't taken a stand in the breach and confronted him, to turn his anger away" (cf. Ps 106:23). I dare say to pastors and leaders of the Church: When, in prayer, you feel that God is angry with those he has given into your care, don't side with God but with the people! That's what Moses did, to the point of protesting that he himself wanted to be blotted out of the book of life with them (cf. Ex 32:32) and the Bible gives us to understand that this was exactly what God wanted, because "He gave up the idea of harming his people." But in front of the people you must side with God with all your strength. A little later as he approached the camp, Moses blazed with anger: he ground the golden calf into powder which he scattered on the water and made the Israelites drink it (cf. Ex 32:19 f.). *Is this the return you make to God? O people brainless and unwise!* (Dt 32:6) he cried to Israel. Only he who has defended the people before God and borne the weight of their sins has the right—and would have the courage—to then shout against them in defense of God, as Moses did.

In the Bible we find this lovely eulogy of the intercessor Jeremiah, which the liturgy has applied to certain saintly pastors and which now re-echoes for us as a good wish and programme: *This is a man who loves his brothers, and prays much for the people and the holy city* (2 M 15:14).

X. Let Love Be Sincere

The excellent way of charity

In outlining the new life in the Spirit, St. Paul shows, in chapter eight of the Letter to the Romans, a singular oscillation of thought and expression. At the beginning this new life seems to be an accomplished fact, a gift received: *The law of the Spirit which gives life*—he says—*set you free from the law of sin and death* (Rom 8:2). We are, therefore, already free, already living in the Spirit. *You*—it adds—*live not by your natural inclinations, but by the Spirit* (Rom 8:9). But later on we find that the Apostle makes a different assertion: *If by the Spirit you put to death the habits originating in the body, you will have life* (Rom 8:13). At the beginning life is presented as something acquired, here it is something to be acquired; in the first case the verbs are in the past or present tenses, in this case they are in the future tense ("you will have life"). If we pass from the theme of "living in the Spirit" to its related one "putting on a new self" this oscillation becomes more obvious and significant. In one passage the Apostle says: *You have stripped off your old behaviour with your old self, and you have put on a new self which will progress towards true knowledge the more it is renewed in the image of its Creator* (Col 3:9-10). Here the passage from the old self to the new self has already come about, and is behind us, in so far as it was historically accomplished by the death of Christ and sacramentally, by Baptism; but if we look at the Letter to the Ephesians we realize that to put off the old self and put on the new self is, instead, in the imperative, something that is before us and must be accomplished throughout life. In fact, it says: *You were to put aside your old self which belongs to your old way of life and is corrupted by following illusory desires. Your mind was to be renewed in spirit so that you could put on the New Man that has been created on God's principles, in the uprightness and holiness of the truth* (Eph 4:22-24). The same oscillation is repeated where "being clothed in Christ" is concerned, which is another way of saying the same thing. At times this seems to have already been accomplished in Baptism: *Every one of you that has been baptized has been clothed in Christ* (Gal 3:27); at other times, instead, it is a command, something to be done: *Clothe yourselves with the Lord Jesus Christ* (Rom 13:14).

What is the meaning of this double series of expressions? That maybe St. Paul is contradicting himself? On the contrary it is a fundamental teaching telling us that the passage from a life based on natural inclinations to life in the Spirit, from the old self to the new self, is, at one and the same time, both God's work and our work, an accomplished thing and something still to be accomplished.

Having contemplated and assimilated by faith what God worked for us in Christ, we have reached the point where we must answer with our life and our choices: having received the gift of the Spirit, we must produce the "fruits of the Spirit." The fundamental teaching in the Letter to the Romans is not so much in the various things it presents as in the order in which they are presented. The Apostle doesn't first deal with the *duties* of the Christian (charity, humility, service, etc.) and then with *grace*—almost as if this were a consequence of the first—but, on the contrary, he first deals with justification and grace, and then with the obligations that these give rise to. For "we do not come to faith from virtue but from faith to virtue" (St. Gregory the Great *In Ez* II, 7; PL 76, 1018). *It is by grace*—he writes—*that you have been saved, through faith: not by anything of your own, but by a gift from God; not by anything that you have done, so that nobody can claim the credit. We are God's work of art, created in Christ Jesus for the good works which God has already designated to make up our way of life* (Eph 2:8-10). We are God's work: that is the main thing; the "good works" follow and are made possible and necessary because of it. We are not saved, in fact, *because of* our good works, but we cannot be saved *without* good works.

There is a change in both style and literary genre as we pass from the first to the second part of the letter to the Romans, from the *kerygma* to the *parenesis* or exhortation: *I urge you, then, brothers, remembering the mercies of God* . . . , is how chapter twelve begins. We pass from what God has done "for us" to what he wants to do "with us." We know, in fact, that "He who created us without us, will not save us without us" (cf.

St. Augustine, *Ser.* 169, 13). In this way we are helped, as I said in the introduction, in restoring one of the most important and difficult balances to keep; the balance between the mysteric element and the ascetic element of our spiritual life, between Christ as a "gift" and Christ as "model." "As—it has been written—the idea of Christ as model was overemphasized in Medieval times, so Luther emphasized the other aspect, affirming that Christ is a gift and this gift can only be accepted through faith (S. Kierkegaard, *Journals*, X1 A 154). By following the way outlined by Paul in the letter to the Romans, we can bring together these two aspects of the faith in a catholic and ecumenical unity. The Apostle teaches us that we mustn't start with "imitation" but with "faith" (and we are grateful to Luther for his recall on this point) but he also teaches us that we mustn't stop at "faith only" because "imitation" (good works) must follow as the only real true expression of our correspondence and gratitude and as a true and total expression of faith itself. "If we really love—St. Augustine says—we will imitate. In fact, we couldn't give in exchange a more exquisite fruit of our love than imitation" (*Ser.* 304, 2; PL 38, 1395 f.).

The aim of imitation is not simply to be "like" to Christ, to do the things he did; it is to be "clothed" in Christ, that is, to be filled with Christ, to be transformed into him so as to form with him "one only spirit" (1 Cor 6:17). "The aim of Christian life—said a Russian saint going straight to the point—is the acquisition of the Holy Spirit!" (St. Seraphin of Sarov, *Conversation with Motovilov*). Christian virtues are not an aim in themselves and neither is their end the moral perfection of he who practises them, nor his "heroism" in practising them (the concept of "the heroism of virtue" was unknown in the Christian language up to the XVI century!), but their end is God. This is where they differ from pagan virtues, even when called by the same name. Practised for pagan or natural reasons, virtue has a *negative* end—impassibility or *apatheia,* that is the quenching of passion—and a *human* end—to live according to reason. The evangelical practice, instead, has a *positive* end—the acquiring of the Holy Spirit—and a *divine* end—to live according to Christ. Before going on to point out the various fields of christian commitment and the different virtues, the Apostle himself explains the "end" of all this: to offer one's life as "a living sacrifice, dedicated and acceptable to God" (Rom 12:1).

1. Sincere Love

Love is the first of the fruits of the Spirit, or christian virtues, that the Apostle lists in Galatians 5:22. And it is with love that the exhortation to virtue starts in our letter. The whole of chapter 12 is one exhortation after the other on charity: *Let love be without any pretence . . . In brotherly love let your feelings of deep affection for one another come to expression and regard others as more important than yourself* (Rom 12:9 f.). Chapter 13 contains the well-known statements of principle on charity as a summary and fulfillment of the law: *The only thing you should owe to anyone is love for one another, for to love the other person is to fulfil the law* (Rom 13:8-10). Chapter 14 recommends charity in its particular form towards the weak and towards those of the community who think differently on any point. In Chapter 8 the Apostle spoke of charity in so far as it is the "law of the Spirit," that is, an infused disposition which makes us capable of loving; now he talks of charity as being "fruit of the Spirit," that is, a virtue acquired through the constant effort of our free will collaborating with grace.

To grasp the spirit that unites all these recommendations and Paul's basic idea, or rather, sentiment, on charity, we must start with the opening words: *Let love be without any pretence!* This is not one of the many exhortations but the matrix from which all the others are derived. It contains the secret of charity. With the help of the Spirit let us try to grasp this secret. The original term used by Paul and which is translated as "without pretence" is *anhypokritos,* that is, without hypocrisy. This word is a sort of pilot light. Actually, it is a rare term and is almost exclusively used in the New Testament to define christian love. The expression "love without hypocrisy" (*anhypokritos*) is again repeated in 2 Cor 6:6 and in 1 Pt 1:22. This last text enables us to grasp, without any doubt, the meaning of the term in question, because it is explained through a periphrasis: genuine love—it says—consists in loving each other intensely "from the heart."

St. Paul, therefore, with the simple statement: "Let love be sincere," gets to the root of charity, which is the heart. Love should be genuine, true and without pretence. Just as wine has to be crushed from the grapes to be "genuine" so love has to be crushed from the heart. Also in this, the Apostle faithfully echoes the thought of Christ. He had, in fact, repeatedly and forcefully indicated the heart as being the "place" in which the value of man's actions is decided, what is pure or impure, in a person's life: *For from the heart come evil intentions* (Mt 15:19). We could talk of a Pauline intuition where charity is concerned which consists in revealing that behind the visible and exterior world of charity made up of works and words lies an entirely interior world which in relation to the first is what the soul is for the body. This intuition is also present in that great text on charity that 1 Cor 13 is. A careful reading of this text shows that all of what St. Paul says refers to this interior charity, to the disposition and sentiments of charity: charity is patient and kind, it is never jealous, it does not take offence or store up grievances, it is always ready to make allowances, to trust and to hope . . . There is no direct mention of *doing* good or of doing works of charity, but the whole passage is a recall to the root of *loving*. Benevolence comes before beneficence. It is the Apostle himself who makes the clear distinction between the two spheres of charity, saying that the greatest act of exterior charity (to give all one's possessions to the poor) would be of no use if interior charity were lacking. It would be the opposite to "genuine" charity. Hypocritical charity is, in fact, that which does good to others without loving them. It shows exteriorly something that has no corresponding sentiment in the heart. We then simply have something that looks like charity, which may, in the worst of cases, be a cover up for egoism, self-seeking, the taking advantage of a brother or just simple remorse of conscience.

It would be a fatal error to set charity of the heart and charitable works one against the other, or to take refuge in interior charity, so as to find a sort of alibi for the lack of active charity. We know how strongly the words of Jesus (Mt 25:34 f.), of James (2:16 f.) and of St. John (1 Jn 3:18) urge us to active charity. We know the importance St. Paul himself gave to the collections for the poor of Jerusalem. On the other hand, to say that without charity even the giving of all one has to the poor "will do me no good whatever," doesn't mean to say that this is useless and of no value to anyone; it means, rather, that it is of no good "to me" whereas it may be very good for the needy person receiving it. It is not, therefore, a question of taking from the importance of works of charity, so much as giving them a secure base against egoism and its numerous tricks. St. Paul wants all Christians to be "planted in love and built on love" (Eph 3:17), that is, that charity be the root and foundation of all. Jesus himself established this principle when he said: "Love your neighbour *as yourself!*" (Mt 22:39). God couldn't have secured love of our neighbour to a more firmly fixed pillar than this; he wouldn't have obtained the same results even if he had said: "Love your neighbour as your God!" because man can still deceive himself about the love of God—that is, about what loving God means—whereas he cannot do so about love of himself. Man knows what it means to love himself at all times; it's a mirror which is always in front of him.

Genuine love is loving at this depth, where it is no longer possible to deceive because you are alone with yourself. Alone, in front of the "mirror," with God looking down on you. In this way my neighbour enters into my innermost being, into what Scripture calls the "interior man"; he truly and entirely becomes "neighbour," because I keep him in my heart, even when I'm alone with God and with myself. My neighbour (*proximus*) actually becomes intimate (*intimus*). This is the greatest dignity a person can grant another person and it is through charity that God found the way of accomplishing such a sublime state which preludes the final communion of saints, when one will be, through love, in all and all in one and the joy of each one will be multiplied by the joy of all. This is a sign of what has always come about in God; God, in fact, keeps us in his heart; he *did* good to us because he *wants* our good.

2. Divine Love

To be genuine, christian love must, therefore, start from the interior, from the heart. However, we must immediately make it clear that we are dealing with something that goes deeper than simple "interiorization," or just shifting the emphasis from the exterior practice of charity to an interior practice. This is only the first step. Man's depths are no longer purely psychological; through the presence of the Holy Spirit, he also has theological depths, the depths of God! Herein lies the mystery of charity; herein is the newness created in us by the new life in the Spirit. If we haven't grasped this, we've understood nothing and remain within the old and natural horizon in which the quality of christian love is no different to other types of love. "Moral" charity is based on "theological" charity. Interiorization touches on the divine. A Christian—St. Peter said—is he who loves with "all his heart": but with a new heart! Once, man, under the law, invoked a new heart! *God, create in me a clean heart!* (cf. Ps 51:12); God himself had promised him a new heart (cf. Ezk 36:26). Now this new heart has been created and is present in every baptized person. All we have to do is to get it to work, to exercise it. This is what the Apostle's exhortation aims at.

When we love "from the heart," it is God, present in us with his Spirit, who loves in us; God's own love passes to others through us. Our acting is truly made divine. To "share the divine *nature*" (2 Pt 1:4) means, in fact, to share the divine *action* (the divine action of loving because God is love!). It is not we who deduce such a great thing through some complicated process of reasoning; it is clearly contained in the New Testament: *The love of God*—it is written—*has been poured into our hearts by the Holy Spirit* (Rom 5:5). When Jesus says: *Love one another as I have loved you* (Jn 15:12), this "as" couldn't mean "in the same way," or "to the same extent" (which would be impossible), but "with the same love with which I have loved you." In fact, immediately after he prays to the Father that the love he has received from him may be in his disciples (cf. Jn 17:26). It's the same as for consolation: *God*—writes St. Paul—*comforts us in all our affliction, so that we may be able to comfort those who are in any affliction, with the comfort with which we ourselves are comforted by God* (2 Cor 1:4). We comfort with the comfort with which we are comforted by God, we love with the love with which God loves us. Not with a different one. This explains the apparently disproportionate resonance that a simple gesture of love, often even unexpressed, has, and the newness and hope it gives rise to. It's because it's the sign and channel of another love, something like, in proper proportion, the Eucharist being the sign of another food. Christian love can, therefore, be distinguished from all other types of love by the fact that it is the love of Christ: "It is no longer I that love but Christ loves in me!" The *Agape* that comes from the eternal source of the Trinity, which in Jesus Christ was clothed in a human shape and heart, now longs to spread itself so as to irrigate all the earth; it wants to circulate in hearts like honey in the honeycombs. It is at this deep and hidden level that the real transformation of the world comes about. The source of egoism is blocked and the source of love reopened. Creation starts again! Divine love is truly the substance of the new world.

I too can be a radiating centre of God's love. There is nothing exalting or intoxicating in this thought. It is the most "sober" of thoughts, because "what have you got that wasn't given to you?" (cf. 1 Cor 4:7). It is the most sober of thoughts also because in order to put the new heart in motion, it is necessary to silence the old one; one must die to oneself.

3. Let Us Stop Passing Judgement

While meditating on the Apostle's exhortation on charity, at a certain point I was forcefully reminded of the words of the prophet Jeremiah: *Clear the ground that lies neglected, do not sow among thorns . . . apply circumcision to your hearts* (Jr 4:3-4). In the framework of the genuine love presented by the word of God, I had a clear-cut vision of my heart as being like neglected soil, full of thorns, which is waiting to be tilled. But at the same time I was filled with the desire and new need to undertake the work of making my heart a "welcoming" place for my brethren, like the heart of God, who "is merciful to all and nothing that he has made disgusts him" (cf. Ws 11:23 f.).

Once, in Africa, finding myself facing a landscape which must have been similar to the one facing the prophet Jeremiah, I understood what he was alluding to in the words I have just mentioned. During the months of drought the fields are neglected and are literally covered with thorns and brambles. When the rainy season is approaching and it is time to sow the seeds, the peasant goes to his field, gathers together all the brambles and shrubs and burns them, so as not to sow among the thorns. At sunset, many bonfires can be seen burning brightly here and there, in the immense and silent African landscape. We—the prophet says—must do the same with the soil of our hearts. We must "destroy the enmity within us." The Word of God suggests that we make three bonfires in particular.

The first bonfire to be made is that of bad judgements. *Why, then, does one of you make himself judge over his brother and why does another among you despise his brother? . . . Let us each stop passing judgement, therefore, on one another* (Rom 14:10-13). Those hostile judgements, full of aversion and condemnation, are the thorns the prophet Jeremiah was talking about: they must be pulled out from the roots and burnt so as to free our hearts of them. Jesus says: *Do not judge and you will not be judged . . . Why do you observe the splinter in your brother's eye and never notice the great log in your own?* (Mt 7:1-3). These words don't mean: do not judge men and men will not judge you (we know by experience that this is not always true), but, rather: do not judge your brother, so that God will not judge you; even better still: do not judge your brother because the Lord has not judged you. It is not a question of utilitarian morality but of kerygmatic morality. God compares our brother's sin (the sin that has been judged), whatever it is, to a splinter, against the sin of the person who judges (the very fact of judging others) which is a log. The log is the simple fact itself of judging, so serious is it in the eyes of God.

St. James and St. Paul each give their own reasons for this prohibition to judge. The first says: *Who are you to give a verdict on your neighbour?* (Jm 4:12). He means: Only God can judge because he knows the secrets of the heart, the why, the intention and the aim of each action. What do we know of what is in the heart of another man when he behaves in a certain way? What do we know of all the conditioning he is subject to through temperament and type of education? And what do we know of the implications of his actions? Wanting to set ourselves up as judges is dangerous; it's like throwing an arrow with shut eyes, not knowing where it is going to land; we expose ourselves to being unjust, relentless and obtuse. It is sufficient to notice how difficult it is for us to understand and judge ourselves and how many shadows confuse our thoughts, to understand that it is not possible for us to reach the depths of another person, his past, his present, the sorrow he has experienced: *After all, is there anyone who knows the qualities of anyone except his own spirit, within him?* (1 Cor 2:11). One day, an old monk, on hearing that one of his brethren had sinned, said: "What a terrible thing he has done!" Then, during the night an angel brought the soul of the brother who had sinned before him and said: "There you are, the person you have judged is dead. Do you want me to send him into the Kingdom of God or into eternal punishment?" The old monk was so shocked that he passed the rest of his days in groans and tears and toil, begging God to forgive him his sin (cf. Dorothea of Gaza, *Instructions*, VI, 71; SCh 92, p. 272).

St. Paul's reason is that he who judges behaves in the same way as the one being judged! *So no matter who you are, if you pass judgement you have no excuse. It is yourself that you condemn when you judge others, since you behave in the same way as those you are condemning* (Rom 2:1). We have probably realized the truth of this ourselves, at our own expense, each time we have judged someone and then had the chance of reflecting on our own behaviour. It is typical of human nature to judge and condemn in others what is particularly displeasing in ourselves but which we lack the courage to face; the miser condemns meanness, the sensuous sees sins of lust everywhere and there is no one more able than a proud man to notice sins of pride around him.

But the question of judging others is a delicate and complex one and cannot be left incomplete if it is not to seem unrealistic. How can we, in fact, live without ever judging anyone at all? Judgement is implicit in us, even in a glance. We cannot observe, listen, live, without forming an opinion, that is, without judging. Indeed, it is not so much from judging others that we must free our hearts as from the venom with which we judge! That is, from the resentment and condemnation in us. In Luke's writings, the command given by Jesus: *Do not judge and you will not be judged,* is immediately followed by: *Do not condemn and you will not be condemned* (Lk 6:37) as if to clarify the meaning of the command. In itself, judging is a neutral act, the judgement can end either in condemnation or absolution and justification. It's the negative judgements that are reproached and banished by the Word of God, those that condemn both the sin and the sinner at the same time. A mother and an outsider can judge a child for the same fault which, objectively speaking, the child possesses; but how different the two judgements are! The mother, in fact, suffers as if the fault were hers, she feels equally as responsible and is determined to help the child. She doesn't go about talking of her child's fault to the four winds. Well, then, our judgements on our brethren must be like those of the mother because "we are all joined to one another" (Rom 12:5). The others are "ours."

Sometimes, depending on one's office or the type of sanctity one is called to, God may exact—and at the same time grant the necessary grace—that a person completely stops judging others. But this is not usually the case; whoever is responsible for others, parents, superiors, confessors, judges, must judge. At times, passing judgement is the type of service one is called to give to society or the Church. The strength of christian love lies in this: it is capable of turning a negative judgement into something positive and of turning an act of non-love into one of love. In our Letter St. Paul judges—and with what clarity and severity—his Hebrew countrymen (Rom 2:17 f.). But he can also say: *This is the truth that I am speaking in Christ, without pretence, as my conscience testifies for me in the Holy Spirit; there is great sorrow and unremitting agony in my heart. I could pray that I myself might be accursed and cut off from Christ, if this could benefit the brothers who are my own flesh and blood* (Rom 9:1-3). And he can say this because he knows before God and his own conscience that he loves them. This is genuine love without any pretence.

Here, then, are some practical suggestions. Do not judge unless you can say what St. Paul says, or—if you are obliged to judge without having reached this level of charity—humiliate yourself, acknowledge it and do not be surprised if the correction does not give immediate and obvious results. God wants to correct us while we are correcting others;

that is, he wants to correct us also while we have to correct others. Sometimes, after trying at length and in vain to make a subject or brother understand something, we might realize that the problem lies in our not loving him wholeheartedly, so that we must start again in a different way. Jesus speaks clearly: we must first take the "log" out of our own eye and then we will be able to see clearly enough to take the "splinter" out of our brother's eye (cf. Mt 7:5). We must get rid of resentment and non-love and then the observation will be accepted and the brother will, perhaps, get rid of his "splinter." He will trust us. Who would allow another person to violently put his finger into his eye to remove a splinter as if he were getting ready to pull out weeds from soil?

Esteem is another qualifying point of interior charity and it is strictly connected to the preceding one: *Regard others as more important than yourself* (Rom 12:10). But here we are again touching that sore point where love is at odds with its enemy, egoism. To hold a brother in esteem means not to have too much self-esteem, not to be always sure of oneself. It is necessary—the Apostle says—"not to have too high consideration of oneself" (cf. Rom 12:3). He who has too high a consideration of himself is like a man who keeps a strong light in front of his eyes at night: he cannot see anything else but that light; he cannot see the light of his brothers, their good points and their value.

The second bonfire to be made is, therefore, that of thoughts and sentiments of disregard and scorn for our brothers. We must learn to "relativize" in our relations with others, that is we must neither give too much importance to our merits nor to the faults of our neighbours as we often tend to do. We must learn to keep our "ego" under constant observation as if it were on the prisoner's bench; as soon as it makes a move to sit on the judge's bench, we must lead it back gently but firmly. This is how true compunction of heart can be acquired which helps us to grow in both humility and charity at the same time.

The obstacle that can impede us in this work of acquiring genuine charity is dwelling on the importance to what others think of us ("he has no regard for me, he despises me! . . ."), because, in the light of the Gospel, this is entirely out of place. The new law of love doesn't consist in doing to others what they do to you (as was the case in the old law of retaliation), but in doing to others what God did to you: *The Lord has forgiven you; now you must do the same* (Col 3:13). It's true that others might serve as a criterion of measure, but even then it is not a question of what they *do* to you, but of what you *would like* them to do to you! (cf. Mt 7:12). You must, therefore, measure yourself against God and yourself, not against others. You must concern yourself only with how you treat others and with how you accept their treatment of you; the rest is simple distraction and is of no importance to the question. It concerns the others.

4. Avoid Evil Words

Between the interior sphere of sentiments, judgements and regard, and the exterior one of the works of charity, there's the in-between sphere of words which has a little of the one and the other. The mouth is the spy of the heart, for *words flow out of what fills the heart* (Mt 12:34). It is true that our love must not be just "words or mere talk" (1 Jn 3:18), but we must *also* love with words and talk. "The tongue—St. James says—can boast of great things," both in good and in evil; it can "set fire to a huge forest," it is "full of deadly poison" (Jm 3:1-12). How many deaths are caused by the tongue! In community and family life, sharp and ruthless words can close us up in ourselves and quench all confidence and fraternal atmosphere. The most sensitive are literally "mortified" by harsh words, that is, killed, and perhaps we, too, have a few of these deaths on our conscience . . . It is true that we mustn't just aim at hypocritically changing our language without a change of heart which is its source (St. James says that "a spring of salt water cannot produce fresh water"), but it is also true that one helps the other. That's why St. Paul gives this precious rule for speech: *Let no evil talk come out of your mouths, but only such as is good for edifying, as fits the occasion, that it may impart grace to those who hear it* (Eph 4:29). These words, on their own, could become a spiritual programme for Lent; in fact, they involve quite a healthy form of fasting: fasting from evil words! If one were to decide to make a rule of the Apostle's words, he would very soon experience a circumcision of the lips and then of the heart, which Jeremiah spoke about earlier on. This is the third bonfire to be made: that of all our evil words.

It is easy to learn to recognize evil words and good ones; all that's necessary is to follow, or foresee the path they are taking and where they are leading to: whether they lead to our own glory or to the glory of God and of our brother, whether they serve to justify, commiserate and assert my reasons, or those of my neighbour. Evil words will, at first, be spoken and must be taken back, pardon sought and reparation made; then, little by little, the words will be held back, as if on the tip of the tongue, until they begin to disappear and make room for good words. What a gift this is for our brothers, and what a contribution to fraternal charity! A good word from the heart is like balm for our brother, it is a gift from God himself because, as we have seen, when we love from the heart, it is God that loves in us. God made the word his favourite means of consoling, of illuminating, of giving life to the world and of revealing his love in the Bible. According to the ancient Fathers of the Church, Jesus himself is the "good Word" coming from the Father's heart which is spoken of in Psalm 45: *My heart overflows with a good word* (Ps 45:2 Vulg.).

5. Look on Your Brother in a New Light

Love is truly the universal solution. It is difficult to establish the best thing to do in each single case: whether to keep silent or speak out, to let things take their course or correct someone . . . But if you have love, whatever you do will be right, *because love can cause no harm to your neighbour* (Rom 13:10). In this sense, St. Augustine used to say: love and then do what you will. "This short rule is given to you once and for all: love and do what you will. If you keep silent, do so out of love; if you speak, do so out of love; if you correct someone, do so out of love; if you forgive, do so out of love. Let the root of love be in you, because only good can come from this root" (*In Ep. Joh.* 7,8; PL 35, 2023).

Love is the only thing we owe to anyone: *The only thing you should owe to anyone is love for one another* (Rom 13:8). Each person that approaches you is a creditor coming to collect what you owe him. Perhaps he'll ask you for something you can't give him or must definitely refuse him; but even if you must send him away with a refusal, be careful not to send him away without paying him his debt of love. God, in Christ, gave you love to share with your brothers; this love does not belong to you; your brother has every right to demand his share. You are the debtor of a never ending debt, because whatever you may do, you will never get near to sharing the same measure of love you have received. This is the "ration of food" which the master, on leaving, entrusted to his servant to be given to his household at the proper time (cf. Mt 24:45 f.).

This interior charity which the Apostle has spoken of so far is a type of charity that we can all practice at all times. Exterior works of charity must necessarily be interrupted but charity needn't be. This is not a type of charity that some must practice and others receive; it is not the charity that distinguishes the rich from the poor or the healthy from the sick. We can all practice it, the poor as well as the rich. It often reverses the situation established by fate and human injustice and makes the poor the truly rich and truly donators.

Apart from being universal, this type of charity is also very practical. In fact, it's not a question of undertaking an abstract battle against one's thoughts but starting to see the people and situations around us in a new light. We don't have to go in search of occasions to carry this out as they are always there. They are the people we have to deal with today itself. All you have to do is make up your mind to look on a person with that genuine love and you will be amazed to see how your attitude towards him has completely changed. It's as if you had a new eye, totally different to the natural one. All one's relationships change. There is no situation in which we cannot do something to take a step forward in this work. Let us take an example. You may be in bed, sick or sleepless and you cannot pray all the time. The word of God suggests a task of extreme importance to you: to alternate prayer and fraternal charity. You could—through faith—welcome into your room the persons whom God puts into your mind at that moment. These will probably be the people towards whom you most need to change your attitude. While they are there in front of you, or rather, within your very heart, you could begin to see each one with the eyes and heart of God just as you would like God to look on you. You will find that, as if by miracle, all the resentment, the reasons for prejudice and hostility, disappear; you will see the person as a poor suffering creature, fighting his weaknesses and limits just like yourself and everyone else, as "one for whom Christ died" (Rom 14:15). You'll be amazed that you hadn't seen this sooner and you'll take leave of him in peace as you would take leave of a brother. You can continue in this line for as long as the grace you have been given assists you. No one knows what is going on; if anyone should enter your room they'll notice no change except, perhaps, your countenance might be a little more radiant; but in the meantime the kingdom of God has been within you. Queen Charity paid you a visit! A little of the new heaven and earth took over from the old earth and the first to benefit from this will be the brothers with whom you have become reconciled. Because *love is what builds* (1 Cor 8:2). That world, reconciled, in peace—in which each man's dignity and place is recognized and which we all desire and hope for—began to be accomplished that day around your bed. In fact, that world will never be accomplished outside of man, if it is not first accomplished in some way within him, in his heart.

Let us conclude by making ours the prayer which the liturgy of the Church raises to God during the special Mass "to ask for the virtue of charity": "Father, inflame our hearts with the Spirit of your love, so that we may think and work according to your will and love you in our brothers with sincerity of heart. Through Christ our Lord."

XI. Don't Think Too Highly of Yourselves

Humility as truth

The pearl-diver of the south seas diving in search of precious pearls experiences something unique, which, in a smaller sense, is experienced by any swimmer who has tried to go deep underwater. With all its force, the water tends to push him back up. This is Archimedes' principle of fluid pressure, that is, the pressure exerted from below towards the surface on a body immersed in fluid. The bigger and more voluminous the body, the greater the mass of water being moved and the greater the force exerted towards the surface. Everything, therefore, tends to keep the pearl-diver at surface level or to push him back up. But he is drawn down by hope and often by need because he earns his living by this work. So, powerfully and skillfully, he heads straight down towards the bottom of the sea. The effort is enormous but it gives way to un-restrained joy as soon as he catches sight of a half-open shell at the bot-tom of the sea through which he can glimpse a shining pearl.

The search for humility is an adventure somewhat similar to that of the pearl-diver. In fact, we must go down; we must dive below the calm water of our self-illusions and keep on going down until we reach the solid ground where the truth concerning us lies. And this must be done while a stronger force than the sea—that of our innate pride—tends to push us "up," to make us "emerge," to lift us above ourselves and others. But the pearl that awaits us at the end, hidden in the shell of our hearts, is far too precious for us to desist from the undertaking and give in to ourselves. In fact, we have to overcome the illusory sphere of what seems or what we believe of ourselves so as to approach our true being, because—as St. Francis of Assisi used to say—"man is worth what he is worth before God and nothing more."

Man—it has been pointed out—possesses two very different kinds of life: his real life and the imaginary one which he lives in his own mind or in the opinion of others. We labour unceasingly to embellish and preserve our imaginary existence and we neglect the real one. If we have a virtue or merit, we take great pains to make it known in one way or another and thus enrich our imaginary being through this virtue or merit. We are even ready to sacrifice something of ourselves for it, to the point, sometimes, of being vile in order to seem brave and even to give our life, so long as others talk of this (cf. B. Pascal, *Pensées* 147 Br.). To work at becoming humble is, therefore, an undertaking for our "true self" and, as such, it affects us as men even before affecting us as believers. It's human to be humble! Man (*homo*) and humility (*humilitas*) both come from the same Latin word (*humus*) which means earth, ground. Nietzche bitterly fought against christian morality because it preaches humility; he fought against it for one of the most beautiful gifts it gave the world. Let us, therefore, place our trust in the Word of God; through the power of the Holy Spirit it will make fishermen of us who cannot and no longer want to do other in life than search for that precious pearl.

1. Humility as Soberness

St. Paul's exhortation to charity dealt with in the preceding chapter is enclosed within two short exhortations on humility which clearly refer one to the other, thus forming a sort of framework to the discourse on charity. Omitting what's in between, a straight reading of the two exhortations states: *I bid every one among you not to think of himself more highly than he ought to think, but to think with sober judgement . . . Do not be haughty but associate with the lowly; never be conceited* (Rom 12:3,16).

These are not just ordinary recommendations to moderation and modesty; in these few words the apostolic exhortation opens a very wide horizon of humility to us. Alongside charity, St. Paul sees humility as the second fundamental value, the second course to be worked at to renew our life in the Spirit. Also in this case the secret lies in a spiritual reading of the Word of God. This spiritual reading doesn't only consist in reading what came about *first* in the light of what came *after,* that is, prophecy in the light of fulfilment, the Old Testament in the light of the New Testament and vice versa, but it consists in reading a *part* in the light of the *whole,* in reading each single word or phrase while keeping in mind other words from Scripture on the same topic, knowing that the same Spirit that inspired that word, inspired all the rest too. The first aspect of spiritual reading (which we can call diachronic) stresses more the *continuity* of Scripture while the second aspect (which we can call synchronic) stresses more the globality or *unity* of Scripture. When a person with an ear for music and a knowledge of harmony hears a note, he can immediately feel its "overtones," that is the notes that "accord" with it. The same thing happens when a person has become familiar with the Bible. Each word calls to mind other words which complete it and make it form a unity. Thus the Word of God takes shape and means much more than it says. It's as if it started off a familiar tune that someone knows and is able, therefore, to continue by himself. The word is "abbreviated," condensed. It's the ever new miracle of the Word of God. Thus, we find that there's no surer and more effective method than to read the Bible with the Bible.

The overtones—the harmonics!—of the passage we've just listened to belong in part to the Old Testament and in part to the New Testament. The most significant of that from the Old Testament is from Ecclesiasticus: *My child, be gentle in carrying out your business . . .The greater you are, the more humble you should behave, and then you will find favour with the Lord . . . Do not try to understand things that are too difficult for you or try to discover what is beyond your powers* (Sir 3:17-21).

Where the New Testament is concerned, the passage certainly recalls the evangelical parable in which Jesus exhorts his disciples not to seek the first place, but the last, and which ends with the well known words: *Everyone who exalts himself will be humbled and he who humbles himself will be exalted* (Lk 14:7-11). Life in the christian community—of which the Apostle is tracing the outline—is really the "feast" the parable talks about. In it, believers are invited to put the word of Jesus into practice: not to aspire to the highest places but to choose the humblest places for themselves, if they can.

St. Paul, therefore, applies to the life of the christian community the traditional biblical teaching on humility which is continuously expressed in the space metaphor of "raising" oneself and "lowering" oneself, tending upwards and tending downwards. One can "aspire to things that are too high" either through the intelligence in trying to get too much to the root of things without keeping to the apostolic Kerygma, or with the will, by aspiring to positions and jobs of prestige. The Apostle has both these possibilities in mind and, at any rate, his words strike at both one and the other at the same time: the *presumption* of the mind and the *ambition* of the will. In doing so though—that is in transmitting biblical traditional teaching on humility—St. Paul gives a partly new and original motivation to this virtue which is a step ahead of biblical doctrine on humility. In the Old Testament, the motive or reason that justifies humility, is associated with God who "scorns the proud and shows favour to the humble" (cf. Pr 3:34; Jb 22:29). However, the reason why God "raises the humble and abases the proud" had not yet been explicitly said. The fact that God "abases the proud"—noticed also by other religions and cultures—can be explained in different ways: for example, by the jealousy or "envy of God," as certain Greek authors taught, or simply the divine will to punish human arrogance (*hybris*). The decisive concept which St. Paul introduces into the discourse on humility is the concept of *truth*. To what we may call the theological motive associated with God he adds another motive associated with man, which we may call anthropological. God loves a humble person because a humble person possesses the truth; he is a true man. He punishes pride, because pride, before being arrogance, is untruth. The Greek philosophers lacked this certainty and while they knew all other virtues and exalted them, they knew nothing of humility. The word humility (*tapeinosis*) always had the mainly negative meaning for them of lowness, meanness, wretchedness, pusillanimity. They lacked the two important points through which it is possible to associate humility and truth in man: the idea of creation and the biblical idea of sin. The idea of creation, in fact, establishes the certainty that all that is good and beautiful in man comes from God, nothing excluded ("He made us, we didn't make ourselves," said psalm 100 in the *Vulgate*). The biblical idea of sin establishes the certainty that all that is really morally wrong and evil in man comes from his freedom, from himself. Biblical man is urged to humility by both the good and the evil he discovers in himself.

I mentioned a new aspect introduced by St. Paul in his discourse on humility. If, however, we do not find the link between humility and truth *defined* in the Old Testament, we find that it is *lived*. It is a typical sentiment of humility-truth that urges the just men of the Bible to repeat almost in every page: "For you are upright in all that you have done for us for we have sinned" (Dn 3:28 f.; Ba 1:15 f.). It is the same sentiment that inspires psalm 51 from beginning to end: *For I know my transgressions . . . against thee, thee only have I sinned . . . Behold thou desirest truth in the inward being; therefore teach me wisdom in my secret heart . . .*

But let us now examine the Apostle's thought. The word he uses in the text we are dealing with to indicate humility-truth is soberness or wisdom (*sophrosyne*). He exhorts Christians not to form a wrong and exaggerated idea of themselves (*hyperphroneim*) but, rather, to judge themselves rightly, soberly (*sophronein*), we could almost say objectively. In verse 16, where the exhortation is taken up again, the equivalence to "each one thinking of himself with sober judgement" is found in the expression "associate with the humble" or "choose what is humble" (*tapeinois*). He is saying that a man is wise when he is humble and humble when he is wise. In abasing himself, man draws close to truth. This reason for humility, which I have called anthropological, is, however, in itself also a theological reason, because it concerns God and not only man. "God is light," St. John says (1 Jn 1:5), he is the truth, and can only meet man in truth. He gives his grace to the humble because only a humble person is capable of recognizing grace: he doesn't say: "My arm or my wisdom has done this!" (Cf. Dt 8:17; Is 10:13). St. Theresa of Avila wrote: "One day I was wondering why God so loves the humble when it suddenly and unexpectedly struck me that this must be because he is the supreme Truth and humility is truth" (*Interior*

Castle VI, 10). The Saint had reached the same conclusion as St. Paul; God had taught her the truth of his word by interior enlightenment.

2. In the Prison of our Nothingness

We have, thus, started our descent to the bottom, towards the "pearl" we spoke about at the beginning. The Apostle is neither vague nor superficial now concerning the truth about ourselves. Some of his concise phrases in other letters which belong to this same order of ideas, leave us with no escape and make us go really deep down in our search for truth. One of these phrases says: *What have you that you did not receive? If then you received it, why do you boast as if it were not a gift?* (1 Cor 4:7). There is only one thing I did not receive, which is all mine and only mine, and that is sin. I know and feel that this comes from me, that it has its origin in me, or, at any rate, in man and in the world and doesn't come from God. All the rest—including my acknowledgement that sin comes from me—is from God. Another phrase says: *If anyone thinks he is something, when he is nothing he deceives himself!* (Gal 6:3). The "right judgement" of ourselves lies, therefore, in acknowledging our nothingness! This is the solid soil humility moves towards! The precious pearl is precisely the sincere and serene conviction that on our own we *are* nothing, we can *think* nothing, we can *do* nothing. *Cut off from me you can do nothing*, says Jesus (Jn 15:5) and the Apostle adds: *Not that we are sufficient of ourselves to "think" anything* . . . (2 Cor 3:5). We can, as the occasion needs, use either one or the other of these words to put a sudden end to a temptation, a thought of self-complacency, like a real "sword of the Spirit": "What have you that you did not receive?" We experience the efficaciousness of God's Word above all when we apply it to ourselves more than when we apply it to others.

There was a time in the history of spirituality (the XVII century) during which, in certain circles, there was a lot of talk about this sentiment of one's own nothingness, to the point of giving rise to the suspicion that it contained a good dose of self-satisfaction, making a greater soberness desirable where humility itself was concerned. This happens when the descent towards one's nothingness is seen as an ascetic or psychological process of introspection or self-conviction, not when it is the pure strength of the Word of God guiding us towards an acknowledgement of the real situation. In other words, not when it is an objective process of docility and obedience to the truth in allowing ourselves to be "taught by God." In this case, it is the Holy Spirit who leads us to the discovery of the "whole truth" about ourselves and "convinces" us of our nothingness.

But how can the Apostle say that we are in fact "nothing" if, in the order of creation, the Bible exalts man saying that God made him "a little less than God," that he "crowned him with glory and honour" and "put all things under his feet" (cf. Ps 8), and if, in the order of redemption, God himself affirms that we are "enriched in him with all gifts," that we are "not lacking in any spiritual gift," that we are actually children of God and heirs of Christ (cf. 1 Cor 1:5, 7; Rom 8:17)? These are the very things that exact humility! Man has nothing of *his own*, nothing he can boast about. It is man's boasting that humility excludes, not his acknowledgement nor his gratitude.

This is the way for us to discover the true nature of our nothingness, which is not a pure and simple nothingness, an "innocent trifle." We can glimpse the end the Word of God is leading us to which is to acknowledge what we really are: a *proud nothingness*! I am that someone who "believes he is something," whereas I am nothing; I have nothing I haven't received, but I am always ready to boast—or tempted to boast—about something, as if I hadn't received it! This is the misery of everyone and not just the condition of a few. It is the exact definition of the old self: a nothing that believes it is something, a proud nothing. The Apostle himself confesses what he discovered when he, too, descended to the bottom of his heart: "I find within me—he says—another law . . . I see that sin dwells within me . . . wretched man that I am! Who will deliver me?" (cf. Rom 7:14-25). For St. Paul that "other law," that "indwelling sin" is, as we know, above all self-glorification, pride, boasting of oneself.

At the bottom of our descent, it is not, therefore, humility that we find but pride. Yet it is exactly in this discovery that humility lies—that we are radically proud and not through God's fault but our own, because we became so through making ill use of our freedom—as this is the truth. To have discovered this finishing line, or even just glimpsed it from a distance through God's Word, is a great grace. It gives a new kind of peace. It's like discovering, in war time, that there's a safe air-raid shelter right under your house which you can reach from inside and which is completely beyond the reach of bombs. A great spiritual teacher, Blessed Angela of Foligno, exclaimed on her deathbed: "Oh unknown nothingness, oh unknown nothingness! There is no better vision in this world for the soul than to contemplate its own nothingness and live in it as if in a prison cell" (B. Angela da Foligno, *Il libro,* Quaracchi 1985, p. 737). The same saint used to exhort her spiritual sons to do their best to retreat back into that cell as soon as they had left it for any reason. We should be like certain timid little animals who never move too far from the entrance to their burrows so that they can quickly get back into it at the first sign of danger.

This advice hides a great secret, a mysterious truth that can be experienced if we try. We realize then that this cell truly exits and that we can really enter into it whenever we want to. It consists in the serene and tranquil sentiment that we are nothing, a proud nothing. In this prison cell we no longer see our neighbours' faults, or we see them in a different light. We realize that, through grace and practice, it is possible to accomplish what the Apostle says and which, at first sight, might seem extreme: "Count others better than yourselves" (cf. Ph 2:3). At least we can understand how this was possible for the saints. Closing oneself in this prison is, therefore, anything but closing oneself in oneself; on the contrary, it is an opening out to others, to being, to the objectivity of things. It is the opposite of what the enemies of christian humility have always thought. It is a closing *to* egoism, not *in* egoism. It is a victory over narcissism, one of the evils that even modern psychology judges disastrous to the human being.

And, moreover, the enemy cannot penetrate that cell. One day, Anthony the Great had a vision; in a flash he clearly saw the countless traps of the enemy and groaning, he exclaimed: "What could ever avoid all these traps?" and a voice answered him: "humility!" (*Apoph.Ant.* 7; PG 65,77).

But the greatest secret of that cell is that God visits it. There is no other place in the world where God prefers to meet his creature. That dark cell of a humble and contrite heart is, in fact, full of light for him, because truth shines there. It is God's favourite dwelling place where he loves to "come and linger" as he did in the garden of paradise before sin existed. The prophet Isaiah gives us this sublime soliloquy: God looks at the heavens and says: "It is my throne!"; he looks at the earth and says: "It is my footstool!" And he goes on to say: *What is the place of my rest? All these things my hand has made, and so all these things are mine. But this is the man to whom I will look, he that is humble and contrite in spirit!* (Is 66:1 f.; cf. Is 57:15). Everything in the universe belongs to God. There is nothing new for him anywhere, nothing surprises him; his omnipotence has done and can do all things. But, mysteriously, there is one thing his omnipotence alone cannot or will not do which is to make a man's heart humble itself and acknowledge his sin. To obtain this, God needs our free cooperation. A humble heart is always something new to God, a surprise that makes him start with joy. Truly "God does not despise a humble and contrite heart!" (cf. Ps 51:17). The cell of self-knowledge also becomes the cell of the knowledge of God which the Canticle calls "the banqueting house" (Song 2:4). *I thank thee, Father,* Jesus said . . . *that thou hast hidden these things from the wise and understanding and revealed them to the babes* (Mt 11:25). God has revealed Jesus, the secret of secrets, to the babes, who are the humble.

3. The Humility of Mary

The Gospel gives us Mary as an insuperable model of this kind of humility we are looking at. God, Mary sang in the *Magnificat, regarded the low estate (humility) of his handmaiden* (Lk 1:48). But what did the Virgin mean by "humility"? She did not mean the *virtue* of humility but her humble *state*, or at the most, the fact that she came from the humble and poor *class* mentioned in the rest of the Canticle. This is confirmed by the direct reference to the canticle of Anna, Samuel's mother, where the same word used by Mary (*tapeinosis*) clearly refers to Anna's sterility and not to her sentiment of humility. But the fact is clear in itself. How can we think that Mary exalts her own humility, without destroying Mary's humility? How can we think that Mary attributes God's choice of her to her humility without thereby destroying the gratuity of such a choice and making Mary's whole life incomprehensible from her conception on? And yet, much is still rashly said about Mary who didn't boast of any other virtue other than her humility, as if, in so doing, great honour were being paid to this virtue instead of doing it great harm. The virtue of humility has a special code of its own. He who doesn't believe he has humility, has it, while he who believes he has, is without it. Only Jesus can call himself "humble of heart" and truly be so. This, as we shall see, is an exclusive characteristic of the humility of the man-God and it cannot exist in anyone else.

Did Mary, therefore, not possess the *virtue* of humility? Of course she possessed it and at the highest degree, but only God knew this. She was unaware of it. In fact, the point of merit that cannot be equalled of true humility is that it is known only to God and not to the person possessing it. In all the languages the Bible was written in before it came down to us, Hebrew, Greek, Latin and English, the word "humility" had two fundamental meanings: an objective one indicating *lowness*, smallness or actual misery, and a subjective meaning indicating the *sentiment* of one's lowness. Mary pronounced the word humility in the objective sense and God listened to it in the subjective sense! Herein lies the ineffable mystery of humility. Where Mary saw only lowness, God saw only humility. This was certainly a "merit" on Mary's part but it consisted precisely in her acknowledging that she had no merit.

The same is true of the lives of the Saints. One day Brother Masseo, one of St. Francis of Assisi's companions, unexpectedly asked the Saint why it was that all the world was running after him and wanted to see him. Did St. Francis answer that perhaps it was because God hadn't found anyone more "humble" than himself? No; he said it was happening because God had found no one "less worthy" than himself. "Do you want to know—he asked with great fervour of spirit—why all the world runs after me? It's because the eyes of the most high God haven't found anyone more vile among sinners, anyone less worthy or more sinful than I am" (*Little Flowers*, c. X). St. Bernard stated all this in a few words: "A really humble person always wants to be considered vile and not be called humble" ("Verus humilis semper vult vilis reputari, non humilis praedicari") (*Ser. XVI in Cant.* 10; PL 183, p. 853).

In the new situation created by her divine maternity, Mary's soul, free from all real and sinful concupiscence, moved quickly and naturally to its centre of truth, her nothingness, and nothing or no one could change this. It makes the humility of the Mother of God appear to be a unique miracle of grace. Even Luther felt forced to praise her, saying: "Even if Mary welcomed God's great work in her, she nevertheless preserved such a low sentiment of herself as to never raise herself above the least of men . . . In this we extol the wonderfully pure spirit of Mary who, while she was being so greatly honoured, never permitted herself to be tempted but, as if unseeing, remained on the right path" (*Comm. on the Magnificat*; Weimar edit., 7, p. 555f.). Mary's soberness is beyond all comparison even among the saints. She resisted against the tremendous tension of the thought: "You are the mother of the Messiah, the mother of God! You are what every woman of your people would have wanted to be!" On seeing her, Elizabeth exclaimed: *Why is this granted me, that the mother of my Lord should come to me?* and Mary answered: *He has regarded the humility of his handmaiden!* She withdrew into her nothingness and praised God alone saying: *My soul magnifies the Lord.* The Lord, not the handmaid. Mary is truly the masterpiece of divine grace.

Mary, I have just said, withdrew into her nothingness before God and remained there in spite of all the tempests she faced. This is seen from the way she stayed by her Son, always aside, silent and unpretentious. She didn't even claim the right to be in the foreground listening to her Son as he preached to the crowds. She remained "outside," to the extent that she had to ask the help of others when she wanted to speak to him (cf. Mt 12:46 f.). Although she was the Mother of God, Mary didn't consider the fact of being so close to God as a treasure to be jealous of or a right to be affirmed. She stripped herself and took on the name and attitude of a servant, thus becoming the same as every other woman . . . Mary is the perfect incarnation of St. Paul's teaching on humility; she didn't aspire to higher things, but bowed to what was humble.

4. Humility and Humiliation

Mary was humble, yet she wasn't spared humiliation. What should we say about ourselves then? We, who are but a proud nothing always inclined to emerge and leave truth behind? We mustn't deceive ourselves into thinking that we are humble just because God's word has led us to an understanding of our nothingness. At the most we now have a certain knowledge of humility but not humility itself. We can judge the degree of humility we have reached when the initiative is taken by others, that is when others and not ourselves realize our faults and failings; when we are not only able to be truthful with ourselves but willingly allow others to tell us the truth about ourselves. Our state of humility is seen, in other words, in how we accept rebukes, correction, criticism and humiliation. To expect to root out our pride ourselves without anyone else intervening would be like wanting to remove a tumour by ourselves. There are people (and I certainly count myself one of them) who are capable of sincerely saying all the bad in the world about themselves; people who, in confession or prayer, accuse themselves with admirable frankness and courage, but the trouble starts as soon as anyone else begins to take their confession seriously or dares to utter even a small part of what they themselves have said. There is obviously still a long way to go to reach true humility and humble truth.

Sometimes, the unpleasant truth about ourselves comes to light independent of our will or that of others and we should know how to behave in these situations so that they may become a source of humility for us. Maybe we've "given vent to our feelings" in a conversation or discussion; we've let others see our hidden sentiments; we've expressed judgements and feelings of ill-will, and then realized that we were not doing ourselves any honour but just showing our weak side. It's as if we had given free rein to the evil in our hearts, especially where faults against charity and patience are concerned. How we wish we'd never spoken! This, however, is sorrow not for *having been* evil but for *having shown* ourselves to be so. It's not the truth we love, but our good reputation. We are more concerned about our "imaginary being" that the real one. In a certain sense we should be glad about it once it has happened. To compromise and reveal ourselves, above all in our own eyes, for what we really are inside, is more a remedy to sin than a sin in itself unless our speech has given rise to scandal or directly offended someone. In fact, a pseudo-holiness which God detests, is thus shattered. The most dangerous sin is often that which takes place within us without leaving any outer trace so that punishment cannot be inflicted, we cannot be made to feel the consequences of being humiliated. Whenever I show myself to be imperfect or evil, I can always glorify God saying: Thank you, Lord, because I have shown my true nature and besides you and me, others now also know the truth. "It is good for me that I was humbled" (cf. Ps 119:71). I am happy that your glory is flying high on the ruins of my pride.

At other times, praise, the opposite to interior and exterior humility, helps us to measure how far we are from true humility. St. Augustine described his struggles on this point which is often our struggle too. "Can I hide—he said—that I am gratified by praise? It's true that one has to edify one's neighbour and show gratitude. If it is the good of my neighbour that touches my heart when I hear my own praises, why am I less aggrieved when blame is unjustly laid at another's door than when it is laid at mine? Why do insults sting me more when they are offered to me than when I hear them offered to others with equal injustice?" And again he wrote: "When men hold certain offices in human society it is necessary that they should be loved and feared by other men. This is why the old enemy of our true happiness gives me no peace. He sets his traps about me baiting me with tributes of applause in the hope that our greed for praise will catch us off our guard and divorce my joy from the truth and place it in man's duplicity and we are pleased to be loved and feared by others not for your sake but in your place" (cf. *Conf.* X, 36-37; *Ser* 339, 1; PL 38, 1480).

When I seek glory from a person for something I've done or said, that person is almost certainly seeking glory from me for what he has done or said in return, so that we are both seeking our own glory and neither one of us obtains it. And if by chance it is obtained, it is nothing but "vainglory," that is, empty glory destined to become nothing at death. But just the same the effect is terrible. Jesus actually attributed the impossibility to believe to the search for one's own glory. To the Pharisees he said: *How can you believe who receive glory from one another and do not seek the glory that comes from the only God?* (Jn 5:44). When we find ourselves trapped by thoughts and aspirations to human glory, let us throw the words of Jesus into this confusion of thoughts as a burning torch: *I do not seek my own glory!* (Jn 8:50). These have an almost sacramental power to fulfil what they mean and thus to dissipate such thoughts.

But it is not enough not to seek one's own glory and praise; it is necessary to be able to accept the lack of this glory and praise and to live without glory or prestige, to accept, all told, the radical solution of the problem which deprives us even of the opportunity of being self-satisfied. This happened to Jesus. He not only didn't seek his own glory but accepted that his glory be destroyed by man and that he should be "despised and rejected by man" (Is 53:3). He "despised the shame" (cf. Heb 12:2). So as to be able to say "stop!" to the dangerous search for self-glory, it is necessary to become familiar with the thought of living without consideration and the many "well done"s we could gather along the way.

As we can see, humility is a life-long struggle and involves every aspect of life. Pride can be nourished by both good and evil and survive, therefore, in any situation. Actually, differing from other vices, it is good and not evil that is the preferred breeding place of this terrible "virus." "Vanity—wrote B. Pascal—is so anchored in man's heart that a soldier, a soldier's servant, a cook, a porter brags and wishes to have admirers. Even philosophers wish for them. And those who write against vainglory want it to have the glory of having written well, and those who read it desire the glory of having read it; and I who write this have perhaps this desire; and maybe those who will read it, will do the same" (*Pensées* n. 150 Br.). Vainglory is capable of transforming our very reaching for humility into an act of pride. But through grace, we can emerge victorious from the terrible battle. If, in fact, the old self can transform our very acts of humility into acts of pride, we, through grace, can transform our acts of pride into acts of humility by acknowledging them—by humbly acknowledging that we are a proud nothing. So God is glorified even by our pride.

In this battle God usually comes to the aid of those who love him with an efficacious and unique remedy: *To keep me from being too elated by the abundance of revelations*—St. Paul wrote—*a thorn was given me in the flesh, a messenger of Satan, to harass me, to keep me from being too elated* (2 Cor 12:7). To "keep man from becoming elated," that is to keep him from being driven back up to the surface once he has found the pearl, God sort of anchors him to the earth; he fixes "burdens on his sides" (cf. Ps 66:11). We don't exactly know what this "thorn in the flesh," this "messenger of Satan" was for Paul, but we know well what it is for us! Anyone who wants to follow the Lord and serve the Church has one. These are humiliating experiences which constantly recall us, often day and night, to the harsh reality of what we are. It may be a defect, an illness, a weakness, an impotence, which the Lord doesn't take from us in spite of all our supplications. It may be a persistent and humiliating temptation, perhaps even that of pride! Or a person we are obliged to live with and who is a real thorn in the side in spite of the good will of both parties, and who is capable of exposing our frailty and of demolishing our presumption. Sometimes it may even be a more difficult situation where the servant of God has to witness the failure of all his efforts and face things too great for him, which makes him see clearly his own nothingness of sinful creature. It is above all in such cases that he learns what it means to "humble oneself under the mighty hand of God" (cf. 1 Pt 5:6).

In this chapter we have aimed at locking ourselves into the prison of our own nothingness. However, before concluding this meditation we must note that contemporary philosophy has also tried to lock man into the prison of his own nothingness. But what a different and terrible prison this second one is, a prison from which God is excluded! It must be mentioned to realize what an abyss faith saves us from.

The most celebrated philosopher of our century asked himself what was the real and impassable concrete entity to which conscience recalls man and upon which he must build his existence if he wants to be authentic. And the answer was: his nullity! All human possibilities are, in fact, impossibilities. Every effort to project oneself and raise oneself starts in nullity and ends in nullity. "Existential nullity has by no means the character of privation, where something is lacking in comparison with an ideal which has been set up but does not get attained; rather the Being of this entity is already null as projection; and it is null in advance of any of the things which it can project and which it mostly attains." (M. Heidegger, *Being and Time*, § 58). Thus, an authentic existence enfolds the basic nullity of existence knowing it "exists to die." The only possibility left to man is to resign himself to this nullity making, as the saying goes, a virtue of necessity.

Secular thought which at one time fought against christian preaching on humility now proposes a form of humility and soberness no less radical than the christian one, even if unlike this, it is a dead end in itself—not "virtue" in fact but "necessity." Also according to the Gospels we have seen that we on our own have no possibility—either to think or to want or to act—but we know and practically experience that in Christ, God offers us every possibility since "all is possible to him who believes" (Mk 9:23). The good thing that emerges from this brief comparison with contemporary existential thought is the unsuspected confirmation that humility is truth and that no one is "authentic" if he is not humble and this urges us to love and nourish this evangelical virtue even more.

I spoke at the beginning of the "harmonics" in the Pauline text on humility. One of these is certainly Psalm 131, with which we shall now terminate this teaching in prayer:

> O Lord, my heart is not lifted up,
> my eyes are not raised too high;
> I do not occupy myself with things
> too great and too marvellous for me.
> But I have calmed and quieted my soul,
> like a child quieted at its mother's breast;
> like a child that is quieted is my soul . . .

The man who has discovered the calm and serene sentiment of his own nothingness is like a happy child resting on its mother's breast.

XII. Choose What Is Humble
Humility as service

We have seen that in his exhortation on humility, St. Paul stresses such a special link between humility and charity that it could be said that if the "text" presents humility as truth, the "context" presents it as charity and service. Christian humility would seem incomplete if we didn't take the second aspect into account which makes it not only an individual virtue for ourselves but also a community virtue open to others. The christian community and the Church are the setting for all the exhortations in the Letter to the Romans: *For as in one body*—says the Apostle—*we have many members, and all the members do not have the same function, so we, though many, are one body in Christ, and individually members one of another, having gifts that differ according to the grace given to us* (Rom 12:4-6). Together charity and humility are the means of preserving unity in this diversity of gifts and charisms, so that they may serve to build, and not to destroy, the one body: *Outdo one another*—the Apostle therefore recommends—*in showing honour. Live in harmony with one another, do not be haughty, but associate with the lowly* (Rom 12:10, 16). A different and perhaps better translation of the last sentence is: *Choose what is humble!*

In this case too, as in the preceding one, we must look for the "harmonics" to be able to bring the Apostle's real and complete thought to light. The text I have in mind is from Paul's Letter to the Philippians and in many ways it could be defined as a parallel text to that of Romans: *Complete my joy by being of the same mind, having the same love, being in full accord and of one mind. Do nothing from selfishness or conceit, but in humility count others better than yourselves. Let each one of you look not only to his own interests but also to the interests of others. Have this mind among yourselves, which you have in Christ Jesus . . .* (Phil 2:2-5). Besides numerous and almost literal similarities this text, nevertheless, presents new aspects which are of great interest to us as they enrich our understanding of biblical humility.

1. Humility as the Imitation of Christ

The first new element lies in the *term* itself by which humility is named. While in the Letter to the Romans the technical term, so to say, of humility is still missing, in this passage it is given great importance. We are no longer talking simply of soberness (*sofrosyne*) (cf. Rom 12:3), but also of humility (*tapeinofrosyne*) (cf. Ph 2:3). By using this compound term, which means to be humble (*tapeinos*) minded (*fronein*) and which he seems to have coined himself, the Apostle gets rid of all the ambiguity present up to then, and which still exists today, in the term humility (*tapeinosis*). This term, in fact, can have both an objective meaning where it refers to social position (like in the phrase "of humble origin"), and a subjective meaning, where it refers to being *humble-minded*. With the new term St. Paul clearly places the accent on interior humility, or humility of the heart, that is, on what we would call the virtue of humility.

The other new aspect concerns the *reason* or grounds for humility; in other words the "why" of humility. In the Letter to the Romans the answer was: we must be humble because humility is truth. This is still a fully valid reason but a totally new reason has been added to it: the imitation of Christ: "Have this mind among yourselves which you have in Christ Jesus who . . . *humbled* himself" (Phil 2:8). Here, the principal reason for humility is no longer an idea but a person; it is no longer an abstract principle but an event: "he humbled himself." In this, at a particular point, we see the whole magnificent process of the christianising of virtue being accomplished. Virtue is no longer so much commended by the principle of "right reason" as by the actual person of Christ himself and his Paschal mystery; it is no longer based on philosophy but on history; it is not based on wisdom (*sophia*), to use St. Paul's language, but on the *kerygma*. It is thus that the law becomes the Gospel and works become grace. From being the work of man humility has now become the work of God which man must imitate. God has treated us like a father who wants to help his child to do something, for example to draw a house. At first the father gives the child some hints, a sheet of paper and some coloured pencils . . . The child tries again and again but can't manage it. Then the father takes the paper and with the child looking on makes a drawing of a house; then he tells the child to trace it. That's what God has done with us: at first, in the law, he gave humility as a work to be accomplished, but later, in the Gospel, he gave us humility as a work to imitate. God no longer says to man, as he said under the law: "Go and take the last place!" but: "Come and take the last place!" He doesn't just urge him towards humility, but draws him: *Learn from me*—he says through Christ's words—*for I am meek and humble of heart!* (Mt 11:29).

But then, is humility no longer a search for truth? Certainly it is a search for truth but for the new truth of man, Jesus Christ. It is no longer only a rational or existential truth, but it is also objective and historical. We know from dogma that Christ is "true man" or the "perfect man" and this means that he is the fulfilment of true humanity. Jesus is the true and perfect man who "restored God's power to him," who does not seek his own glory and is, therefore, pure "praise to the glory of God" (cf. Eph. 1:14). He is the true and perfect "image of God" (Col 1:15).

In Christ we find all the reasons for humility brought together. There are, as I have already mentioned, at least two reasons for being humble: one lies within ourselves and the other in God, an anthropological reason, so to say, and a theological one. The anthropological negative reason is based on the knowledge of self and one's own nothingness which I have dealt with in the preceding chapter. The theological positive reason is based on the knowledge of God, on his infinite majesty, goodness and holiness. When God reveals himself to someone, the person becomes aware of his nothingness and spontaneously becomes humble. This is the type of humility experienced by Isaiah when he saw the vision of God's glory in the temple. The prophet didn't need to carry out a long and deep reflection on himself to learn what he was; the simple presence of the majesty of God suddenly placed him in a state of humility and he exclaimed: *Woe on me! For I am lost; for I am a man of unclean lips* (Is 6:5). When, on Lake Gennesaret, Simon Peter saw Jesus' divine power at work in the miraculous fishing, he also entered into this state of supernatural humility and said: *Depart from me, for I am a sinful man, O Lord* (Lk 5:8). Mary's humility was also "divinely" brought about. Mary saw herself as being so small and insignificant, simple and poor in front of her God, that this reverent fear filled her with humility. This is the perfect reason for humility and it will last forever. The Blessed in heaven are not humble because of the vision of their wretchedness and sin but because of their vision of the overwhelming perfection and holiness of God.

There are, therefore, according to the Bible, two reasons coming from opposite directions for humility: one comes from God and the other from man, one consists in self-knowledge and the other in the knowledge of God. These two reasons, both anthropological and theological, have become fused. In Christ Jesus, who is God and man in the same person, we have the complete and definitive reason for humility which is the christological reason.

2. Humility as Service

With the imitation of Christ as the new reason for humility, we have a corresponding new field of action of humility which we must now learn about from the Word of God. In the Gospel, Jesus says: *Learn from me for I am meek and humble of heart* (Mt 11:29). But wherein does Jesus tell us to imitate his humility? In what was Jesus humble? In the Gospel there is never the slightest admission of guilt on the lips of Jesus either when he is talking to men or with God. This, by the way, is one of the most hidden but most convincing proofs, of Christ's divinity and of the absolute uniqueness of his conscience. There is not a saint or a great historical personage, nor a founder of a religion in whom we find such sentiment of innocence. All of them are aware, more or less, of having committed some mistakes and of being in need of pardon, at least from God. Gandhi, for example, was very acutely aware of having taken the wrong stand on certain occasions; he, too, suffered from remorse. But not Jesus. He can address his adversaries saying: *Which of you convicts me of sin?* (Jn 8:46). Jesus proclaims that he is "Lord and Teacher" (cf. Jn 13:13), to be more than Abraham, Moses, Jonah and Solomon.

Therefore, where is the humility of Jesus that makes it possible for him to say: "Learn from me for I am humble"? We discover something important here. Humility doesn't principally consist in *being little* because it's possible to be little without being humble; neither does it consist in *feeling little* because it's possible to feel little and really be so and this would be objectivity and not yet humility, without considering that an inferiority complex can be the cause of feeling small and can lead to a withdrawal into oneself and to despair rather than to humility. Therefore, humility, in itself, in its most perfect state, does not consist in being little or feeling little but in *making oneself little!*

Perfect humility consists, therefore, in constantly making oneself small, not for the sake of some personal need or benefit, but for the sake of love, to "elevate" others. That's what the humility of Jesus was like; he made himself so small as to "annihilate" himself for us. What the Apostle says of the poverty of Jesus also throws light on his humility: *Though he was rich, for your sake he became poor, so that by his poverty you might become rich* (2 Cor 8:9). As we can see the humility Jesus revealed to us is a lowering of himself, not so much in thought, word or sentiment as in deed. In alluding to our text from Philippians 2:6 f., Tertullian says that in the Incarnation, God acted like the king who possessed a precious gem set in a gold ring, which one day fell into a sewer. The king put on slaves clothes and plunged into the foul sewage, got hold of his ring, washed it in water and put it on his finger so that it could shine there again. The gem, the author explains, is man's soul and the ring is his body, both fallen into the sewage of sin; Jesus is the king who dressed as a slave, descended into the world of sin and found man, washed him in the water of Baptism and lead him back to the Father (Tertullian, *Framm.* IV; CCL 2, p. 1335). In the preceding chapter I mentioned the example of the pearl-fisher. We could say that Jesus, too, became a pearl-fisher but what he was seeking in lowering himself was man and not himself. What drew him down was not like us the need for truth but love.

The humility of Jesus is the humility that comes from God and whose supreme model is God and not man. God, in fact, *is* not little; he doesn't *feel* little but he *made* himself little and he did this out of love. The Fathers of the Church used the word "condescension" (*synkatabasis*) which indicates two things: God lowering himself and stooping to man and, at the same time, the reason urging him to do this which is his love for man. God, in his position, cannot "elevate" himself; nothing exists above him. If God does something outside the Trinity it can only be to lower himself and make himself little. In other words, it cannot be other than humility. In this light the whole history of salvation appears as the history of the humiliations of God one after the other. When God created the earth he lowered himself; when he adapted himself to stammering a poor human language and inspiring the Bible, he lowered himself; when God became incarnate it was the supreme humiliation of God which crowned all the others: "Look, brothers, at God's humility!," St. Francis of Assisi exclaimed in wonder. "He humbles himself every day as when from his royal throne he descended into the womb of the Blessed Virgin" (*Admonition* I and *Letter to the Gen.* Chapter 28). In the handwritten "Laud to the most High God" which are kept in Assisi, St. Francis while listing the perfections of God ("You are Holy, You are Mighty, You are Triune and One, You are Love, Charity. You are Wisdom, You are Beauty") at a certain point adds: "You are Humility!" The saint thus gave one of the simplest and most beautiful definitions of God: God is indeed humility! God alone is truly humble. We must be humble for this deepest reason of all: to be similar to our Father and not to the "father of untruth," the liar, who, instead, always tends to "elevate himself" and place his throne in heaven (c. Is 14:13).

Now we know what Jesus meant when he said: "Learn from me for I am humble of heart." It is an invitation to make ourselves small for love, to wash, as he did, our brothers' feet. However, in Jesus we realize the seriousness of this choice. It is not a question of stooping and making himself small every once in a while, like a king who, out of generosity, deigns every now and then to go among his people and maybe even serve them in something. Jesus made himself small in the same way that he became flesh, that is, permanently and to the very end. He chose to belong to the category of the small and humble. To be "meek and humble of heart" also means to belong to the humble and poor people of God.

This new side of humility can be summarized in the word *service*. One day, the Gospel tells us, the disciples had discussed with one another who was the "greatest" among them. Then Jesus "sat down"—as if to add solemnity to what he was going to teach them—called the Twelve to him and said to them: *If anyone would be first, he must be last of all and servant of all* (Mk 9:35). Who would be "first" must be "last," that is, he must humble himself; but then, he immediately explained what he meant by last: he must be the "servant" of all. The humility proclaimed by Jesus is, therefore, service. In St. Matthew's Gospel we find an example to reinforce this: *Even as the Son of Man came not to be served but to serve* (Mt 20:28). How many new things these simple words on humility contain! The two virtues of humility and magnanimity are perfectly reconciled. The Greeks—and not only the Greeks—despised humility because they thought it was contrary to magnanimity, that is, to the desire to do great things and excel. Throughout the centuries this question continued to trouble christian writers, who sometimes fell back on awkward and makeshift solutions, as if humility were halfway between magnanimity and pusillanimity. They sometimes even placed the virtue of magnanimity above humility. According to the Gospel, humility is the measure for magnanimity: "Whoever would be first . . . ," "whoever would be great among you . . ." (Mt 20:26): therefore it is lawful to want to be first and do great things. Just that, in the Gospel, the way of accomplishing this has changed. It no longer takes place at the expense of others, dominating them as the powerful in nations do, but to the advantage of others. The Gospel completely changed the scale of values with respect to the old scale which was established and consolidated by sin. What happens between wisdom and foolishness happens between magnanimity and humility: it is necessary to become foolish to be wise (cf. 1 Cor 3:18); it is necessary to make oneself small to become truly great. The saints practised this new and superior magnanimity which is not only measured on things done but above all on the intention with which they are done, that is on love. They weren't magnanimous in human terms but in divine terms.

3. Humility and Charisms

The Apostle tells us that the best place in which to practise the humility-charity revealed by Christ is, as I have already said, the christian community. Not to seek one's own interests but those of others, not to aim at pleasing oneself but others and to place others first are all statements that recall the words of Jesus about becoming the servant of all. The change from humility to charity comes about, above all, through the right use of charisms: *We have gifts that differ according to the grace given to us* (Rom 12:6). Humility-charity is the condition for these graces given to each one and they should not be dispersed but used to build the "one body of Christ" (Rom 12:5). *As each has received a gift (charism), employ it for one another* (1 Pt 4:10). As charisms are given for service, they can only be protected by humility. At this point, I should like to talk first about how humility protects charisms and then about how, on the contrary, charisms protect humility.

First of all, let us look at how *humility protects charisms*. For as in one body we have many members, so—the Apostle says—even if we are spiritually one body only, we have different charisms. At this point he lists some of these charisms: some have the gift of prophecy, others of service and still others of teaching or admonition; there are those that preside, those who do acts of mercy and so on (cf. Rom 12:6-8). These are not just ordinary gifts or simple human talents. Charisms are the work of the Holy Spirit, sparks of God's fire entrusted to us for the Church. Yet, although we have this treasure, we are still just poor creatures. How can we manage not to spoil ourselves and this treasure? That is where humility comes in. It is through this virtue that the grace of God passes and circulates in the Church and in humanity without being dispersed or contaminated. Humility is the "insulating" wire of the Church. Insulating wire is very important and essential to progress in the field of electricity. In fact, the higher the tension and the stronger the electric power passing through the wire, the more resistant the insulator must be to impede the discharging of the current and short circuits. There would be no progress in the field of electricity if there was no corresponding progress in the technology of the insulator. In the spiritual life, humility is the means of insulation which impedes the dissipation of the current of divine grace, or even worse, of the sparking off of the flames of pride. The stronger the current of grace is in a person due to personal holiness or the office he holds, the stronger his humility must be. *We have this treasure in earthen vessels*—the Apostle said—*to show that the transcendent power belongs to God and not to us* (2 Cor 4:7). The "clay" is the insulator protecting and preserving the treasure. It preserves it from the two most frequent dangers to which God's gifts are exposed: selfishness and conceit. In the text quoted at the beginning the Apostle said: *Do nothing from selfishness or conceit, but in humility count others better than yourself.* Humility appears to be the antidote to ambitions, or rivalry and vainglory. St. Francis of Assisi loved to say: "Even though the Lord, the Blessed Virgin and God are honoured and remembered through wooden statues and painted images, the wood and paintings do not claim praise for this. God's servant too is like a picture, a creature made in God's image, in whom God is honoured in all his benefits. God's servant, therefore, just like the wooden statue, must claim nothing for himself; the honour and glory belong to God alone, while the servant claims only shame and sorrow, because, as long as we live, our flesh is in rebellion against the Lord's grace" (*Legenda Perugina,* 104). In a community there are always important tasks to be done which are attractive to the "old" self and humble tasks that no one—if we gave in to the flesh—would want to do. How can we get round this? Humility helps us not to aspire to great things but "to choose what is humble" (Rm 12:16).

It is easy, therefore, to understand how humility protects charisms. But how do *charisms protect humility*? Don't they rather put humility in danger because of the lustre and power they confer? Nothing ennobles man so much as contact with God; the most important positions and the greatest honour and talents are nothing compared with what directly concerns God and his Spirit. Yet these very things that might seem a danger to the humility and soberness of the believer can help him to be humble. In other words, charisms give us another and very strong reason for being humble. Let us see how this happens. St. Paul said that "we all have different gifts" and he listed some of these; the text of Romans 12 gives us one of the many lists of charisms. The fact that we have different gifts means that we don't possess all the gifts, that we are not all apostles or prophets and so on. The direct consequence is that each of us is not the whole but, always and fundamentally, only a part of the whole.

The doctrine on charisms is a formidable ever present reason for humility. It is, in fact, in practising a ministry or in holding an office that we realize that without others, that is, without the rest of the body, we would be nothing. In the text from Romans 12 the Apostle briefly mentioned this but he more amply developed the comparison in his first Letter to the Corinthians (cf. 1 Cor 12:12-17). The body, he explains, has many members and each member has its own function and each one depends on the other. The eye, for example, is a noble and very precious member of the body but it cannot say to the hand: "I do not need you!" What would happen if the whole body were an eye? It would simply be grotesque. The eye, therefore, is nothing in itself and on its own. It needs the other members to support it and make it worthwhile. It needs a face to exist in, an eyelid to protect it and a brain to control it . . . It needs the other members not only to be useful to the body but to be itself. The same is true of the hand, the foot and even the heart. In the spiritual sphere, each one of us is like a small cell that would immediately perish if separated from the rest of the body.

What a wonderful invention of God's wisdom! God, in giving man his gifts, at the same time gave him something extra to help him reach truth and soberness. We could say that charisms begin with building humility and then, together, they build the Church. It is therefore when exercising a charism or practising a ministry that we realize how thoroughly we depend on others and how, without them, we would be suspended on nothing. Thus we are reminded of the basic truth at every moment: that God alone is all and that only the Church is "the fullness" (Eph 1:23) of the Spirit, whereas each one of us is just a small part. We can only draw near to the fullness through others. Our self-sufficiency is thus struck at the roots. A charism, St. Paul says, is "a *particular* manifestation of the Spirit for the *common* good" (1 Cor 12:7); it is like a detail in an immense picture. In the Church there are those competent in Canon Law, others in theology, in government, in administration, in culture and still others in works of mercy . . . With the passing of time it is easy to become sort of hypnotized by one's own sphere of competence, ending up seeing it as the only really important thing in the Church and nothing else matters.

How useful it would be, at times, to widen one's horizon and see one's work and charism in the light of the whole: the whole of today, the whole of centuries! One would immediately get back a sense of proportion and feel very very small. It's like boarding an aeroplane; before the take-off, the buildings of the airport seem huge; then as the plane takes off into the sky, the buildings become smaller and smaller until they disappear altogether. So, those in authority would be encouraged to acknowledge that authority is not everything; there is also doctrine, prophecy, preaching, contemplation, works of mercy. Those with the gift of doctrine would be encouraged to acknowledge that doctrine is not everything even when it is sublime: there is also authority, prophecy, charity and so on. Charisms tend towards the Church with the same dynamism that the part tends towards the whole and drops of water tend to join other drops of water to make a stream.

St. Augustine, commenting on this doctrine point of St. Paul's, makes an illuminating reflection. On hearing all these charisms mentioned, he says, somebody might think that he doesn't even possess one of them and feel sad and excluded. "But, take heed—he adds—if you love, you possess no little thing. If, in fact, you love unity, everything that is possessed by someone else is also possessed by you! Get rid of envy and what is mine will be yours, and if I get rid of envy what you possess will be mine. Envy separates, love unites. The eye is the only member of the body that can see; but does the eye see only for itself? No, the eye sees for the hand, for the foot and for all the other members. In fact, if the foot is about to bang into something, the eye certainly doesn't turn elsewhere omitting to warn it. Only the hand acts in the body, but does it act only for itself? No, it acts also for the eye. If, in fact, a blow of some sort is aimed at the face, does the hand say: I shall not move because the blow isn't aimed at me? In this way, the foot, walking, serves all the other members. In this way, the tongue talks for all the other members which are silent. We have, therefore, the Holy Spirit if we love the Church and we love the Church if we keep ourselves within the unity and love of the Church. Indeed, after stating that men have been given different gifts just as the members of the body have been assigned different tasks, the same Apostle continued to say: *I will show you a still more excellent way* (1 Cor 12:31) and he goes on to talk about charity." (St. Augustine, *In Ioh.* 32, 8; CCL 36, 304f.).

Thus the secret of charity is revealed, which is also the secret of humility, that which makes it "a more excellent way." It makes me love unity—that is, in reality, the Church or the community in which I live—and in this unity all the charisms present and not just a few of them are mine. In fact, better still, if you love this unity more than I do, the charism that I possess is more yours than mine. Let us suppose that I have the charism of evangelist, that is, the charism to proclaim the Gospel; I could be pleased with myself and boastful but I would then be "a clanging cymbal" (1 Cor 13:1). I gain nothing from my charism, the Apostle warns me, while you, listening to me, continue to gain from it in spite of my sin. Through humility-charity, what is so dangerously mine, is yours without any risk. Humility-charity multiplies charisms; it makes the charism of one become the charism of all. But for this to happen it is necessary, as Augustine said, "to get rid of envy," that is, to die to our individualistic and egoistic "self" which seeks its own glory, and to take on the wonderful and great "self" of Christ and his Church. It is necessary to live "for the Lord" and not "for oneself."

The first teaching on humility ended with psalm 131 which is about the peace of the humble and gives the image of the child at its mother's breast. Let us end this second teaching with other peaceful and tranquil words: *Learn from me for I am meek and humble of heart*—says the Lord—*and you will find rest for your souls.*

XIII. By One Man's Obedience

Christian obedience to God

In outlining the virtues that must distinguish the new life of those reborn in the spirit—"what is good and acceptable to God and perfect" (Rom 12:2)—St. Paul, having spoken of charity and humility, now speaks of obedience in chapter 13 of his Letter to the Romans: *Let every person be subject to the governing authorities. For there is no authority except from God and those that exist have been instituted by God. Therefore he who resists the authorities resists what God has appointed* (Rom 13:1). The remainder of the passage where the sword and taxes are spoken of, together with other passages of the New Testament (cf. Tit 3:1; 1 Pt 2:13-15), clearly show that the Apostle is not talking about authority in general, or just about any kind of authority, but exclusively about state and civil authority as, in fact, is pointed out by all modern translations and exegetical studies. St. Paul deals with a particular aspect of obedience which was of particular relevance at the time he was writing and maybe even to the community he was writing for. It was the time when the Zealot rebellion against Rome was growing within Palestinian Judaism and which was to end a few years later with the destruction of Jerusalem. Christianity had sprung from Judaism. Many members of the christian community, even in Rome, were converted Jews. The problem of whether to obey the Roman state or not was relevant also for Christians. The Apostolic Church was faced with a crucial decision. St. Paul, just as the whole of the New Testament, solved the problem in the light of the words of Jesus, especially his words on paying taxes to Caesar (cf. Mk 12:17). The kingdom preached by Christ "is not of this world," it is not, that is, a national and political kingdom. It can, therefore, exist under any kind of political regime, accepting the advantages (such as Roman citizenship), but also the laws. The problem is solved, really, in the sense of obedience to the state. Obedience to the state is a consequence and an aspect of a much more important and wider obedience which the Apostle calls "obedience to the Gospel" (cf. Rom 10:16).

We cannot, of course, limit obedience only to the aspect of obedience to the state which was, at that time at least theoretically speaking, much more strongly felt than it is for us today. St. Paul indicates where the christian discourse on obedience comes in but he doesn't say everything about this virtue in this particular text. He just draws the consequences of principles stated previously in the same Letter to the Romans and elsewhere, and it is these principles we must search for if we want to understand obedience in a way that is useful and relevant to us today. We must discover the "essential" obedience from which all particular forms of obedience spring, including obedience to civil authority. There is in fact a type of obedience which concerns everyone, superiors and subjects alike, religious and lay people. This is the most important of all and it rules and gives life to all other types of obedience. It is not the obedience of "man to man" but the obedience of man to God. And this is the obedience we want to discover from the Word of God. It has been written that, "if obedience constitutes a problem today, it is not one of docility to the Holy Spirit—on whom, indeed, all seem willing to call—but rather that of submission to a hierarchy, to a humanly expressed law or authority." I am personally convinced that this is the case. But it is precisely to make this obedience to law and authority possible and relevant again that we must start from obedience to God and his Spirit. It is, therefore, to the Spirit that we entrust ourselves so that he may take us by the hand and guide us in our quest to rediscover the great secret of obedience.

1. The Obedience of Christ

It is relatively easy to discover the nature and origin of christian obedience: it is sufficient to understand on the basis of which concept of obedience Jesus is defined in Scripture as "the obedient." It is thus immediately obvious that the true basis of christian obedience is not an idea of obedience, but an *act* of obedience; it is not an abstract principle ("the inferior must be subject to the superior"), but an event; it is not founded upon a "constituted natural order," but it itself constitutes a new order; it is not found in reason (the "recta ratio"), but in the *kerygma*. It is based on the fact that *Christ became obedient even unto death* (Ph 2:8); that

Christ *learnt to obey through suffering and having been made perfect he became for all who obey him the source of eternal salvation* (cf. Heb 5:8-9). The luminous focus, which sheds light on the whole discourse on obedience in the Epistle to the Romans, is Rom 5:19: *By one man's obedience are many to be made upright.* The obedience of Christ is the immediate and historical source of justification; both are closely connected. Anyone who knows the importance of the justification in the Epistle to the Romans can then understand the importance of obedience in this text. In the New Testament, the obedience of Christ is not only the most sublime *example* of obedience, but it is its very *foundation.* It is the "constitution" of the Kingdom of God!

Let us try to understand the nature of that "act" of obedience on which the new order is built; let us try, in other words, to understand what the obedience of Christ consisted in. Jesus, as a child, obeyed his parents. Then, as an adult, he submitted himself to the mosaic law, to the Sanhedrin, to Pilate . . . But St. Paul is not thinking of any of these obediences; he is thinking instead of Christ's obedience to the Father. The obedience of Christ is, in fact, considered to be the exact antithesis of the disobedience of Adam: *As by one man's disobedience many were made sinners, so by one man's obedience are many to be made upright* (Rom 5:19; cf. 1 Cor 15:22). Also in the hymn of the Epistle to the Philippians the obedience of Christ "even to death and death on a cross," is tacitly contraposed to the disobedience of Adam who wants to be "equal with God" (cf. Ph 2:6 ff.). But who was it that Adam disobeyed? Certainly not his parents, a government, laws . . . He disobeyed God. Disobedience to God is at the root of every disobedience and obedience to God is at the root of every obedience.

St. Irenaeus interprets Christ's obedience in the light of the songs of the Servant of the Lord as an interior, absolute submission to God, carried out in an extremely difficult situation. "That sin—he writes—which came about on wood was abolished by the obedience of wood because in obeying God, the Son of man was nailed to wood, thus destroying the science of evil and introducing the science of good into the world. Evil is disobedience to God, just as obedience to God is the good. Thus says the

Word, through the prophet Isaiah: *I have not resisted and I have not turned away. I have offered my back to those who struck me, my cheeks to those who plucked my beard, I have not turned my face away from insult and spitting* (Is 50:5-6). Therefore, by virtue of that obedience unto death hanging from a cross, he dissolved the ancient disobedience which came about on wood" (St. Irenaeus, *Epid. 34*).

Obedience covers the whole life of Jesus. If St. Paul and the Epistle to the Hebrews give importance to the place of obedience in the *death* of Jesus (cf. Ph 2:8; Heb 5:8), St. John and the synoptics complete the picture by giving importance to the place obedience played daily in the *life* of Jesus. *My food*—says Jesus in St. John's Gospel—*is to do the will of the Father*; and again: *I always do what pleases Him* (Jn 4:34; 8:29).

The obedience of Jesus to the Father is carried out above all through the obedience to the written word. When Jesus was tempted in the desert, his obedience consisted in recalling the Word of God and keeping to it. "It is written!" God's words, under the present action of the Holy Spirit, become vehicles of the living will of God and reveal their "binding" nature as orders from God. Herein lies the obedience of the new Adam in the desert. After the last "It is written" said by Jesus, Luke goes on to tell us that the "devil left him" (Lk 4:12) and that Jesus returned to Galilee "filled with the Holy Spirit" (Lk 5:14). The Holy Spirit is given to those who "obey God" (Acts 5:32). St. James says: *Give in to God, resist the devil, and he will run away from you* (Jm 4:7). That is what happened when Jesus was tempted. Jesus bases his obedience, in a particular way, on the words written about him and for him "in the law, in the prophets and in the psalms," which he, as man, gradually discovers as he advances in understanding and fulfilling his mission. The perfect concord that exists between the prophecies of the Old Testament and the acts of Jesus, as seen in the New Testament, cannot be explained by saying that the prophecies depend on the acts (that is, that the prophecies were later applied to the acts already carried out by Jesus), but by saying that the acts depend on the prophecies: Jesus "fulfilled" in perfect obedience what was written of him by the Father. When his disciples want to oppose his capture, Jesus says: *But then how would the Scrip-*

tures be fulfilled that say this is the way it must be? (Mt 26:54). The life
of Jesus seems to be guided by an invisible luminous trail formed of the
words written for him; it is from the Scriptures that he takes the "must
be" which governs his whole life.

The greatness of the obedience of Jesus is measured *objectively* "by
what he suffered" and *subjectively* by the love and freedom with which
he obeyed. Filial obedience is radiant in Jesus to the highest and most
perfect degree. Even in the most extreme moments, as when the Father
offers him the chalice of the passion to drink, this filial cry "Abba!" was
always on his lips. *My God, my God, why have you abandoned me?* he
exclaimed from the cross (Mt 27:46); but, according to Luke, he immediately added: *Father, into your hands I commend my spirit* (Lk
23:46). On the cross Jesus abandoned himself to the God who was abandoning him! This is what obedience unto death means; this is the "rock
of our salvation."

2. Obedience as Grace: Baptism

In chapter 5 of the Epistle to the Romans, St. Paul presents Christ as
the head of the obedient, in contrast to Adam who was the head of the
disobedient. As we have said, Christ's obedience, in life and in death,
constitutes the new basis and the criterion on which the virtue of
obedience is founded. In the chapter that follows the Apostle reveals
how we come to be part of this event through baptism.

St. Paul first of all lays down a principle: if you freely place yourself
under the jurisdiction of someone, you are then bound to serve and obey
him: *You know well that if you undertake to be someone's slave and
obey him, you are the slave of him you obey; you can be the slave of
either sin which leads to death, or of Obedience which leads to saving
justice* (Rom 6:16). (In this quotation, I have used a capital letter for
obedience, because we are no longer dealing with abstract obedience but
with the obedience of Christ, or more exactly, with the obedient Christ).
Now, once the principle has been established, St. Paul recalls the event.
Christians, in fact, placed themselves under the jurisdiction of Christ on
the day when, through baptism, they accepted him as their Lord. *Once*

you were slaves of sin, but thank God you have given wholehearted obedience to the patterns of teaching to which you were introduced, and so, being freed from serving sin, you took uprightness as your master. (Rom 6:17). With baptism there has been a changeover of master, a changeover of sides: from sin to justice, from disobedience to obedience, from Adam to Christ. The liturgy expresses all of this, in the contrasting "I renounce—I believe," statements. In ancient times dramatic gestures were used in some baptism rituals to make this interior event visible. The one being baptised first turned towards the west, considered the symbol of darkness, and made signs repudiating and banishing Satan and all his works; then he turned towards the east, the symbol of light, and bowing deeply saluted Christ as his new Lord, as if he were a soldier abandoning the tyrant's army for that of the liberator in a war between two kingdoms.

Therefore, in christian life obedience is something essential; it is the practical and necessary turning-point in accepting the lordship of Christ. There can be no real and effective lordship without man's obedience. In baptism we accepted a Lord, a Kyrios, but an "obedient" Lord, one who became Lord precisely because of his obedience (cf. Phil. 2:8-11), one whose Lordship, so to say, consists in obedience. Obedience, from this point of view, is not so much subjection as likeness. To obey such a Lord is to be like him, because he, too, obeyed.

We find a splendid confirmation of the Pauline thought on this point in Peter's first letter. The faithful—the letter tells us at the beginning—*have been chosen in the foresight of God the Father, to be made holy by the Spirit, in order to obey Jesus Christ* (cf. 1 Pt 1:2). Christians were chosen and sanctified "to obey"; the christian calling is a call to obedience! A little further on in the same letter, the faithful are defined rather suggestively as "obedient children," or better and more literally as "sons of obedience," born out of the obedience of Christ (*tekna hypakoes*) (1 Pt 1:14).

From this we discover that obedience, before being a virtue, is a gift and before being law, it is grace. The difference is that the law tells us to do something, while grace makes it possible for us to do it. Obedience is above all the work of God in Christ, which is then pointed out to the believer, so that he, in turn, will faithfully imitate it in his life. In other words, we have not just the *duty* to obey but we also have the *grace* to obey! Christian obedience is, therefore, rooted in baptism; through baptism all Christians are "vowed" to obedience; they have, in a certain sense, made a "vow" of obedience.

The rediscovery of this biblical idea, founded on baptism, meets the most important needs of the *laity* in the Church. Vatican Council II announced the principle of a "universal call to holiness" of the people of God (*Lumen gentium*, 40) and, as there is no sanctity without obedience, to say that all those baptised are called to holiness is to say that all are called to obedience. However, it is now necessary that those baptised be offered a type of holiness and obedience made to their measure, without a particular character, state or tradition attached to it which would be too far from their way of life. And this holiness, objectively seen, can be nothing other than that essential holiness traced out by the Word of God and founded on baptism.

3. Obedience as "Duty": The Imitation of Christ

In the first part of the Epistle to the Romans, St. Paul presents Jesus Christ to us as a "gift" to be accepted with faith, while in the second or parenetical part, he presents Christ as a "model" to imitate in life. These two aspects of salvation are also present within the single virtues or fruits of the Spirit. In every christian virtue there is a mysteric and an ascetic element, a part that depends on grace and another part that depends on freedom. There is an "impressed" obedience in us and an obedience "expressed" by us. Now it is time to consider this second aspect, that is, our actual imitation of Christ's obedience, obedience as a duty. Thanks to the coming of Christ, the law became "grace," but later on, thanks to the coming of the Holy Spirit, grace became law, the new "law of the Spirit."

Going through the New Testament, trying to find out what the duty of obedience consists in, it is surprising to discover that obedience is almost always obedience to God. All the other forms of obedience are certainly mentioned: obedience to parents, masters, superiors, governing powers, "to every human institution" (1 Pt 2:13), but much less so and much less solemnly. The noun "obedience" (*hypakoe*)—which is the strongest term in the Greek New Testament—is used always and only to indicate obedience to God or, at the most, to instances connected with God, except in one passage in the Epistle to Philemon, where it indicates obedience to the Apostle. St. Paul speaks of obedience to *faith* (Rom 1:5; 16:26), of obedience to the *teaching* (Rom 6:17), of obedience to the *Gospel* (Rom 10:16; 2 Thess 1:8), of obedience to *truth* (Gal 5:7), of obedience to *Christ* (2 Cor 10:5). We also find the same language elsewhere: the Acts of the Apostles speak of obedience to *faith* (Acts 6:7), the First Letter of Peter speaks of obedience to *Christ* (1 Pt 1:2) and of obedience to *truth* (1 Pt 1:22).

But is it still possible and meaningful to talk of obedience to God, after the living will of God, manifested in Christ, has been completely expressed and objectified in a series of laws and hierarchies? Is it permissible to think that, after all this, there are still new "free" manifestations of God's will to be accepted and fulfilled? If the living will of God could be captured and thoroughly and definitely expressed in a series of laws, norms and institutions, that is in an "order" instituted and defined once and for all, the Church would end up paralysed. The rediscovery of the importance of obedience to God is a natural consequence of the rediscovery, started by Vatican Council II, of the charismatic and spiritual dimension, along with the hierarchical dimension, of the Church, (cf. the constitution *Lumen Gentium*), and of the supremacy of the Word of God in the Church (cf. the constitution *Dei Verbum*). In other words, obedience to God can be understood only when it is clearly affirmed—as in *Lumen Gentium*—that "the Holy Spirit guides the Church to the whole truth, it unifies it both in communion and ministry, instructs and directs it through the various hierarchical and charismatic gifts, adorns it with its fruits and constantly renews it and leads it to perfect harmony with its Spouse (*Lumen Gentium* 4). Only by believing in the present and specific Lordship of the Risen Christ over the Church, only by being deeply convinced that also today, as one of the Psalms says, *the Lord is speaking, God of Gods and will not be silent* (Ps 50), then and only then are we capable of understanding the necessity and importance of obedience to God. Obedience is listening to God who talks in the Church through his Spirit, who illuminates the words of Jesus and of the whole Bible, conferring authority on them and making them channels of the living will of God for us.

Obedience to God and the Gospel was necessarily put a little in the shade when the Church was thought of above all in terms of an institution, as a "perfect society," furnished from the beginning with all the means, powers and structures required to lead men to salvation without the need of any other specific and timely intervention by God. From the moment when the Church is again clearly seen as "mystery and institution" together, obedience returns again to being, as it was for St. Paul, not only obedience to the institution but also to the Spirit, not only to men, but also and first of all to God.

But just as in the Church institution and mystery are united and not opposed to one another, we must now show that spiritual obedience to God, rather than detracting from obedience to visible and institutional authority, actually enhances it. It strengthens and vivifies it to the point that obedience to man becomes the criterion for judging whether obedience to God exists or not in a person and whether it is genuine or not. In general, an act of obedience to God comes about like this. You feel flashes of the will of God in your heart; this is an "inspiration" which usually springs from the Word of God listened to or read in prayer. The source of a certain thought is unknown to you, but it is there like a frail bud which can very easily be suffocated. You feel you are being questioned by that word or inspiration; you feel it is asking something new of you and you say "yes." It is still a vague and confused "yes" as to what has to be done and how it should be done, but clear and firm in substance. It is like receiving a sealed letter from someone you love and which you welcome with all its contents even before opening it, thus making your act of faith. Thereafter, the interior clarity perceived at the moment of inspiration often disappears; the reasons why you should do something, so clear at first, become confused. Only one thing remains, and you cannot doubt this even if you want to: that one day you

230 Life in the Lordship of Christ

received an order from God and you answered "yes." What should we do in such circumstances? All the reflections and discernment possible are of little use. This inspiration does not come from the "flesh," that is from your intelligence, and you cannot therefore find it again through your intelligence; it came from the "Spirit" and can only be found again in the Spirit. However, the Spirit no longer talks, as at first, directly to your heart. He is silent and refers you to the Church and her instituted channels. You must place your call in the hands of your superiors or of those who in some way exercise a spiritual authority over you, and believe that if it is from God he will make his representatives recognise it as such. Here the experience of the Magi come to my mind. They saw a star and felt a call in their heart. They set out on their journey, but in the meantime the star had disappeared. They had to go to Jerusalem and question the priests from whom they learnt their precise destination, that is Bethlehem! After this humble search, the star reappeared. They were thus to be a sign also for the priests of Jerusalem.

But what should be done when conflict arises between the two obediences and the human superior asks you something different or opposed to what you believe God wants from you? Just ask yourself what Jesus did in such circumstances. He accepted the external obedience and submitted himself to man and in so doing he did not deny obedience to the Father, but rather he fulfilled this obedience, for this was exactly what the Father wanted. Without knowing or wanting it, sometimes in good faith and at other times not in good faith, men—as with Caifas, Pilate and the crowds—become instruments so that the will of God, not theirs, may be accomplished. Yet this is not an absolute rule: the will of God and his freedom may demand that a person obeys God rather than man as with Peter before the order of the Sanhedrin (cf. Acts 4:19-20).

You can always obey God. We might have to obey visible orders and authorities only every now and then—I mean to obey orders of a certain seriousness—maybe only three or four times in our life; but there are numerous obediences to God. The more we obey, the more numerous God's orders become, because he knows that the most beautiful gift he can give us is what he gave to this beloved son Jesus. When God finds a person determined to obey him, he takes the life of that person in his hands, like the helm of a boat or the reins of a horse. Not just in theory, but in reality, he becomes Lord, that is, he who rules and governs. One could say that minute by minute he defines the gestures and words of that person, his way of making use of his time, in short everything. The person ends up behaving like a good religious subject of other times, who asked his superior's permission, or "obedience" as it was once called, for every little thing.

There is nothing mystical or extraordinary in this; it is something open to all those who are baptised. It consists in "presenting the question to God" (cf. Ex 18:19). I may decide by myself to make or not to make a journey, to do a job, to make a visit, to buy something, and once I have decided, I pray to God for a good outcome. But if love of obedience to God grows in me, I'll first ask him, by the simple means of prayer, which is at everyone's disposal, if it is his will that I make that journey, do that job, make this visit, buy that object, and then I'll act or not. But whatever the decision, it will be an act of obedience to God and no longer a free initiative of mine. It is clear that normally I shall hear no voice in my short prayer and I shall not be told explicitly what to do, or, at least, this is not necessary to make my action an act of obedience. In so doing, I have submitted the question to God. I have emptied myself of my own will. I have renounced deciding for myself and I have given God the chance to intervene in my life if he so wishes. Whatever I now decide to do, based on the ordinary criteria of discernment, will be obedience to God. Just as a faithful servant never takes an order from an outsider without saying: "I must first ask my master," so the true servant of God undertakes nothing without saying to himself: "I must first pray a little to know what my Lord wants of me!" The will of God thus penetrates one's existence more and more, making it more precious and rendering it a "living sacrifice, holy and acceptable to God" (Rom 12:1).

If this rule of "presenting the question to God" is valid for the little things of everyday life, it is much more so for the big things, such as the choice of one's vocation: whether to marry or not to marry, whether to serve God in matrimony or in the consecrated life. The word "vocation" itself, seen on the part of God, in an active sense, means call, whereas seen on the part of man, in a passive sense, means to answer a call, that is obedience. In this sense, the vocation is the fundamental obedience in life, that which realizes baptism and creates a permanent state of obedience in the believer. Those who marry must also do so "in the Lord" (1 Cor 7:39), for obedience. Matrimony thus becomes obedience to God in a liberating and not in a constricting sense, as is the case when one marries to obey one's parents or for some other necessity. It is no longer an exclusively personal choice which is presented to God only on second thoughts so that he might bless and approve it. It is a choice made with him in filial obedience to his will, which is certainly a loving will. When difficult situations arise it is no small difference to be able to say that this is God's will, that the choice was not made alone and therefore God will not fail to give his help and grace.

Real and concrete obedience to God is not simply the privilege of religious in the Church but it can be practised by all baptised persons. Lay people have not got a superior in the Church to whom they owe obedience, at least not in the sense that religious and clerics do. They have, however, a Lord to obey! They have his Word! From its remote Jewish origin the word "obey" means to listen and in particular to listen to the Word of God. The Greek term for obedience in the New Testament (*hypakouein*) literally translated means "to listen carefully" or "pay attention," and the Latin word "oboedientia" (from *ob-audire*) means the same thing. In its original significance, therefore, obedience means submission to the Word, recognising its real power over us. It is easy therefore to understand how a rediscovery of obedience must be kept in mind while we are in the process of rediscovering the Word of God in the Church today. You cannot cultivate the Word of God without also cultivating obedience. Otherwise, you become disobedient ipso facto. Disobedience (*parakouein*) means listening carelessly, with distraction. We could say it means listening in a detached or neutral way without feeling in any way obliged to act on what is being listened to and thus reserving one's own power of decision. The disobedient are those who listen to the Word but, as Jesus says, do not act on it (cf. Mt 7:26). They do not even feel obliged to act on it. They study the Word but without the idea of having to submit to it; they dominate the Word, in the sense that they master the critical tools and rules of analysis, but they do not want to be dominated; they want to maintain the neutrality proper to every scholar with regard to the object of his science. On the contrary, the way of obedience is open to those who have decided to live "for the Lord"; it is a need that is released by true conversion. Just as the book of the "Rules" to be observed is given to a newly professed religious, so a newly converted Christian to the Gospel, in the Holy Spirit, is given this simple rule: "Be obedient! Obey the Word!" Salvation lies in obedience. In the constant struggle between the two kingdoms only the ranks of the obedient will be saved and their password will be: "Obedience to God!"

4. "Behold, I come, O God . . ."

To overcome the present crisis of obedience in the Church, it is necessary to fall in love with obedience, because whoever falls in love with obedience will then easily find the way to practise this virtue. I have tried to throw light on a few points to help in this task. But there is one thing that speaks to our hearts more than all the rest and that is God the Father's favour and delight. Obedience is the key to God's heart. When Abraham came back from Mount Moriah, God said to him: "I will shower blessings on you . . . All nations of the earth will bless themselves by your descendants, *because you have obeyed my command!* (Gn 22:18). The tone of these words makes us think of one who has had to hold back long and with difficulty but who can, at last, freely pour out what is in his heart. This is repeated with Jesus on an infinitely higher level: because Jesus became obedient to death, the Father raised him high and gave him the name which is above all other names (cf. Ph 2:8-11). The favour and delight of God the Father is not just a metaphorical expression, lacking in real meaning; it is the Holy Spirit! As Peter says in the Acts of the Apostles, God gives the Holy Spirit to those who obey him (cf. Acts 5:32).

If we want to enter into God's favour and delight, we too must learn to say, "Here I am!." This little expression resounds throughout the whole Bible. It is among the simplest and shortest words in human language but among the most dear to God. It expresses the mystery of obedience to God. Abraham said: "Here I am!" (*Hineni*) (Gen 22:1); Moses said: "Here I am!" (Ex 3:4); Samuel said: "Here I am!" (1 Sam 3:1); Isaiah said: "Here I am!" (Is 6:8); Mary said: "Here I am!" (Lk 1:38); Jesus said: "Here I am!" (Heb 10:9). It sounds like a roll-call during which those called answer "present" one by one. These men really answered God's "roll-call"!

Psalm 40 describes a spiritual experience which can help us to form a "proposal" at the end of this meditation. One day, full of joy and gratitude for the benefits of his God ("I waited, I waited for Yahweh, then He stooped to me . . . ; He pulled me from the seething chasm . . ."), the psalmist, in a true state of grace, asks himself what he could do to respond to such goodness: should he offer holocausts, victims? He immediately realises that this is not what God wants of him; it is too little to express what is in his heart. At this point it is revealed to him that what God wants of him is a generous and solemn decision to do, from that moment on, what God asks of him, to obey him in everything. Then he exclaims:

> Lo, I come,
> In the roll of the book it is written of me;
> I delight to do thy will, O my God;
> Thy law is within my heart.

When Jesus came into the world he made these words his own saying: *Lo, I have come to do thy will, O God* (Heb 10:5). Now it is our turn. The whole of life, day by day, can be lived in the spirit of these words: "Lo, I come to do your will, O God!" In the morning before beginning a new day, on keeping an appointment, before meeting someone or starting a new job: *Lo, I come to do your will, O God!"* We do not know what that day, that meeting, that job holds in store for us. We are certain of one thing only: that, whatever the situation, we only want to do God's will. None of us knows what the future holds for us; but how wonderful it is to go towards it with these words on our lips: "Lo, I come to do your will, O God!"

XIV. Let Us Put
on the Armor of Light
Christian purity

In our reading of the Letter to the Romans, we've come to where it says: *The night is far gone, the day is at hand. Let us then cast off the works of darkness and put on the armour of light; let us conduct ourselves becomingly as in the day, not in revelling and drunkenness, not in debauchery and licentiousness, not in quarrelling and jealousy. But put on the Lord Jesus Christ and make no provision for the flesh, to gratify its desires* (Rom 13:12-14).

In his *Confessions*, St. Augustine tells us the part this passage played in his conversion. His acceptance of the faith was almost complete; his objections had been demolished one after the other and God's voice had become ever more pressing. But something held him back: the fear of not being able to live chastely: "The folly of follies and vanity of vanities held me back—he wrote—these old attachments of mine, drawing me back to the flesh and whispering: Are you going to dismiss us? and then: We'll no longer be with you again, for ever and ever? and again: From this moment you will no longer be allowed to do this thing or that, for evermore? What was it, O my God, that were they insinuating when they whispered this or that thing!" On the other hand he felt the ever more pressing recall of his conscience inviting him to trust in God saying: "Cast yourself upon God's arms, and have no fear. He will not draw back and let you fall. Cast yourself upon him without fear. He will welcome you and set you free!" (*Conf.* VIII, 11). He was in his host's garden, a prey to this interior battle, weeping all the while, when all at once he heard coming from a nearby house what sounded like a child's voice repeating: "*Tolle, lege!*, take it and read; take it and read!" He took these words to be a divine command and as he had the book containing St. Paul's Epistles at hand, he opened it at random, decided to accept the first passage on which his eyes should fall as being God's will for him.

His eyes fell on the passage we have just read. A light of confidence flooded his heart and all the darkness of doubt was dispelled. He knew that with God's help he could be chaste (cf. *Conf.* VIII, 12).

What the Apostle calls "works of darkness" in the passage are the same as what he defines elsewhere as "desires or works of the flesh" (cf. Rom 8:13; Gal 5:19) and what he calls the "armour of light" is what he elsewhere calls "works of the Spirit" or "fruit of the Spirit" (cf. Gal 5:22). Two terms (*koite* and *aselgeia*) are used for these works of the flesh to underline sexual dissoluteness compared to the armour of light which is purity. In the passage we are dealing with, the Apostle doesn't dwell too long on this aspect of christian life but from the list of vices placed at the beginning of the Letter (cf. Rom 1:26 ff), we know how important it was in his eyes. If he doesn't explicitly explain purity here, at least he says this is where it should be done. We are dealing with the third fundamental relation that the Spirit wants to restore; the relation with ourselves after that with God and that with our neighbour, restored respectively by obedience and charity. St. Paul establishes a close connection between purity and sanctity and between purity and the Holy Spirit: *For this is the will of God, your sanctification; that you abstain from immorality; that each one of you know how to control his own body in holiness and honour, not in the passion of lust like heathens who do not know God; that no man transgress and wrong his brother in this matter, because the Lord is an avenger in all these things . . . God has not called us for uncleanness but in holiness. Therefore whoever disregards this, disregards not man but God, who gives his Holy Spirit to you* (1 Thess 4:3-8). Let us try, therefore, to make also this "exhortation" of God's word ours by carefully examining purity, as a fruit of the Spirit.

1. Christian Reasons for Purity

In his Letter to the Galatians St. Paul wrote: *The fruit of the Spirit is love, joy, peace, patience, kindness, goodness, faithfulness, gentleness, self-control* (Gal 5:22). The original Greek term, translated as "self-control," is *enkrateia* which has a wide range of meanings. In fact, self-control can be practised in eating, talking, holding back one's anger, etc.

Here, however, as is almost always the case in the New Testament, it means self-control in a very precise sphere of the person, the sexual sphere. We deduce this from the fact that just a little earlier on, when listing the "works of the flesh," the Apostle uses the term *porneia*, that is impurity, as the opposite to self-control.

We have, therefore, two key terms to help us understand the reality we want to talk about, a positive term (*enkrateia*) and a negative one (*porneia*). One describes the fact and the other describes its absence or its opposite. I've said that the term *enkrateia* literally means self-control, control over the body and especially over the sexual instinct. But what does *porneia* mean? (Let us first try to get all the possible meanings from the simple names of things before going beyond this). In modern translations of the Bible this term is sometimes given as prostitution, other times as immorality, and still other times as fornication or adultery or as something else. The basic idea of the term *porneia* is, however, to "sell oneself," to alienate one's body and therefore, to prostitute oneself. (The word comes from the verb *pernemi* which means "I sell myself".) In using this term to indicate almost every manifestation of sexual disorder, the Bible says that every sin of impurity is, in a certain sense, prostitution or a selling of oneself.

The terms St. Paul uses tell us, therefore, that two opposing attitudes are possible towards one's sexuality, one is fruit of the Spirit and the other is fruit of the flesh; one is a virtue and the other a vice. The first attitude is to keep one's self-control and control of one's body; the second attitude is, instead, to sell or alienate one's body, that is use sexuality for one's own pleasure, for utilitarian purposes different to those for which it was created, making the sexual act a venal act even if the benefit is not always in terms of money as in ordinary prostitution, but in egoistical pleasure and an end in itself.

When speaking of purity and impurity in simple catalogues of virtues and vices without going deeply into the matter, the New Testament language doesn't differ too much from that used by pagan moralists, for example, the stoics; they also fluently used the terms *enkrateia* and *porneia*, self-control and impurity. The simple terms themselves, therefore, give us no specific biblical and christian meaning. Pagan moralists also exalted self-control but only in view of interior peace and impassibility (*apatheia*). Among them purity was governed by the principle of "right reason." In fact, though, these two old pagan words hold a completely new meaning which comes as usual from the *kerygma*. This is obvious in our text of Romans 13:12-14, where sexual dissipation is significantly contrasted with "putting on the Lord Jesus Christ." The first Christians were able to grasp this new meaning because it was the subject of teachings in other contexts.

Let us now look at one of these specific teachings on purity to discover the real christian motives for this virtue which came down to us from the death and resurrection of Christ. The text is 1 Corinthians 6:12-20. It seems that the Corinthians, maybe through a misinterpretation of what the Apostle said, lived by the principle that: "All things are lawful for me" to justify sins of impurity also. The Apostle's answer contained an absolutely new reason for purity which springs from the mystery of Christ. It is not lawful, he said, to be immoral or to sell oneself or to dispose of oneself for one's own pleasure simply because we no longer belong to ourselves but to Christ. We cannot dispose of what is not ours. *Do you not know*—he says—*that your bodies are members of Christ . . . and that you are not your own* (1 Cor 6:15, 19). Pagan motivation has been reversed in a certain sense; the supreme value to be safeguarded is no longer to be masters of ourselves but to let Jesus be our master. *The body is not meant for immorality but for the Lord!* (1 Cor 6:13). The final motivation for purity is, therefore, that "Jesus is the Lord!" In other words, christian purity doesn't consist so much in establishing the control of the reason over instinct as in establishing Christ's control over the whole person—reason and instincts. The most important thing is not that I have self-control but that Jesus has control over me. The leap in quality between the two perspectives is almost infinite. In the first case purity is in function of myself, I am the scope; in the second case purity is in function of Jesus, Jesus is the scope. We should certainly make every effort to acquire self-control but only to offer it to Christ. This christological reason for purity becomes more pressing from what St. Paul adds in the same text: we do not only "belong" to Christ generically speaking, we are not simply his property or something that belongs to him but we are the very body of Christ, his members! This makes the whole question immensely more delicate because it means that by committing an act of impurity, I prostitute the body of Christ committing a sort of hateful sacrilege; I commit an "outrage" against the body of God's Son. *Shall I therefore take the members of Christ*—the Apostle says—*and make them members of a prostitute?* (1 Cor 6:15). The enormity of such a hypothesis is enough to strike us with terror.

To this christological reason, another pneumatological one is immediately added which concerns the Holy Spirit: *Do you not know your body is a temple of the Holy Spirit within you?* (1 Cor 6:19). To abuse of one's body is therefore to profane the temple of God; but if one destroys God's temple, God will destroy him (1 Cor 3:17). To commit an act of impurity is to "grieve the Holy Spirit of God" (cf. Eph 4:30).

Together with the christological and spiritual reasons, the Apostle also mentions an "eschatological reason" referring to man's ultimate destiny: *God raised the Lord and will also raise us* (1 Cor 6:14). Our bodies are destined to be resurrected; they are destined to participate, one day, in the beatitude and glory of the soul. Christian purity is not based on contempt for the body but on the greatest esteem for its dignity. In fighting against the gnostics, the Fathers of the Church said that the Gospel does not preach salvation "away from" the flesh but the salvation "of" the flesh. Those who consider the body something "foreign" destined to be abandoned here on earth do not have the same reason as Christians do for keeping it in holiness. The libertine trends in history almost always started within the movements that preached a radical spiritualism, like the Cathars. A Father of the Church wrote: "As the body is united to the soul in every action, it will also be the soul's companion in whatever happens in the future. Let us therefore respect our bodies brethren and let us not misuse them as if they were foreign things; let us not say, as heretics do, that the body is something foreign to us but let us respect it as something belonging to our person. We must account to God for everything we have done through the body" (St. Cyril of Jer., *Cat* XVIII, 20; PG 33, 1041).

The Apostle ended his teaching on purity with a vibrant invitation: *So glorify God in your body!* (1 Cor 6:20). The human body is, therefore, for God's glory and it expresses this glory when man lives his sexuality and his bodily state in loving obedience to God's will, which is the same as saying in obedience to the real meaning of sexuality, its intrinsic and original nature which is not that of selling oneself but of giving oneself. This glorification of God through the body doesn't necessarily exact a renunciation of one's sexuality. In the next chapter, that is, in 1 Corinthians 7, St. Paul explains, in fact, that this glorification of God can be expressed in two ways and through two different charisms: either through matrimony or through virginity. The virgin and celibate both glorify God in their bodies but those who marry also glorify God so long as each one lives the requirements of his state.

2. Purity, Beauty and Love of our Neighbour

In the new light springing from the paschal mystery of Christ which St. Paul has so far illustrated to us, the ideal of purity holds a privileged place in every synthesis on christian morality in the New Testament. We could say that there isn't a Letter of St. Paul's in which he doesn't dedicate space to it when he describes the new life in the Spirit (cf., for example, Eph 4:17-5:33; Col 3:5-12). This fundamental necessity for purity is specified, according to the different states of life of Christians. The pastoral Epistles show how purity must be manifested in young people, women, married couples, the elderly, widows, presbyters and bishops; purity is presented in its various forms of chastity, conjugal fidelity, soberness, continence, virginity and modesty. As a whole, these aspects of christian life define what the New Testament, especially the pastoral Epistles, calls "beauty" or the "beautiful" (*kalòs*) aspect of the christian vocation, which together with goodness (*agathòs*), forms the one ideal of the "good beauty" or the "beautiful goodness," so that we can talk indifferently of both good works and beautiful works. In calling purity the "beautiful virtue," christian tradition grasped this biblical view which expresses a deep truth in spite of the misuse and too unilateral emphasis that have sometimes been placed on it. In fact, purity is something beautiful!

Such purity is more a style of life than a single virtue. It has a range of manifestations that go beyond the mere sexual sphere. There is purity of the body but also purity of the heart which shuns not only acts but also evil thoughts and desires (cf. Mt 5:8, 27-28). Then there is purity in word which consists, negatively, in abstaining from foulness, silly talk and levity (cf Eph 5:4; Col 3:8) and positively, in frankness and sincerity in talking, that is in saying "yes, yes" and "no, no" in imitation of the immaculate Lamb "on whose lips no guile was found" (cf. 1 Pet 2:22). Finally there is purity of the eyes and glance. Jesus said: "The eye is the lamp of the body. So if your eye is sound, your whole body will be full of light" (cf. Mt 6:22 f.; Lk 11:34). St. Paul uses a very suggestive image for this new style of life. He says that Christians, born of the paschal mystery of Christ, must be "unleavened bread of sincerity and truth" (cf. 1 Cor 5:8). The term used here by the Apostle, *eilikrinéia,* contains in itself the image of "solar transparency." In our text of Romans 13:13 he talks of purity as being the "armour of light!"

There is a tendency nowadays to oppose sins against purity with sins against one's neighbour and only sins against one's neighbour tend to be considered as real sin. Sometimes there's a lot of irony about the excessive cult associated in the past with the "beautiful" virtue. In part, this attitude is understandable; moral teaching had too unilaterally over emphasized sins of the flesh to the point of creating, at times, real and true neurosis to the detriment of paying attention to duty towards one's neighbour and to the detriment of the virtue of purity itself which was thus impoverished and reduced to being almost only a negative virtue, the virtue of being able to say no. Now we have passed to the opposite extreme and tend to minimize sins against purity to the advantage (often only verbal) of attention to our neighbour. The basic error lies in opposing these two virtues. The Word of God, far from putting in contrast purity and charity, strongly links them. It would suffice to read the continuation of the text of 1 Thessalonians quoted at the beginning, to realize how interdependent these two virtues are according to the Apostle (cf. 1 Thess 4:3-12). The ultimate aim of purity and charity is to be able to lead a life "full of dignity," that is complete in every relation, both in relation to oneself and in relation to others. In our text the Apostle sum-

242 Life in the Lordship of Christ

marized all of this in the expression: "Let us conduct ourselves becomingly as in the day" (cf. Rom 13:13).

Purity and love of one's neighbour together have the same meaning as self-control and the gift of oneself to others. How can I give myself if I am a slave to my passions and don't own myself? How can I give myself to others if I haven't yet understood what the Apostle has told me, that I don't belong to myself and that my very body is not mine but the Lord's? It's an illusion to believe that true service to others which always requires sacrifice, altruism, forgetfulness of self and generosity can go hand in hand with a disorderly personal life geared towards gratifying myself and my passions. The inevitable end would be making use of others just as I make use of my own body. He who cannot say "no" to himself cannot say "yes" to others.

In people's minds, one of the excuses that greatly contributes to favouring the sin of impurity and emptying it of all responsibility is that, after all, it doesn't harm anyone, it doesn't violate anyone's rights and freedom, unless we are dealing with a case of rape. But apart from the fact that it's a violation of God's fundamental right to give his creatures a law, this excuse is also false where our neighbour is concerned. It is not true that the sin of impurity ends with the sinner. There is a solidarity among all sins. Each sin, no matter where it is committed or by whom, infects and defiles man's moral environment. Jesus calls this infection "scandal" and he uses some of the most terrible words in all the Gospel to condemn it (cf. Mt 18:6 f.; Mk 9:42 f.; Lk 17:1 f.). Even the evil thoughts stagnating in the heart defile man and the world according to Jesus: *For out of the heart come evil thoughts, murder, adultery, fornication . . . These are what defile a man* (Mt 15:9-20). Every sin causes an erosion of values and all sins together create what St. Paul defined "the law of sin" whose terrible power over all men he illustrated (cf. Rom 7:14 f.). In the Hebrew *Talmud* we find a story which is a good illustration of the solidarity in sin and the harm that each sin, even personal, causes to others. "Some people—we read—find themselves on a boat. One of them takes a drill and starts boring a hole directly beneath himself. When the other passengers see this they ask him what he is doing and he answers: 'What does it matter to you? Am I not making a hole under my own seat?' But they answer: 'Yes, that's true, but the water will get in and we'll all be drowned!"

It must be added that purity doesn't just predispose us to a right relation with ourselves and others but also to an intimate and familiar relation with God. Both the Old and New Testaments underline this continuously. It's impossible to pray with an impure heart; experience itself shows that this can't be done. We can't "raise" ourselves to God who is spirit if we are held prisoners of the flesh, which is matter. It would be like a bird trying to take flight when it has been trapped and is fixed to the ground by a wire. St. Peter wrote to the first Christians: *Keep sane and sober for your prayers* (1 Pet 4:7). If St. Paul advises even those who are married to abstain sometimes from their intimate relations, which are right and holy, so as to dedicate themselves more freely to prayer (cf. 1 Cor 7:5), because of the present state of human nature, what must be said of disorderly sexual acts? They make prayer practically impossible, unless there is a sincere will to fight against and overcome one's weaknesses.

3. Purity and Renewal

A study of the history of the origins of Christianity clearly shows us that two principal means helped the Church to transform the pagan world of that time: the preaching of the Word, the *kerygma,* and the testimony of the life of the Christians, the *martyria.* In the sphere of the testimony of christian life two factors again, more than anything else, amazed and converted the pagans: brotherly love and the purity of their morals. Even Peter's first Letter mentioned the amazement of the pagan world on seeing the very different way of life of the Christians. He wrote: *Let the time that is past suffice for doing what the Gentiles like to do, living in licentiousness, passions, drunkenness, revels, carousing and lawless idolatry. They are surprised that you do not join them in the same wild profligacy* (1 Pet 4:3-4). The Apologists—the christian writers who defended the faith in the first centuries of the Church—stated that the pure and chaste life of the Christians was something "extraordinary and unbelievable." One text tells us that "they marry and have children as all others but they do not abandon their children. They share the same table but not the same bed; they live in the flesh but not according to the flesh; they live on earth but, in fact, they are citizens of heaven" (Anonymous, *Letter to Diognetum*, 5, 5). Especially the reform of families had an extraordinary impact on the pagan society. The authorities had been wanting to reform the family for some time but they had been impotent in preventing its break-up. St. Justin, the martyr, had used this argument as the basis for the Apology he had addressed to Emperor Anthony the Pius: the Roman emperors are preoccupied with reforming custom and the family and they try to issue suitable laws for this scope which, however, turn out to be insufficient. Well then, why not acknowledge what the christian laws have been able to obtain from those who have accepted them and see the help they could also be to civil society? Some wonderful christian girls, who died martyrs, showed how far christian strength went on this point.

We mustn't think that the christian community was entirely exempt from sexual disorders and sins. St. Paul had even had to reprimand a case of incest in the Corinthian community. But these sins were seen as such and were condemned and corrected; it wasn't required to be without sin in this matter, as in other matters. What was important was to struggle against sin. Adultery, together with homicide and apostasy, was considered one of the three greatest sins, so much so that there was much discussion for some time in certain environments about whether it could be remitted by the sacrament of Penance.

Let us now leave the origins of Christianity and look at the present-day situation. What is the position of purity in our present world? The same as it was then, if not worse! We live in a society which, custom-wise, has sunk back into full paganism and the complete idolatry of sex. The tremendous condemnation St. Paul made of the pagan world at the beginning of his Letter to the Romans, could be applied, point by point, to the present world, especially to the so-called affluent society. *God—* he wrote—*gave them up to dishonourable passions. Their women exchanged natural passions for unnatural and the men likewise gave up natural relations with women and were consumed with passion for one another, men committing shameless acts with men* . . . *Though they know God's decree that those who do such things deserve to die, they do not only do them but approve those who practise them* (Rom 1:26-27, 32). Also today, not only are such things and even worse being practised but every effort is being made to justify them—to justify, that is, every moral licence and sexual perversion—so long as, it is said, no harm is being done to anyone and no one's freedom is being violated. It's as if the whole thing had nothing to do with God! Whole families are destroyed and we ask what harm is being done.

Doubtlessly certain traditional moral opinions on sex needed to be revised and modern science has contributed to clarifying certain mechanisms and conditionings of the human psyche which take from or diminish the moral responsibility in certain types of behaviour considered sinful in the past. But this progress has nothing in common with the pansexualism of certain pseudo-scientific and permissive theories which tend to deny every objective norm of sexual morals reducing the whole matter to a spontaneous evolution of customs, that is to a question of culture. If we took a close look at what is called the sexual revolution of our times we would be terrified to note that it is not just a simple revolution against the past but that it is frequently a revolution against God also. The battle in favour of divorce, abortion and other similar things are usually carried out under the slogan: "I belong to myself! My body is mine!," which is the exact antithesis of the truth established by the Word of God, that we are not ours, we do not belong to ourselves because we "belong to Christ." This is therefore the voice of revolt against God; it's a pretension of absolute autonomy.

Today, unfortunately, there is even a more serious situation than in St. Paul's time. Some of these permissive theories have penetrated the Church itself. Certain environments and publications reach the point of justifying, without too much distinction, homosexuality and other disorders clearly condemned by the Word of God. It's possible to hear on the lips of those who should be teaching people sound doctrine, considerations which leave one dumbfounded for their superficiality like what I personally heard once with my own ears: "God loves you as you are; God wants your fulfilment above all; therefore if you are 'like that' and feel that this fulfills you, go ahead and don't torment yourself. God is a Father!" As if it were possible to fulfil oneself outside the will of God, through sin! In this way one sins through a lack of faith in God's power. Instead of a weak and sick brother being told: "God loves you and God is stronger than your weakness!" he is told that his sin and weakness are stronger than God.

4. Pure of Heart!

I don't wish to dwell too long on describing the situation around us which we are all well aware of. In fact, what I want is to discover and communicate what God wants from us Christians in this situation. God is calling us to the same task to which he called our first brothers in faith, that is to "go against this torrent of wild profligacy." He is calling us to carry out the purification of the temple of the Holy Spirit which is our body and the body of the whole Church. He is calling us to make the "beauty" of christian life shine anew in the eyes of the world. He is calling us to fight for purity. To fight tenaciously and humbly. It is not necessary for all of us to be immediately perfect. This is as old a battle as the Church itself. But today the Holy Spirit is calling us to do something new, to be witnesses to the world of the original innocence of creatures and things. The world has sunk very low; sex, it has been written, has gone to our heads. Something very strong is necessary to break this kind of narcotization and intoxication with sex. It's necessary to reawaken in man that nostalgia for innocence and simplicity his heart yearns for even if this heart is all too often immersed in mire. Not the innocence of creation which no longer exists but the innocence of redemption which was restored to us by Christ and which is offered to us in the sacraments and in the Word of God. St. Paul indicated this programme when he wrote to the Philipians: *Be blameless and innocent, children of God without blemish in the midst of a crooked and perverse generation, among whom you shine as lights in the world, holding fast the word of life* (Phil 2:15 f.). This is what the Apostle calls "putting on the armour of light!"

Modesty is an important aspect today of this vocation to purity, especially for the young. Modesty in itself proclaims the mystery of the human body which is united to a soul; it proclaims that there's something in our bodies that goes beyond the body and transcends it. Modesty is respect for oneself and for others. When the sense of modesty is lacking, human sexuality is fatally banalized, stripped of all spiritual light and easily reduced to a consumer good. Today's world makes fun of modesty and goes all out to see who will go the farthest. By using real violence on them, it induces young people to be ashamed of what they should be proud and jealous of. It is necessary to put an end to this. St. Peter recommended to the women of the first christian community: *Let yours be the adorning of the hidden person of the heart with the imperishable jewel of a gentle and quiet spirit which in God's sight is very precious. So once the holy women who hoped in God used to adorn themselves* (1 Pet 3:4 f.). It's not a question of condemning every exterior ornament of the body and every effort to make the most of one's image and make it more beautiful, but this should be accompanied with clean sentiments of the heart. It should be done more for others, especially for one's fiance or husband and children than for oneself; it should be done to give joy rather than to seduce.

Modesty is the most beautiful ornament of purity. It has been written that "the world will be saved through beauty" but the same author immediately added that "there is only one absolutely beautiful being in the world whose apparition is a miracle of beauty: Christ" (F. Dostoevsky). Purity is what allows the divine beauty of Christ to manifest itself and shine on the face of a young Christian. Purity is a splendid testimony for the world. We are told in an authentic account of her martyrdom that the young Perpetua, one of the first christian martyrs, was tied to a fierce cow in the arena and thrown into the air but on falling, bleeding, back to the ground, "she arranged her dress, more worried about her modesty than the pain" (*Passio SS. Perp. et Fel.*; PL 3, 35). Such examples contributed to changing the pagan world and giving it regard for purity.

A purity made up of fear, taboos, prohibitions, mutual avoidance between man and woman as if one were always and necessarily a danger for the other and a potential enemy rather than a "help" would not be enough. In the past, purity was often reduced to this complex of taboos, prohibitions and fears as if the virtue should be ashamed of the vice and not the vice of the virtue. Thanks to the presence of the Spirit within us, we must aspire to a purity that is stronger than its opposing vice, a positive and not just a negative purity, through which we can experience the truth of the Apostle's words: *To the pure all things are pure!* (Tit 1:15) and again from Scripture: *He who is in you is greater than he who is in the world* (1 Jn 4:4).

We must start with healing the "heart" which is the root, because it is from the heart that comes all that defiles a person's life (cf. Mt 15:18 f.). Jesus said: *Blessed are the pure in heart, for they shall see God* (Mt 5:8). These will truly see, that is they will see the world and God through new eyes, limpid eyes able to discern what is beautiful and what is ugly; what is truth and what is falsehood; what is life and what is death. Eyes like those of Jesus! With what freedom was Jesus able to mention any topic: children, women, pregnancy, birth . . . Eyes like Mary's. We must love beauty, real beauty. The beauty creatures received from God and which is revealed to the pure of heart. Purity no longer consists then in saying "no" to creatures but in saying "yes" in so far as they are God's creatures and as such good. To be able to say this "yes" means to accept the suffering of the cross, since after sin came into the world, our way of looking at creatures has become turbid. Concupiscence has exploded within us. Sexuality is no longer a peaceful thing. It has become an ambiguous and threatening force dragging us away from God's law against our own will.

5. The Means: Mortification and Prayer

I have thus suggested the means for acquiring and preserving purity. The first means is, in fact, mortification. True interior freedom which makes it possible to approach every creature in the light, to listen to and become acquainted with all kinds of misery without becoming defiled ourselves is not just the fruit of being used to evil. Purity is not obtained by savouring everything and trying to immunize ourselves, inoculating ourselves with small doses of the germ of the evil we want to combat, but by curing the core of the infection. It is obtained through mortification: *If by the Spirit you put to death the deeds of the body you will live* (Rom 8:13).

We must do all in our power to free the word "mortification" from the suspicion that has been weighing on it for some time. Today, man has yielded to the call of the "old" man without realizing it; he has created a special philosophy to justify and even exalt the indiscriminate gratification of his instincts or, as we like to say, his natural impulses, seeing it as the way to self-fulfilment, as if man needed a special philosophy for such things and his corrupt nature and human egoism weren't sufficient! Mortification, it's true, is vain and carnal if done for itself and not in a spirit of freedom or, even worse, if done to claim privileges from God or gain praise from others. This is the idea many Christians have of it and the reason they shy away from it, maybe because they've come to know freedom of the Spirit. But the Word of God tells us of a new way to consider mortification, a completely spiritual way because it comes from the Holy Spirit: *If by the Spirit you put to death the deeds of the body you will live.* Such mortification is the fruit of the Spirit and it is for life.

Speaking of purity it is necessary to mention a special type of mortification: mortification of the eyes. The eye is called the mirror of the soul. When there's a whirlwind scattering dust and leaves about no one leaves his windows wide open to get everything full of dust. He who created the eye also created the eyelashes to protect it . . . Talking about the mortification of the eyes we cannot by-pass the television, which is the new great danger of our times. Jesus said: *If your right eye causes you to sin, pluck it out and throw it away* (Mt 5:29) and he said this about the purity of our glance. Television is certainly not any more necessary to us than the eye is, so we must say of it: if your television is a cause of sin to you, throw it away! It would be much better to appear ignorant of the latest happenings and entertainments in the world than to be well informed about everything but to have lost the friendship of Jesus and spoiled your heart. If you see that in spite of all your proposals and efforts, you cannot limit yourself to what is useful and suitable to a

Christian, it is your duty to get rid of your television. Many christian families have eliminated the television set because they realized that the benefit didn't compensate the harm that was being done on a christian and human level and they are really disconcerted when they realize through the odd hint that a priest or consecrated person has seen certain programmes, the content of which they are well aware of. How can a priest or religious fill his eyes and mind for hours and hours at night with images that deride the evangelical beatitudes and especially purity, and then early the next morning expect to celebrate the praises of the Lord, proclaim his Word, absolve from sins, break the body of Christ and receive it in communion?

Let us therefore have recourse to mortification and let us have recourse to prayer. Purity is, in fact, much more "fruit of the Spirit," that is, a gift of God, than fruit of our own efforts—even if these are indispensable. St. Augustine described his own personal experience in this matter in the text mentioned earlier on: "My lack of experience led me to believe that continence depended on one's own efforts and I knew I didn't possess the strength. I was foolish enough to ignore what is written, that is, that no one can be continent if you do not grant him the grace (cf. Wis 8:21). And you would certainly have granted me this if with the groans of my heart I had begged it of you and with firm faith had thrown my worries upon you . . . You want me to be pure; well then, grant me what you want and then ask me what you will!" (*Conf.* VI, 11; X, 29). And we know that he obtained chastity in this way.

As I said at the beginning, there's a strong link between purity and the Holy Spirit. The Holy Spirit, in fact, gives us purity and purity gives us the Holy Spirit! Purity draws the Holy Spirit to us as it drew the Spirit to Mary. In Jesus' time the world was swarming with "impure" spirits who acted undisturbed among men. When, full of the Holy Spirit after his baptism in the Jordan, Jesus entered the synagogue in Capernaum, a man possessed of an unclean spirit cried out: *What have you to do with us, Jesus of Nazareth? Have you come to destroy us? I know who you are, the Holy One of God!* (Mk 1:24). Who knows how long that man had been in the synagogue, undisturbed, without anyone realizing anything! But when Jesus, who radiated the light and fragrance of the Spirit, stepped into the synagogue, the impure spirit was unmasked. He became agitated and couldn't bear the presence of Jesus and came out of the man. This is the great silent exorcism that Jesus is calling us to work around us: to drive out impure spirits and the spirit of impurity from ourselves and those around us, giving our brothers, especially the young, the joy to fight for purity.

Conclusion

"Let Us Live for the Lord"

Towards the end of his Letter, while the Apostle is concentrating on giving practical advice on the particular problem of whether or not to eat the meat sacrificed to idols, at a certain point the tone of his speech suddenly becomes so elevated and solemn that it seems to be an already existing profession of baptismal faith or a hymn to Christ invented by the Apostle himself. The words go well beyond the problem relating to the Roman community and have a universal meaning investing the whole of christian existence. We can see in them the crowning point of the whole Letter and of our pilgrimage. *None of us lives to himself and none of us dies to himself. If we live, we live to the Lord, and if we die, we die to the Lord; so then, whether we live or whether we die, we are the Lord's. For to this end Christ died and lived again, that he might be Lord both of the dead and of the living* (Rom 14:7-9).

St. Paul took us by the hand at the beginning of our journey while we were still immersed in impiety, "deprived of God's glory" and living "for ourselves" and he has led us to this new state in which we no longer live for ourselves but for the Lord. To live for oneself is to live as if self were the beginning and the end; it means living "in" oneself and "for" oneself. It indicates an existence locked within itself, intent only on one's own satisfaction and glory with no prospect of eternity. On the contrary, to live for the Lord means to live "of" the Lord, that is of the life that comes from him, of his Spirit, and it means to live "for" the Lord, that is for his glory. It's a question of substituting the main principle; no longer "I" but Christ: *It is no longer I who live, but Christ who lives in me* (Gal 2:20). It means decentralizing ourselves to make Christ the centre. It's a sort of Copernican revolution carried out in the little world or microcosm that man is. In the ancient ptolemaic system, it was held that the earth was at the centre of the universe while the sun moved round it as its vassel and servant, to illuminate and heat it. But Copernicus reversed this theory stating that the sun stays still in the centre and

252

that the earth moves round it for light and heat. To carry out this Copernican revolution in our own little world, we must pass from the old to the new system. In the old system it's my "self"—the earth!—that wants to be at the centre and dictate the laws, assigning each thing to where it best suits me, keeping things and people I like close to me and things and people I don't like distant. In the new system it's Christ—the Sun of justice!—who is at the centre and reigns while my "self" humbly turns towards him to contemplate him, serve him and receive the "Spirit of life" from him.

It is truly a question of a new existence. Even death loses its character of irreparability and defeat. The greatest contradiction man has ever experienced, that between life and death, has been overcome. The most radical contradiction is no longer between living and dying but between living for oneself and living for the Lord. Now, living for oneself has become the real death. For those who believe, life and death in the physical sense are only two phases and two different ways of living for and with the Lord; the first is lived in faith and hope—a taste almost of what is to come; the second when, through death, we come into full and definite possession. *For I am sure*—the Apostle wrote—*that neither death nor life . . . will be able to separate us from the love of God in Christ Jesus our Lord* (Rom 8:38). Actually, seen in this light, death could even seem a "gain" because it allows us to be more fully "with Christ" (cf. Phil. 1:21 f.).

The Apostle's words are not mere expressions of religious enthusiasm. There is a pressing message underlying them. We, he said, belong to the Lord (Rom 14:8) and the reason for this is that "Christ died and lived again that he might be Lord" (Rom 14:9), that is to ransom us and have authority over us. *As we belong to the Lord, let us therefore live for the Lord!* The first part of the sentence summarizes the whole kerygma, while the second part summarizes the whole "parenesis."

The reason why we should live for the Lord is given here in the fact we belong to him. We are his. He "gave his flesh in return for our flesh and his soul in return for our souls" (St. Ireneus, *Adv. Haer.* V,1,1); He completely ransomed us. No man has ever been able to buy the will of another together with the body, for even the will of slaves is free. This wasn't the case with Christ. Even more than anything else our will belongs to him. Therefore, every time we make use of our will for ourselves we are taking it away from its right owner.

But justice is not the only reason; there is also a reason of love. St. Paul said: *The love of Christ controls us because we are convinced that one has died for all. And he died for all, that those who live might live no longer for themselves but for him who for their sake died and was raised* (2 Cor 5:14 f.). The love more than the right of the Lord urges us to make a decision. *Christ loved us and gave himself up for us* (Eph. 5:2). He loved us "while we were yet helpless," "while we were enemies" (Rom 5:6, 10). He loved each one of us taken individually: *He loved me and gave himself for me!* (Gal 2:20). He would still have died if I had been the only person on earth to save. Christ's love is infinite because it is the love of a God and the infinite cannot be divided into parts. Therefore, on his part he loves each one of us with the same intensity with which he loves the whole of humanity. Just as in the Eucharist his body is present in each one of the innumerable particles consecrated in the Church, so his love is wholly present in each redeemed person. These words of God are addressed to each one of us: *You are precious in my eyes, and honoured, and I love you* (Is 43:4).

The love of God really "controls" us and besieges us on all sides. In ancient times whenever a lord bought a slave, he didn't do so for the slave's sake and benefit but for his own sake, to enjoy the slave's service and benefit from his work. But with the Lord Jesus everything is the very opposite. "All this was done for the glory of the servants. The Lord didn't pay the ransom to benefit from the ransomed but to make his goods theirs, so that the servants would benefit from the master and the master's work and that the ransomed might completely possess the ransomer. Christ's servants possess their Lord and are heirs to his goods" (N. Cabasilas, *Life in Christ*, VII, 5; PG 150, 717).

The fruit of living for the Lord is *joy*. Whoever lives for himself has only miserably uncertain and finite things to feed his joy on and is therefore inevitably prone to sadness. But he who lives for the Lord has an infinite motive and object for joy, which is divine and always new. The joy of the Lord himself becomes his as Jesus himself stated: *These things I have spoken to you, that my joy may be in you, and that your joy may be full* (Jn 15:11). "If, through some artifice, it were possible to get rid of one's body for a better one, joy would also increase and the better the new body, the greater the joy would be. So, then, when the question is not just of getting rid of a body or a home but of ourselves to welcome God and when God takes the place of body and soul, of home and friends and everything else, this joy must necessarily be greater than any human joy and become the joy of the divine beatitudes" (Cabasilas, *op.cit.*, p.715).

The joy experienced in living for the Lord flows into what St. Paul calls "rejoicing": *We rejoice in our hope of sharing the glory of God* (Rom 5:2). This rejoicing or even "boasting" is a joyful certainty which enables redeemed man to live in a way completely unknown to natural man deprived of faith. It comes from hope in God's glory and endures even in tribulation. It actually transforms tribulation into rejoicing (cf. Rom 5:4), well aware that *the sufferings of this present time are not worth comparing with the glory that is to be revealed to us* (Rom 8:18).

In practice, living for the Lord means living for the *Church* which is his body. Therefore, the decision to serve Christ in a new way must necessarily imply a decision to take our place—or of returning to it if it has been abandoned—in the service of the Kingdom, of being available for the needs of the Parish or religious community we belong to, no longer withholding anything for ourselves and of submitting our will to our superiors in obedience in all things from now on if there has been any hesitation in the past.

Having, therefore, come to the end of our journey of re-evangelization and spiritual renewal, we must now resolve to choose Jesus again as the only Lord of our life. This is what makes baptism "effective"; we "release" the sacrament within us because a new strength flows from it and the charisms given to each one of us for "the common good" (cf. 1 Cor 12:7) can manifest themselves. The simplest way to express this decision is by learning to say "in the Spirit": *Jesus is Lord!* with the force that made it possible for the Apostle Paul to say: *If you confess with your lips that Jesus is Lord and believe in your heart that God raised him from the dead, you will be saved* (Rom 10:9).

To say "Jesus is Lord" in this way and with faith means to mysteriously take part in his death and resurrection. To say "Jesus is Lord" is not only to affirm something but to make a decision; it means to freely enter into his sphere of power and recognize him as one's Lord. It's as if we were saying: "Jesus is *my* Lord, the reason for my existence. I no longer want to live for myself but for him!" What power these simple words contain! Through them the Gospel is at work, which is "God's power for those who believe." They are a powerful bastion against the forces of evil within us and outside us. In the Gospel we note that demons go as far as saying to Jesus: "You are the Son of God!" "You are the Holy One of God!" but they never say: "You are the Lord!" When they say "You are the Son of God" they are, in fact, simply acknowledging something that doesn't depend on them and which they cannot change; but it would be quite a different thing to say: "You are Lord." It would mean they were acknowledging Jesus as Lord and placing themselves under his lordship. If they were to do this, they would immediately cease to be what they are and become angels of light again. The words "Jesus is Lord!" are a watershed between two worlds.

We must hasten our decision. In the midst of his teaching, the Apostle admonishes us: *It is full time now for you to wake from sleep. For salvation is nearer to us now than when we first believed; the night is far gone, the day is at hand* (Rom 13:11 f.). The night is our present life and the day at hand is "the Lord's day" which will fix our destiny for all eternity. A famous author who was condemned to death, even if the death sentence wasn't carried out, described the psychological state of a condemned man while he is being taken to the place of execution: "The condemned man thinks to himself: 'there's a long, long way to go, and at walking pace into the bargain, among thousands of people. Then there's the turning into the second street and we still have to get to the end of that before we reach the tremendous square'. However, as they proceed, the houses remain behind while the cart moves relentlessly forward . . .

'But this is nothing', he thinks, 'the turning into the next street is still a long way off!' And so he boldly looks to the right and left at the thousands of people who are mercilessly staring at him and all the time he feels deeply within himself that he too is neither more nor less a man than they are. Then the turning is reached. 'But, this is still nothing', he thinks again, 'we still have a whole street to go'. And as he proceeds and leaves the houses behind him, he continues telling himself that there are still a number of houses left! And so he goes on towards the end of the street until he comes out into the square" (F. Dostoevsky, *The Brothers, Karamazov,* VII, 9). How often we behave exactly like this man! We deceive ourselves that we still have a long time to live. No matter how quickly time passes we think that we have many more long years to live . . . and in the meantime we also distract ourselves looking to the right and left. The Word of God admonishes us that this world is passing away (1 Cor 7:31). St. Augustine stated that we must pass "from the world" so as not to pass "with the world" (*In Ioh.* 55:1; CCL 36, 464). Everyone passes, even the incredulous and the wicked who deny and hate God. But it's one thing to pass from the world and another to pass with the world. It's one thing to pass "from this world to the Father" and another to pass from this world to the enemy. We must pass from this world with our hearts before our bodies leave it. Let us pass to remain! It's written, in fact, that *the world passes away and the lust of it; but he who does the will of God lives forever* (1 Jn 2:17).

When talking about the law of the Spirit we mentioned the need to "bind ourselves" at the moment we discover love and perceive the risk we run of losing it and changing back to what we were before because of our fickleness. Now is the moment to bind ourselves. This can be done in the form of a renewal of our baptismal promises, religious vows or in the simple form of a strong promise or proposal . . . Not everyone can make the traditional vows but everyone can make the "vow." The religious vows have their origin in the fundamental vow of baptism which means to want to live "for the Lord," totally "vowed" and dedicated to him in life and in death. God wants us to place our freedom in his hands to do great things with us.

In the life of Blessed Angela of Foligno, that great mystic we are acquainted with at this stage, there is an episode that might help us to understand this. She had left the world and sin behind some time earlier and was living a very austere life, having renounced all her possessions. But one day she realized that there was still something she could do, that God wasn't really everything for her because her soul, in part, wanted God but it also wanted other things besides God. Then she felt as if her whole being was forming a unity, as if her body was forming a unity with her soul, her will with her intelligence and one only will was being formed in her. At that moment she heard a voice asking her: "Angela, what do you want?" and with all her strength she cried out: "I want God!" and God answered her: "I shall fulfil your wish" (*Il libro della B Angela da Foligno*, cit., p. 316). With that cry she consumed her freedom and God worked that wonderful adventure of sanctity in her which, eight centuries later, still illuminates the Church and the world.

"I want God!" are the greatest words a person can pronounce. The strongest words God can pronounce, and which, in fact, he has often pronounced in the Bible are: "I *am* God!" No one else can say these words and to do so is condemned as impiety (cf. Ezek 26:1 f.) but a creature can say: "I want God!" This brings about the unity of the will and the person. Man himself is divided. He is dispersed among countless thoughts, regrets, plans, desires. It would be easier to count the hairs of our head than the thoughts of our heart. We are like a tree of thick foliage which, in autumn, is full of birds making a deafening noise. The cry: "I want God!" that explodes from the whole being is like a shot aimed at that tree causing all the birds to fly off leaving behind deep silence and peace.

That same question is being asked of us now if we know how to listen to it. God is calling us by name in our inmost being and saying: "What do you want?" Blessed forever is he who has the courage to answer with his whole being and with the force only the Holy Spirit can give: "I want God!"

Appendix

Notes on how to use the contents for spiritual exercises,
retreats and seminars for a new life in the Spirit

For spiritual exercises and retreats it is advisable to place emphasis particularly on the two central parts of this spiritual journey which are the negative one of repentance and liberation from sin and the positive one of the renewal of the covenant and the gift of the Spirit ("Repent . . . and then you will receive the gift of the Holy Spirit!"). The following brief notes, based on experience, can help to make these two themes in particular more significant by integrating God's word with some practical initiatives and liturgical celebrations. Other notes deal with prayer in common and the day dedicated to Mary.

1. Penitential Liturgy

For the liturgy of repentance the following scheme is suggested to be used alongside the chapter (VII) on liberation from sin:

a. a biblical reading, for example Hosea 14:2-9 or Luke 15, the parables of mercy;

b. a common examination of conscience using some of God's great words as a "mirror." These are to be said slowly, each one being followed by suitable questions. It could be the decalogue or the passage on the beatitudes ("Blessed are the poor in spirit": am I poor in spirit?; "Blessed are the pure of heart": have I been pure in my body, in what I've looked at, in my intentions. . . ? and so on); another one could be the hymn on charity in 1 Cor 13 ("Charity is patient": am I patient?; "Charity knows no anger," do I? and so on); another could be Ephesians 4:25-5:5, suitable for a rather mixed congregation;

c. after a time of silence, psalm 51, the *Miserere,* is recited together leaving at the end to those who desire it, the chance to

259

say out loud the verse or words of the psalm that best expresses their state of mind and confession of sins. Then some brief passage from Scripture could be read, for example, Micah 7:18-20 ("Who is a God like thee, pardoning iniquity and passing over transgression"), or Zechariah 3:1-7 ("Behold, I have taken your iniquity away from you . . .") with the aim of opening souls to trust and joy in forgiveness.

d. finally, after a hymn and the choral recitation of the "I confess," the head of the assembly invokes God's mercy using the words of the penitential act at the beginning of Mass and then time is allowed to those who wish to complete the penitential act by approaching the sacrament of reconciliation.

The penitential day could be concluded with a gesture of joy and festivity, which could be, for example, a dispensation of silence at meal time or, in the case of young people, an invitation to sing and dance before the Lord as many psalms suggest.

2. Prayer of Liberation and Healing

If it's possible and the circumstances permit, it is advisable on the penitential day to talk about and pray for freedom from those things that are not really and truly sins but which nevertheless hinder true freedom of spirit. It's what also St. Paul suggests in his Letter to the Romans where, together with freedom from sin (ch. 6), he also deals with freedom from slavery to the law (ch. 7) and from fear (8:25). In this God's Word is confirmed and is aided by modern psychology which has enlightened us about the number of things man does for spurious reasons different to those he confesses to himself because he is conditioned by complexes, illusions and neurosis or worried about hiding to himself and others something he often wrongly thinks is dishonourable for him. The Apostle is certainly alluding also to this type of psychological freedom when he says "there is now no condemnation for those who are in Christ Jesus" (Rom 8:1). The teaching of Christ's freedom is completed when, having repented of what is really sin, the believer is helped to free himself also of fears, inhibitions, false guilt complexes, phobias, dangerous scruples, inferiority complexes, deep resentments, traumas and lack of affection in childhood or, if it is not always possible to free himself completely, at least to accept these things with more serenity and freedom. Many people, especially the young, spend a lot of energy on covering up an often exaggerated physical defect which, accepted with simplicity and humour, wouldn't detract anything at all from their personalities but, rather, would even make them more lovable.

3. The Hour of Common Prayer

The hour of common prayer to be made every day, if possible before the Blessed Sacrament exposed, is the time in which we place ourselves with simplicity and faith in the "real" presence of Jesus thus bearing witness to the fact that the mystical body of Christ, which is the Church, is built and renewed only by Christ's eucharistic body from which it gets life and the Spirit. This hour can be centered on the Eucharist trying to arouse a living sentiment of the real presence of Christ ("Behold, *now, here,* there is more than Solomon . . . !"). Another day can be filled with the penitential liturgy already spoken of and still another one can be dedicated to the Holy Spirit while yet another can be dedicated to the Passion of Christ. Each time the time of silence and adoration can be alternated with suitable biblical readings, simple and repetitive hymns, litany acclamations which will allow anyone who wishes to join in the prayer. ("You are Christ, the Son of the living God" and all acclaim: "Glory to you Lord!"; "You are the most beautiful of the sons of men"; "You are the bread of eternal life," and so on. The same can be done for the Holy Spirit or for the Father, making use of the titles and acclamations in Scripture).

4. The Marian Day

In the course of the retreat a day particularly dedicated to venerating the Mother of God shouldn't be neglected, during which a Holy Mass should be celebrated in her honour and the hour of common prayer dedicated to her perhaps by praying the rosary in a solemn way. For the homily of the Mass the following scheme can be followed: Recalling, as

Preface III in honour of the Blessed Virgin in the present day Roman Missal does, Mary's presence in Scripture in the three stages that make up the christian mystery and that is:

a. the *Incarnation* (Lk 1:26 ff.: the Annunciation),

b. *the Paschal mystery* (Jn 19:25-27: "Near the cross of Jesus stood Mary his Mother . . .") and

c. *Pentecost* (Acts 1:14. "All these with one accord devoted themselves to prayer . . . together with Mary the Mother of Jesus"). It should be stressed how Mary through these strong events, besides being the Mother of Jesus also became "mother of the Church in the order of grace" (cf. *Lumen Gentium,* 61) having "conceived" us, that is, "made us welcome" together with Jesus in the Incarnation, given birth to us through suffering of Calvary and having stood for us, so to say, as godmother at baptism, in the cenacle. The comparison between Mary's faith and that of Abraham as suggested by Scripture itself (cf. Lk 1:37 and Gen 18:14), shows us that if Christians don't hesitate to call Abraham "our father in faith," even more so they must not hesitate to call Mary "our mother in faith." Abraham believed in the birth of a son in spite of being old and his wife's sterility; Mary believed in the birth of a son in spite of her virginity; Abraham believed when God asked him to sacrifice his son on Mount Moriah; Mary believed when God asked her to accompany her Son to the sacrifice of death on Mount Calvary; with Abraham God drew back before his son's death whereas with Mary he went even further, asking her to believe even beyond death. Therefore it is clear how, through being so forcefully present on these three occasions, Mary, besides being the "Mother" of the Church became her model and image too: a) a model of obedience to the Word through her "Here I am" at the Incarnation, b) a model of faith and constancy in trial in the Paschal mystery, and c) a model of prayer at Pentecost (Mary, in the cenacle, is the model of any person who, having strongly experienced the Spirit and the cross, places himself at the disposal of others so that they too might experience God; she is the model of apostolic souls but of a truly "spiritual" apostolate based on prayer and the expectation of the Holy Spirit).

5. Invocation of the Holy Spirit

At the end of the retreat, in the place of the usual blessing and "reminders," it would be advisable to make a solemn invocation of the Holy Spirit, preferably during the eucharistic celebration for which the following procedure is suggested. After the liturgy of the Word a brief *homily* could be given. It could start with the words of the Symbol: "I believe in the Holy Spirit, the Lord and *giver of life*," or with the words of Jesus: "It is the Spirit that *gives life*" (Jn 6:63) and show how, throughout the history of salvation, the Holy Spirit is constantly at work each time life is granted or an improvement is realized in the way of living. At creation God breathed "the breath of life" into Adam and he became a "living being" (Gen 2:7); at the Incarnation the Spirit descended on Mary and the New Adam was born; at Pentecost the Spirit descended on the group of frightened disciples and the Church was born; the Spirit descends in the Eucharist, on the altar, on the bread and wine which are natural and inanimate things and these become the living body and blood of Christ, "the bread of life" and the "drink of salvation"; the Spirit descends now again on us and from "dried bones" we are transformed into living members of Christ. We become new men . . . After the homily the Saints are invoked in a short spontaneous litany, baptismal vows are renewed following the scheme proposed by the liturgy at the Easter vigil and, if it is the case, also religious profession could be renewed. Then some singing could be done together and the sequence of the Holy Spirit recited "Veni Sancte Spiritus," leaving some time at the end for those who wish to make theirs the invocation they are most in need of: "Bend what is rigid," "Warm what is cold," "Heal what is wounded." Or some particularly forceful text on the Holy Spirit could be read, such as the prophecy of Ezekiel on the dried bones (Ezek 37) making it real and live in a direct way ("Come from the four winds, O breath, and breathe upon *these* slain, that they may live . . . Behold, I will open *your* graves, O my people . . . ," or it could be John 20:22: "He breathed on them, and said to them: "Receive the Holy Spirit").

6. Seminaries for a New Life in the Spirit

For the "Seminaries for a new life in the Spirit" in the charismatic Renewal movement, seven meditations from the first part of the book could be chosen in the case of a first seminary (God's love, salvation, Christ's passion, the resurrection, the Father, freedom from sin, the law of the Spirit), or else the remaining meditations of the second part (prayer, charity, humility, obedience, purity, living for the Lord) for a second level seminary. Prayer for "a new outpouring of the Spirit" could be placed after the teaching on the "New Pentecost," or at the end, as for retreats.

Works Most Frequently Quoted and Abbreviations

Bl. Angela of Foligno, *Il Libro*, crit. edition Quaracchi, Grottaferrata 1985; Engl. transl. by M.G. Steegman, *The Book of Divine Consolation of the Bl. Angela of Foligno*, London—New York 1909.

N. Cabasilas, *Vita in Christo*, PG 150; Engl. transl. by C.J. de Catanzaro, *Life in Christ*, New York 1974.

P. Claudel, *Corona benignitatis anni Dei*, in *Oeuvre poétique*, Paris 1957, p. 369 ff.

Saint Francis of Assisi, *Writings and Early Biographies. English Omnibus of the Sources for the Life of St. Francis*, Franciscan Herald Press, Chicago 1983.

Julian of Norwich, *Revelations of Divine Love*, trans. into modern English by C. Wolters, London—New York 1982.

M. Heidegger, *Sein und Zeit*, Tübingen 1953; Engl. transl.: *Being and Time*, London 1962.

S. Kierkegaard, *Works*, transl. into English by W. Lowrie, A. Dru, D.F. Swenson, Princeton N.J. and London 1936 ff; *Journals*, transl. by R.G. Smith 1965.

M. Luther, *Works*, crit. edit. by J.C.F. Knaake and others, Weimar 1883 ff. (= Weimar Ausgabe), English transl. by J. Pelikan and H.T. Lehmann, St. Louis, Mo, and Philadelphia, 1955 ff.

K. Marx, *Oekonomisch—philosophische Manuskripte* (1844) (=*Manuscripts of 1844*); in *Gesamtausgabe*, III, Berlin 1932, p. 124; *Zur Kritik der Hegelsche Rechtsphilosophie* (=*Critic of Hegel's Philosophy of Law*), in *Gesamtausgabe* I, 1, Frankfurt a. M. 1927, pp. 614-615.

F. Nietzsche, *Die fröhliche Wissenschaft*, Leipzig 1905; English transl. *The Gay Science*, in *Complete Works*, ed. by O. Levy, New York 1909 ff.

The Cloud of Unknowing, transl. into modern English by C. Wolters, London 1978; by W. Johnston Garden City, New York 1973.

B. Pascal, *Pensées*, crit. edit. by L.C. Brunschvicg; English transl. W. Finlayson—Trotter, London—New York 1956.

Ch. Péguy, *Le Porche du mystère de la deuxième vertue*, in *Oeuvres Poétiques Complètes*, Paris 1975, pp. 327-670.

H. Schlier, *Der Römerbrief*, Freiburg 1977.

CCL = Corpus Christianorum, series Latina, Tournhout 1953 ff.

CSEL = Corpus Scriptorum Ecclesiaticorum Latinorum, Vienna 1866 ff.

DS = Denzinger-Schönmetzer, E*nchiridion Symbolorum et Definitionum*, Herder 1967.

GCS = Die Griechischen Christlichen Schriftsteller, Leipzig-Berlin 1897 ff.

LXX = Septuagint, Greek Version of the Bible.

PG = Patrologia Graeca, ed. J.P. Migne, Paris 1857 ff.

PL = Patrologia Latina, ed. J.P. Migne, Paris 1844 ff.

PLS = Patrologia Latina Supplementum. ed. by A. Hamman, Paris 1958 ff.

SCh = Sources Chrétiennes, Paris 1942 ff.

Vulg. = Vulgate, Latin Version of the Bible.

12:46ff	202
15:7-8	161
15:18f	248
15:19	180
15:19-20	242
16:25	32
18:1-3	46
18:6f	242
19:12	69
20:26	215
20:28	215
22:37ff	150
22:39	181
22:40	146
24:45f	190
25:34f	180
26:24	33
26:39	170
26:54	225
26:65	165
27:43	66
27:46	65, 165, 225
28:19f	vii

Mark
1:15	43, 44
1:24	250
2:7	128
9:23	50, 207
9:35	215
9:42f	242
10:15	46
12:17	221
14:33f	60
14:36	60, 106, 170
15:16-19	63
16:6	76
16:16	vi

Luke
1:26ff	262
1:37	50, 262
1:38	234
1:48	200
2:14	2

3:4-6	43
4:5	26
4:6	31
4:12	70, 224
5:8	212
5:14	224
6:37	186
7:13	18
7:14	85
11:34	241
12:4-5	119
14:7-11	194
15	259
15:21ff	123
16:8ff	85
17:1f	242
17:21	119
18:14	52
22:53	70
22:61f	72
23:28	64
23:39ff	71
23:41	69
23:46	114, 225
24:24	82

John
1:13	26
1:14	11
1:17	153
1:29	62
3:19	29
4:14	171
4:23	172
4:34	166, 224
5:6	59, 125
5:44	205
6:63	263
8:12ff	x
8:29	224
8:46	165, 212
8:50	205
10:17-18	110
11:33, 35	18
11:42	95, 166

Index of Documents and Authors Quoted

Thematic Index

Abraham - Father figure, 105; obedience of, 233; faith of, 262

Atheism - 25f

Baptism - personal faith and, vi; renewal of, 117, 154, 255

Bitter - the ___ waters transformed into sweet, 67

Charisms - and Pentecost, 154; and humility, 216ff; and charity, 219

Charity - fruit of the Spirit and moral virtue, 179ff

Church - the building up of, purpose of apostolic preaching, 209; spiritual
dimension of, 228f

Confession - and remission of sins, 129ff

Contrition - 121f

Conversion - the meaning of ___ in the Old Testament and in Jesus'
preaching, 43ff; of Paul, 47; of the Jews, 43f; of St. Augustine, 235f

Cross - "words from the ___", 54; Jesus on, 65

Dark Night - of the spirit, 61f

Death - nearness of, 256f

Depth Psychology - and the mystery of impiety, 27f; and the meaning of
sin, 123f; contribution of ___ to understanding the passion of Christ, 59;
interior freedom, 260

Despair - sin and, 34

Easter - exodus from sin to grace, 118f; from this world to the Father, 257

Ecumenism - between the East and the West, 89

Emotions - importance of feeling deeply, 18f

Eucharist - and forgiveness of sins, 131f; hour of adoration, 261

Faith - 40ff; comes from hearing, 79ff; as appropriation, 48ff; and works,
46f, 177f; and virtue, 177ff; and imitation of Christ, 178f; and interpretation, 77f